Resolving Environmental Disputes

The Conservation Foundation is a nonprofit research and communications organization dedicated to encouraging human conduct to sustain and enrich life on earth. Since its founding in 1948, it has attempted to provide intellectual leadership in the cause of wise management of the earth's resources. The Conservation Foundation is affiliated with World Wildlife Fund.

Resolving Environmental Disputes

A Decade of Experience

GAIL BINGHAM

 The Conservation Foundation
Washington, D.C.

Resolving Environmental Disputes
A Decade of Experience

Cover design by Sally A. Janin
Typography by Rings-Leighton, Ltd., Washington, D.C.
Printed by R.R. Donnelly & Sons Company, Harrisonburg, Virginia

The Conservation Foundation
1255 23rd Street, N.W.
Washington, D.C. 20037

Library of Congress Cataloging in Publication Data
Bingham, Gail.
    Resolving environmental disputes.
    Bibliography: p.
    Includes index.
    1. Environmental mediation—United States. I. Title.
KF3775.B44 1986   333.7'0973   85-25532
ISBN 0-89164-087-8

Contents

Foreword

The Conservation Foundation made dispute resolution a major priority in 1975. Our Program in Business and the Environment was directed at alleviating the polarization that then was hobbling implementation of a number of environmental laws and programs. The idea was to enlist the adversaries in more forthcoming exchanges on the critical, divisive issues where environmental policies entailed large economic costs and thus were keenly resisted. From the outset, there was wariness among both environmental groups and corporations about mediation, policy dialogues, and related alternatives to the more accustomed avenues: litigation, administrative proceedings, and legislative resolution of conflicts.

Increasingly, the alternative approaches have demonstrated their merit and have won over some skeptics. The number of mediated disputes in the mid-1970s could be counted on the fingers of both hands. Only five organizations were in the business of fostering mediation and negotiation in site-specific conflicts or policy disputes. By mid-1984, a decade after environmental mediation had first been attempted, mediators had been involved in at least 160 environmental disputes. Results of many of those efforts were successful, remarkable for the positive climate of public opinion they fostered and for the sense among the parties that they had won, each of them.

Certainly, mediation has not been the main arena for resolving disputes in the United States. Americans by most measures have become more and more litigious. In our environmental programs, as in health care, automobile safety, and other areas of public policy, the nation has tolerated huge and growing costs of resolving conflicts. Often, though not always, there is a better way. This book offers a timely look at some of the better ways.

A dozen or so years of experience now offer sufficient variety to allow some judgments about what has worked and what has been found wanting, what types of conflicts have been successfully addressed by mediation and what types would have been better approached more traditionally in the courts. This examination is timely because the field has a reasonable body of history to draw on, and because environmental dispute resolution appears to be on the verge of expanding into new areas of formalized decision making.

Dispute resolution procedures are being written into statutes. State agencies are being given responsibilities for managing environmental mediation services, and public officials are being trained in dispute resolution techniques. The mediation profession itself is becoming more self conscious. At this point, then, it seems particularly appropriate to look back at the practice of environmental dispute resolution experiences and ask what has been achieved thus far and what can be learned from the first decade of experience.

In *Resolving Environmental Disputes: A Decade of Experience*, Gail Bingham does just that. She presents the history and growth of environmental mediation, illustrated by several case examples. She raises and evaluates important hypotheses that can provide guidance in understanding what factors in individual disputes are most likely to aid or hinder successful mediation. She also discusses the relative costs and efficiencies of litigation and mediation.

Finally, Ms. Bingham explores the key problems that will face environmental mediation in the future. One major concern, she says, is likely to be funding. Some of the philanthropic institutions that provided the initial support for mediation attempts are now increasingly urging alternative dispute resolution programs to become self-sustaining. Finding the funds to continue and expand mediation programs almost certainly will prove challenging, especially in this era when the government cannot be expected to be a significant source of funds.

The Conservation Foundation continues to give a high priority to the search for more satisfactory means of resolving environmental conflicts. Several of our policy dialogues have resulted in significant achievements. Recently, the Agricultural Chemicals Dialogue Group has helped develop guidelines to reduce the misuse of pesticides in developing countries. The National Groundwater Policy Forum has proposed national and state policies for preventing groundwater contamination, policies that have already been incorporated in pending legislation. Clean Sites, Inc., now engaged in active efforts to resolve liability issues and get cleanup under way at more than a score of the nation's most troublesome hazardous waste sites, is rewarding the confidence of the Foundation's Steering Committee on Hazardous Waste, which conceived it in 1984. Through these hands-on efforts at dispute resolution, as through its research, the quarterly newsletter *Resolve*, and the biennial National Conferences on Environmental Dispute Resolution, the Foundation works to elevate and inform the debate, achieve policy breakthroughs in controversial or stalemated issues, test and demonstrate new approaches, and communicate the possibilities in this new field to the parties engaged in disputes and the growing numbers of mediation professionals.

We are most grateful to the National Institute for Dispute Resolution for generous assistance toward the research for this book. And, to The J.N. Pew, Jr. Charitable Trust, The William and Flora Hewlett Foundation, Charles Stewart Mott Foundation, and Exxon Corporation, I wish to express our particular gratitude for general support of the Foundation's dispute resolution program.

William K. Reilly
President
The Conservation Foundation

Acknowledgments

The idea behind this book arose in a conversation in 1983 between Conservation Foundation president William K. Reilly and the president of the Atlantic Richfield Foundation, which had for the previous five years generously supported the work of RESOLVE: Center for Environmental Conflict Resolution and later The Conservation Foundation, after the merger of RESOLVE into the Foundation. The two presidents wanted to know whether the field of environmental dispute resolution, which the Atlantic Richfield Foundation had wanted to encourage, had in fact grown and produced useful results. Although this study's concept and its weaknesses are my responsibility, this book would not have happened without their vision and support.

This book also would not have been possible without the generous cooperation of my colleagues in the environmental dispute resolution field, who shared their time and their case experience with me. The same is true for the parties to the disputes documented in this report. This book is really their story. The parties to these disputes and the mediators who were called in to assist their negotiations had the insight and the courage to try something new. It is a further reflection of their willingness to take risks that they were willing to share both their successes and their failures with me. I am sorry that I cannot acknowledge them individually, but they have my deep appreciation and respect. This book is dedicated to each of them.

Last, but not least, I would like to thank my colleagues at The Conservation Foundation. To Terry Davies, I am indebted for the standards of quality in research and writing that he demonstrates by example and that he has had the patience to share with me. Bradley Rymph edited the manuscript and made the final product much clearer that it would have been otherwise. Steve Gold spent many hours sorting through files of documents and notes to prepare the appendix. Jenny Billet typed and retyped the many stages of the manuscript and has been of invaluable assistance for the past five years. Among others, Fran Irwin, Grant Thompson, and Toby Clark helped keep my spirits up. Thank you.

Executive Summary

Negotiation, mediation, consensus building, policy dialogue—these and related approaches through which parties can resolve their differences voluntarily are becoming increasingly important in settling environmental disputes. *Resolving Environmental Disputes: A Decade of Experience* documents the development of these dispute resolution alternatives and assesses whether the results have met initial hopes and expectations. What are the different approaches to environmental dispute resolution? What have these approaches sought to achieve, and how successful have they been? What kinds of disputes have been resolved? Who have the parties to these disputes been? How much do these dispute resolution processes cost? How much time have cases taken to be resolved? What other lessons have been learned to date?

The book is intended for anyone interested in finding better ways of addressing controversial environmental issues. It is written particularly for the men and women in government agencies, private corporations, and public interest groups who are responsible for making decisions that affect the environment and who often find themselves in dispute.

As used in this report, the term *environmental dispute resolution* refers collectively to a variety of approaches that allow the parties to meet face to face to reach a mutually acceptable resolution of the issues in a dispute or potentially controversial situation. Although there are differences among the approaches, all are voluntary processes that involve some form of consensus building, joint problem solving, or negotiation. Litigation, administrative procedures, and arbitration are not included in this definition or in this study, because the objective in those processes is not a consensus among the parties. Although environmental dispute resolution processes can occur with or without the assistance of a mediator, only cases that involved a mediator were included in this study.

The interest in alternative approaches for resolving environmental disputes seems to come largely from dissatisfaction with more traditional decision-making processes. Specific complaints about these processes are legion, but most are related to the same problem—the frequent inability of traditional decision-making processes to deal satisfactorily with the real issues in dispute. When a dispute is not adequately resolved, dissatisfied parties may attempt to prolong the dispute, hoping to change the outcome, using whatever means are available. In environmental disputes, the parties often have many such opportunities—through administrative appeals, perhaps in several different regulatory agencies; through litigation; and through political action. The parties often also have the clout to use such opportunities, although the result may only be stalemate.

Although voluntary environmental dispute resolution processes are often characterized as alternatives to litigation—with the presumption that litigation is bad—they are better viewed as additional tools that might or might not be more effective or more efficient in particular circumstances. Litigation and other traditional decision-making processes remain important options. Disputes over environmental issues are so varied that no one dispute resolution process is likely to be successful in all situations. Depending on the circumstances, the parties may prefer to litigate, to lobby for legislative change, to turn to an administrative agency, or to negotiate a voluntary resolution of the issues with one another. This complicated strategic decision is, and should be, affected by applicable laws and regulations, by the experiences and resources of the parties, and by those parties' calculations of how well their interests will be served by different approaches.

Chapter 1 of this report describes the history and growth of the environmental dispute resolution field—the initial experiments with mediation in the early 1970s, the growth of new cases and new organizations based on the earlier successes, and the diversity of issues resolved as case experience has grown. In preparing this study, 161 environmental dispute resolution cases were documented. These cases form the basis for describing the first 10 years of practice and for evaluating the results to date.

There are different points of view and different expectations for what environmental dispute resolution options could and should achieve. In chapter 2, several criteria that can be used to evaluate the success of environmental dispute resolution alternatives are discussed, and some of these criteria are applied to assess the success of these approaches.

In chapter 3, factors that are presumed to affect the likelihood of reaching a successful agreement are explored. Chapter 4 examines the expectation that voluntary dispute resolution processes will be more efficient than litigation, and chapter 5 concludes with a discussion of important issues and questions raised by this first decade of experience with environmental dispute resolution alternatives. For those interested in the case examples that form the basis of this study, short descriptions of some cases are included in an appendix.

1. THE GROWTH OF THE ENVIRONMENTAL DISPUTE RESOLUTION FIELD

In 1973, Daniel J. Evans, then governor of the state of Washington, invited mediators Gerald W. Cormick and Jane McCarthy to help settle a long-standing dispute over a proposed flood control dam on the Snoqualmie River. Since then, the use of environmental dispute resolution alternatives has grown rapidly. Nationally, by the end of 1977, 9 environmental disputes had been mediated. Another 11 were mediated in 1978, and 19 more were mediated in 1979. By mid-1984, mediators and facilitators had been employed in over 160 environmental disputes in the United States. Compared to 1973, when only two individuals were beginning to develop a mediation practice for environmental disputes, there are now organizations and individuals in at least 15 states, the District of Columbia, and Canada offering environmental dispute resolution services. Others, elsewhere, are attempting to establish similar practices.

In addition, and relatively recently, the practice of environmental dispute resolution has grown beyond the resolution of disputes on a case-by-case basis to the institutionalization, by statute, of procedures for resolving environmental disputes. Statutes in Massachusetts, Rhode Island, Texas, Virginia, and Wisconsin authorize or even require negotiation of disputes over the siting of solid waste or hazardous waste facilities. A statute in Virginia specifies procedures for negotiation and mediation of intergovernmental disputes triggered by annexation proposals, and, in mid-1985, the Pennsylvania legislature was considering a bill proposed a few years earlier to authorize mediation of any local land-use or zoning dispute.

Environmental dispute resolution organizations also provide services that are not reflected by the number of cases in which they have been involved. Many conduct training courses in the effective use of environmental dispute resolution techniques. All provide consultation and technical assistance to parties in disputes wishing to explore the feasibility of an alternative approach in a particular controversy. Other services offered include newsletters, conferences, and consulting to various organizations, particularly government agencies, wishing to develop an organizational capability for more effective dispute resolution.

Among the cases that comprise the cumulative track record of the environmental dispute resolution field, there is striking diversity. The primary issues involved in these cases fall into six broad categories, with some cases dealing with more than one primary issue. Some cases involve site-specific disputes over a particular project or plan; others involve disputes over questions of state or national environmental policy.

- *Land-use.* About 70 site-specific and 16 policy-level land-use disputes have been resolved with the assistance of a mediator. They have involved neighborhood and housing issues, commercial and urban development issues, parks and recreation, preservation of agricultural land and other regional planning issues, facility siting, and transportation.
- *Natural resource management and use of public lands.* Mediation has been used in 29 site-specific and 4 policy-level controversies, involving fisheries resources, mining, timber management, and wilderness areas, among others.
- *Water resources.* Among the 16 site-specific cases and 1 policy-level case that involved water resources, the issues in dispute included water supply, water quality, flood protection, and the thermal effects of power plants.
- *Energy.* In this area, 9 site-specific and 4 policy-level cases involved such issues as siting small-scale hydroelectric plants, conversion of power plant fuel from oil to coal, and geothermal development.
- *Air quality.* Odor problems, national air quality legislation, and acid rain were the topics of 6 site-specific cases and 7 policy dialogues.
- *Toxics.* National policy on the regulation of chemicals, plans for removal of asbestos in schools, pesticide policy, and haz-

ardous materials cleanup were among the issues discussed in 5 site-specific cases and 11 policy dialogues.

When people think of environmental disputes, they commonly think of cases in which environmental groups challenge proposals made by private industry. Most environmental dispute resolution cases do not fit that model, however. Environmental groups and private companies were involved in negotiations with each other in only 21 percent of the site-specific cases studied. Many mediated environmental disputes have involved only public agencies. In others, citizen groups were engaged in disputes with their local government, or a mix of government agencies were in dispute with one another and a variety of interest groups.

- Environmental groups were at the negotiating table in only 35 percent of the site-specific cases documented in this book.
- Private corporations were involved in 34 percent of the site-specific cases studied.
- Federal and state agencies and units of local government were involved in 82 percent of these cases.

For the most part, environmental dispute resolution processes have been used on an ad hoc, case-by-case basis. Recently, however, efforts to encourage and routinize the practice have emerged. Negotiation and mediation procedures have been written into statutes governing hazardous waste siting, annexation, and coastal zone management issues. The Administrative Conference of the United States (ACUS) adopted a resolution in 1982 recommending that federal regulatory agencies incorporate negotiation into the rule-making process under certain circumstances, and three federal agencies have experimented with negotiated rule making. In 1984, ACUS recommended that greater use of negotiation be made in the cleanup of abandoned, toxic waste sites. In New Jersey, the state supreme court commissioned a special study and is now sponsoring an experimental effort to explore ways in which the judicial system can encourage the voluntary resolution of environmental issues, among others, that frequently come before that state's courts. In addition, the National Institute for Dispute Resolution (NIDR) has helped establish and fund statewide offices of dispute resolution in five pilot states—Hawaii, Massachusetts, Minnesota, New Jersey, and Wisconsin.

2. HOW SUCCESSFUL HAVE ENVIRONMENTAL DISPUTE RESOLUTION PROCESSES BEEN?

Although people's strategies for resolving environmental disputes may vary depending on their views about social conflict and the characteristics of the dispute itself, individuals and groups care about similar factors. They care about the outcome and the extent to which it satisfies the real issues in dispute, as they see them. They care about the process—how much they are able to influence a decision, the fairness of the process, and its efficiency. And, to the degree that the parties have or wish to have a continuing relationship, they care about the quality of that relationship and their ability to communicate with one another.

An assumption inherent in environmental dispute resolution alternatives is that the parties are good judges of what the real issues are and whether they are resolved adequately. Another is that the voluntary nature of the process, both in deciding whether to participate and whether to concur in an agreement, allows the parties to exercise that judgment freely. In theory, therefore, environmental dispute resolution processes allow broader attention to the real issues in dispute, because the parties set the agenda and because they decide what the terms of the agreement will be. Thus, the first and most simple measure of how successful these processes have been in resolving the issues is how often agreements have been reached.

A second test of how well the agreements reached have resolved the real issues in dispute is the extent to which the parties have supported the agreement through the implementation process. It is during implementation that other problems with the adequacy of a dispute resolution process may emerge. Were all the parties with a stake in the issues involved? If not, although an agreement may have been reached, it may not have addressed the issues of concern to unrepresented parties. These parties may take action to block the implementation of the agreement. Does the agreement satisfy community norms of fairness? Were the parties well informed during the process so that the agreement is technically sound? Was a mechanism established for dealing with unanticipated events after the agreement was reached and the negotiations terminated? How were the parties able to handle disputes that may have arisen during the implementation process?

Other, intangible factors are also likely to be important to parties in dispute. Sometimes, as part of reaching an agreement, and sometimes in spite of *not* reaching an agreement, the participants report that the process itself was valuable. They may feel that they have gained valuable insights into their opposition's point of view on the issues and have created more open lines of communication. For example, in one policy dialogue sponsored by The Conservation Foundation, the parties reported more than a dozen instances in which one or another of them contacted others on issues outside the scope of the dialogue group's discussions. They had not done so in the past, although many had been involved in these issues for many years. Improving communication in itself is the objective in some dispute resolution efforts. And, even when parties have decided not to participate in mediated negotiations, studies have shown that they often believe that the contacts by the mediator have helped them to clarify the issues and to understand better the dynamics of a dispute, thus helping them to deal with one another more effectively through more traditional decision-making processes.

The objectives set by the parties were identified in each case documented for this study, and three categories of objectives were observed—to reach a decision, to agree on recommendations to a decision-making body not directly represented in the dispute resolution process, and to improve communications. In 29 of the 161 cases documented for this study, the parties' principal objective was to improve communications. In 132 of the cases, the parties' objective was to reach some form of agreement with one another. Of these cases, 99 involved site-specific issues and 33 involved policy issues. Overall, agreements were reached in 103, or 78 percent, of the cases; no agreements were reached in the remaining 29 cases.

- Little difference between site-specific and policy-level disputes was evident in the study. The parties were successful in reaching agreement in 79 percent of the site-specific cases and in 76 percent of the policy dialogues or negotiations.
- When the parties at the table had formal decision-making authority, they were able to reach an agreement in 82 percent of the cases. When the agreements took the form of recommendations to a decision-making body that did not participate directly in the negotiations, the parties reached agreement 73 percent of the time.

Reaching an agreement does not mean that it sticks. The problem with litigation and administrative proceedings usually is not that decisions are not reached but that those decisions frequently are appealed. In theory, if the parties themselves have voluntarily agreed to a decision, they are more likely to be satisfied with it. Thus, agreements reached through an environmental dispute resolution process should be more likely to be implemented. How well is this claim borne out in practice?

- For site-specific disputes, of those cases in which agreements were reached and implementation results are known, the agreements were fully implemented in 80 percent of the cases, partially implemented in 13 percent, and not implemented in 7 percent.
- There has been more difficulty in implementing the results of policy dialogues or negotiations than in implementing agreements reached in site-specific disputes. Of the policy-level cases in which agreements were reached and implementation results are known, agreements were fully implemented in 41 percent of the cases studied, partially implemented in 18 percent, and not implemented in 41 percent.

3. WHAT AFFECTS THE LIKELIHOOD OF SUCCESS?

There are few absolutes in predicting whether parties involved in any specific dispute will be successful in reaching an agreement, or, if one is reached, in implementing it. There are several factors, however, that appear to increase the likelihood of success. A few important factors are described below. The first three of these are based on qualitative observations, others are backed up by more quantitative analysis, but all remain hypotheses that require further study.

A particularly important reason for the relatively high success rate in the dispute resolution efforts documented for this study probably is that, as an accepted part of professional practice, the mediators conducted dispute assessments at the beginning of each case as a first step in helping the parties decide whether to proceed with a voluntary dispute resolution process and, if so, what the nature and the ground rules of the process should be. Environmental disputes are so varied that different forms of assistance are appropriate in different cases, depending on the circumstances and the wishes of the parties. Mediators spend time discussing the possibility of a voluntary dispute resolution process with each of the parties, identifying and bringing to the parties' attention those conditions that may make it difficult to resolve the dispute, and helping the parties decide how they wish to proceed. Logically, this initial screening, if done well, will improve the likelihood that, once an informed decision to negotiate has been made, the parties will be successful in reaching an agreement. Until comparable samples of negotiated settlements without the assistance of mediators are available, however, this will remain a hypothesis.

The parties must have some incentive to negotiate an agreement with one another. The willingness of all parties to a dispute to participate is a major factor in the success of a voluntary dispute resolution process, if one expects an agreement reached to be both fair and stable. But the parties are unlikely to participate, let alone agree to a settlement, if they can achieve more of what they want in another way. It is difficult to assess the importance of such incentives, however, because it is hard to measure relative incentives and because this study does not include cases in which the parties lacked sufficient incentives to agree to participate in a dispute resolution effort. Mediators generally do not convene negotiations unless the parties are at least somewhat interested in attempting to resolve the dispute.

The way the negotiation or consensus-building process is conducted also appears to be an important factor in whether agreements are reached. Mediators often refer to the difference between "interest-based" negotiation and "positional" bargaining in discussing what makes negotiations effective. In particular, the ability (and willingness) of the parties to identify the interests that underlie one another's positions, and to invent new alternatives that satisfy these interests, helps enormously in resolving disputes. Again, it is difficult to evaluate how well a negotiation or consensus-building process is conducted. And, at times, the parties can find no common ground regardless of their skill in negotiating with one another or the assistance of a mediator.

Among the factors that can be more easily measured, the likelihood of success is not clearly affected by the number of parties involved in the dispute, the issues themselves, or the presence of a deadline. There is no evidence among the cases studied that a larger number of parties makes reaching agreement more difficult. In fact, the average number of parties for cases in which the parties failed to reach an agreement was lower than the average number of parties in cases in which agreements were reached. It should be noted, however, that the preliminary dispute assessments conducted by most mediators may have screened out many cases in which a large number of parties may have reduced the likelihood of success, thus affecting the sample of cases studied. Also, the evidence does not show that the issues in dispute have a significant effect on the likelihood of success. More study, done perhaps at a more detailed level, may show different results. The influence that the kind of issue has on the likelihood of success also may be linked to other factors, such as whether the particular dispute has precedent-setting implications. Finally, although many mediators report that deadlines are helpful in creating incentives to reach agreement, the data in this study do not indicate that the presence of a deadline by itself affects the likelihood of reaching an agreement.

The most significant, measurable factor in the likelihood of success in implementing agreements appears to be whether those with the authority to implement the decision participated directly in the process. For site-specific disputes, when those with the authority to implement decisions were directly involved, the implementation rate was 85 percent; when they were not, only 67 percent of the agreements reached were fully implemented. Agreements were not implemented in about 7 percent of the cases in both categories. The difference in the implementation results is that when those with the authority to implement the recommendations were not at the table, the terms of the agreement were more likely to be modified. Agreements were partially implemented in about 27 percent of the cases in which those with the authority to implement the agreements were not at the table as compared with 7 percent of the cases in which those at the table had the authority to implement their agreements.

Few factors are absolute preconditions for success. In many situations, the combined positive effect of some factors can offset potentially negative factors. For example, the parties may have sufficient incentives to try to reach agreement even if they have no specific deadline to do so. Also, many factors may be subject to modification by the parties and the mediator before and during the dispute resolution process. For example, for some cases in which the absence of a deadline may be a significant factor, perhaps because other incentives to reach agreement are insufficient, one or more of the parties may be able to create a deadline. If one side lacks sufficient incentives to negotiate, another may raise the ante with positive assurances about implementation, mitigation, or compensation offers contingent on an agreement, or with reminders of ways the dispute could be escalated. If there are an overwhelming number of parties, coalitions, workshop-style meetings, or other changes in the approach may be possible. Or, if those with power to implement the agreement are not direct participants in the process, the mediator may be able to provide an appropriate link between the parties and the eventual decision maker.

4. HOW EFFICIENT ARE ENVIRONMENTAL DISPUTE RESOLUTION PROCESSES?

Perhaps the single most common assertion made about environmental dispute resolution processes—indeed, about alternative dispute resolution processes generally—is that they are cheaper and faster than litigation. There has been little empirical evidence to support this assertion, however. Very little information exists about how long it takes either to mediate or to litigate environmental disputes, and there are several conceptual problems in making comparisons between environmental dispute resolution alternatives and litigation.

Most individuals and organizations involved in environmental disputes can cite at least one occasion in which the parties became so locked in a protracted legal battle that there seemed to be no way out. These stories have helped build the case for the weakness in relying solely on litigation for settling disputes, but they also may have oversimplified common concepts both about litigation and about environmental dispute resolution alternatives. A lawsuit that gocs to trial may take a very long time, but few lawsuits go to trial. Many mediated environmental disputes have been resolved quickly, but voluntary dispute resolution processes are not necessarily fast if the issues are complex. In addition, although mediators generally charge less than attorneys, this does not necessarily mean that one can be substituted for the other. It is also important to consider other costs associated with resolving disputes. The costs of preparing for negotiation, for example, may be as high as or higher than the costs of preparing for some kinds of litigation, particularly for public interest groups.

The major conceptual problem in asking whether environmental dispute resolution processes are really cheaper and faster than litigation is the problem of finding samples of the two approaches that are sufficiently comparable to each other. It also can be misleading to take a case that was first litigated and then mediated and to compare the costs in money and time spent on each approach. One problem, particularly in the latter approach, is that it is unrealistic in many situations to begin counting the costs of mediation at the time that the parties agreed to negotiate, if the previous period of contention, litigation, or clarification of relative power contributed to the parties' willingness to negotiate a voluntary settlement. A simple comparison of costs also leaves out a major part of the equation—the nature and quality of the outcome. A more efficient process may not be more desirable if it leads to significantly poorer decisions in the view of one or all of the parties.

Environmental disputes, on the average, do take longer to resolve through litigation than do civil suits generally, although the median durations of both are relatively short.* For example, the median number of months from filing to disposition of all civil cases in U.S. district courts terminated in the 12-month period ending June 30, 1983, was 7 months, whereas for the same period the median duration of all environmental cases was 10 months. For cases that went to trial, the median duration of civil suits generally was 19 months; for environmental disputes, it was 23 months.

More interesting than the median duration of these lawsuits, however, is the range among the cases: of all civil litigation in this sample 10 percent took more than 28 months from the time of filing to disposition; 10 percent of the environmental litigation took more than 42 months. For those cases that went to trial, 10 percent of the environmental cases took longer than 67 months—or over five and a half years—not counting any possible appeals to a higher court. It is likely, therefore, that it is the *threat* of protracted litigation, not the length of the standard case, that creates the popular conception that mediation is faster than litigation.

In documenting environmental dispute resolution cases for this book, some information was available about how much time the dispute resolution process took. This information is not complete, but one can get a general idea about the duration of cases. Not only

---

*The following data were compiled specially for this study by the Federal Judicial Center.

is this information incomplete, it is definitely *not* comparable to the statistics about litigation given above. Keeping that in mind, the median duration of the environmental dispute resolution cases in this sample was between 5 and 6 months, and 10 percent of the cases took over 18 months to resolve. Information about the costs of these cases is too sparse to report with any confidence.

5. LOOKING AHEAD TO THE NEXT DECADE

During the next 10 years, it will be important to identify and put into practice mechanisms that will encourage the use of environmental dispute resolution processes, increase the likelihood that disputes will be resolved successfully, and protect the parties from potential abuses of these processes. To accomplish this without losing the flexibility that is an inherent part of the strength of voluntary dispute resolution processes will be a challenge. In addition, several important questions remain unanswered. How will the services of mediators be funded? Can citizen groups and public interest organizations afford to use these processes? To whom are mediators accountable, to whom should they be accountable, and how should such accountability be maintained?

In the future, the institutional mechanisms for implementing environmental dispute resolution processes are likely to include: a continuation of the role that independent mediators now play in responding to the needs of parties on an ad hoc basis; court-referred or court-linked programs; mediation services provided by local, state, or federal agencies; and the incorporation of voluntary dispute resolution procedures into state or federal statutes. These options are not mutually exclusive, but the choices do have important implications with respect to who pays the mediator, to how these processes become widely available, to the flexibility of the approach, to the accountability of the mediator, and, ultimately, to how successful voluntary dispute resolution processes will be as an innovation in public decision making for environmental issues.

During the first decade in which mediators helped parties to environmental disputes resolve issues directly with one another, the mediators' services were paid for principally by foundation grants. Corporate donations, government contracts, in-kind support from citizen groups and public interest organizations, and fees made up the rest. For the most part, however, the mediators' services were free of charge to the parties. The question of how these services will continue to be paid is pressing. Foundation officials and others in the field raise a legitimate question: has this first decade of experience established the value of mediation services sufficiently that someone, the government or the parties themselves, is willing to pay for them? The data in this report begin to provide a basis for making such an evaluation. Looking ahead, additional case experience along with institutional mechanisms to encourage the resolution of environmental and other public policy disputes will create a framework for a more detailed assessment of environmental dispute resolution processes.

Introduction

The stories have a familiar ring. A rapidly growing western city finds that, each time it attempts to obtain additional water supplies, the proposed project ignites tremendous controversy. A town's municipal landfill reaches capacity, with the chance of polluting a nearby river; a new site is chosen, but the community adjacent to the proposed new site threatens legal action. A utility company is caught between conflicting pressures—one government agency requiring it to burn coal instead of oil in a power plant, another preventing it from using coal unless expensive air pollution control equipment is installed, and consumer groups protesting rate increases. A large mining company moves to develop an open-pit uranium mine in a national forest and is challenged by environmentalists.

Such controversies make frequent headlines across the United States. These particular stories, however, have an unusual ending. Rather than proceeding to the courtroom or ending in stalemate, the parties to these disputes resolved their disagreements through direct negotiation, with the assistance of a neutral mediator.

Since 1973, when two mediators were invited by the governor of Washington State to help settle a dispute over a proposed flood-control dam,[1] mediators have been employed in over 160 environmental disputes in the United States. Compared to 1973, when only two individuals were beginning to develop a mediation practice for environmental disputes, there are now organizations and individuals in at least 15 states, the District of Columbia, and Canada offering environmental mediation services. Others, elsewhere, are also attempting to establish similar practices.

In addition, and relatively recently, the practice of environmental dispute resolution has grown beyond the resolution of disputes on a case-by-case basis to the institutionalization, by statute, of procedures for resolving environmental disputes through negotiation, mediation, and arbitration. Statutes in Massachusetts, Rhode Island, Texas, Virginia, and Wisconsin authorize or even require negotiation of solid waste and hazardous waste siting disputes.[2] A statute in Virginia specifies procedures for negotiation and mediation of

1

intergovernmental disputes triggered by annexation proposals.[3] And, in mid-1985, the Pennsylvania legislature was considering legislation proposed a few years earlier to authorize mediation of any local land-use or zoning dispute.[4]

The motivation to find alternatives to traditional dispute resolution processes for controversial environmental issues has come principally from the discontent of the parties with certain aspects of traditional adversarial processes. When decisions in a dispute are seen as choices between winners and losers or when decisions are based on narrow procedural grounds, the interests of one, and sometimes all, of the parties to the dispute often remain unsatisfied. Instead, environmental disputes usually need solutions that make both good economic and good environmental sense. Parties also may be dissatisfied with the time and expense of protracted disputes. Some are frustrated when disputes delay new plans and proposals; others are frustrated when disputes delay solutions to environmental problems. Many parties also may be unhappy with their role in the decision-making process and their ability to affect its outcome. Innovation has occurred in environmental dispute resolution processes because of people's desires for more effective and efficient opportunities to find solutions to controversial environmental issues.

Although voluntary environmental dispute resolution processes are often characterized as alternatives to litigation—with the presumption that litigation is bad—they are better viewed as additional tools that might or might not be more effective or more efficient in particular circumstances than traditional processes such as litigation would be. In some cases, a voluntary dispute resolution process such as mediation may be a better alternative than litigation. Environmental dispute resolution approaches also may be useful when litigation isn't even an option. Voluntary dispute resolution processes may not always be appropriate, however, and often they may function better as supplements to legislative, administrative, or judicial processes. Disputes over environmental issues are so varied that no one dispute resolution process is likely to be successful in all situations. Depending on the circumstances and what each party hopes to achieve, the parties may prefer to litigate, to lobby for legislative change, to turn to an administrative agency, to negotiate a voluntary resolution of the issues with one another, or to engage in some combination of these options. This complicated strategic decision is, and should be, affected by applicable laws and regulations, by the experiences and resources of the parties, and by those parties' calculations of how well their interests will be served using different dispute resolution approaches.

This book documents the development of environmental dispute resolution alternatives and assesses whether the results have met initial hopes and expectations. What are the different approaches to environmental dispute resolution? What have these approaches sought to achieve, and how successful have they been? What kinds of disputes have been resolved? Who have the parties to these disputes been? How much do alternative dispute resolution approaches cost? How much time have cases taken to be resolved? What other lessons have been learned from the experience to date?

The purpose of this book is to begin to answer these questions. This is not, however, an evaluation of individual mediators or their practices, nor is it a manual on how to mediate environmental disputes. Rather, it is an attempt to describe and assess the overall track record of innovative dispute resolution processes for resolving controversial environmental issues.

This book is intended for anyone interested in finding better ways of addressing controversial environmental issues. It is written particularly for the men and women in government agencies, private corporations, and public interest groups who are responsible for making decisions that affect the environment and who often find themselves in dispute. It is hoped that information about environmental dispute resolution alternatives and an analysis of how well these approaches have worked in the past will provide them with a better basis for considering new options for engaging in conflict productively.[5]

Some of the most common, and deceptively simple, questions that people ask about the practice of environmental dispute resolution are "Does it work?" "Has it been successful?" and "What are some examples of successful cases?" These questions are particularly difficult to answer, because people have very different expectations about what success means. Individual examples of environmental mediation have shown dramatic results.[6] What about the larger picture, however? What is the overall record?

To do such an assessment first requires identifying the cases that make up the track record of the environmental dispute resolution field. Defining what is or is not an environmental dispute resolution case has been troublesome. The practices among those who call themselves environmental mediators differ significantly in the objectives set and in the style or characteristics of the processes used, although these professionals all are engaged in helping those directly affected by a problem, a project, or a policy to work together toward a voluntary resolution of the issues that divide them. This diversity of practice may be inherent in the attempt to be innovative, which characterizes the field as a whole, but it makes deciding what is and is not part of the history and record of this field more difficult.

Given the variation among environmental disputes, the variation in dispute resolution approaches is not so surprising. Environmental disputes arise over broad policies as well as specific projects. Sometimes, there are two parties; sometimes, dozens. Parties may be well-organized companies, government agencies, or environmental groups, as well as loosely knit associations or coalitions. The relative power of the parties may vary considerably, as may the legal, economic, or political constraints within which they must act. In some cases, the parties may have publicly taken well defined and polarized positions on the issues, while in other cases there may be only the recognition that a problem exists and that agreeing on a solution is likely to be difficult.

Also, the mediators themselves come from different professional backgrounds—law, labor relations, planning, science, natural resource management, and business. Their perspectives on what is needed to improve public decision making in controversial settings influence the dispute resolution approaches they recommend. Many mediators, for example, find the concept of *dispute* resolution itself too limiting, particularly because they often help groups deal with controversial problems before they become disputes.

Finally, the characteristics and objectives of environmental dispute resolution approaches are affected by what the parties perceive will benefit their interests in a specific situation. In some cases, for example, parties have not been willing to engage in formal negotiations but have wanted the opportunity to exchange information with each other and to clarify the issues in a dispute. In other cases, the reverse has been true—at least one of the parties has felt that it was not worth the effort to meet unless the other parties were willing to attempt to reach a binding agreement to settle the dispute.

Although several attempts have been made to develop a conceptual framework that clearly distinguishes different environmental dispute resolution processes,[7] no generally accepted framework has yet been devised. As a result, individuals and organizations involved in this field use different terms for similar approaches and similar terms for different approaches. This report does not attempt to resolve the problem of definitions, however, in part because this problem is not merely one of semantics but, rather, one of how to most usefully understand what the important characteristics of these processes are. It is hoped that this report will add to the foundations on which more clearly articulated theory can be built in the future. Further analytical work that distinguishes, describes, and evaluates different processes is needed.

The term *environmental dispute resolution* is used in this report to refer collectively to a variety of approaches that allow the parties to meet face to face in an effort to reach a mutually acceptable resolution of the issues in a dispute or potentially controversial situation. Although there are significant differences among environmental dispute resolution approaches, all are voluntary processes that involve some form of consensus building, joint problem solving, or negotiation. Litigation, administrative procedures, and arbitration are not included in this definition or in the scope of this study because the objective in these processes is not a consensus among the parties.

Environmental dispute resolution processes can occur with or without the assistance of a neutral "third party." The term *negotiation* is used in this report to refer to direct interactions among the parties. *Mediation* is the assistance of a neutral "third party" to a negotiation. Over the last decade, the number of experienced neutral intervenors has grown considerably. Some call themselves *mediators*; others, *facilitators*. Because the distinctions are very blurred in practice, however, only the term *mediator* is used in this report.

Although cases are not separated in this report by different dispute resolution styles or processes, it is possible to describe and assess cases on the basis of factors other than distinctions among approaches. Useful characteristics for studying cases include, among others, the objectives of the processes, whether the disputes were over site-specific or policy issues, who the parties were, and whether mediators were involved.

Cases are included in this study if the parties had agreed to participate in any dispute resolution process that fit within the general definition above, if there was at least one joint meeting among the parties (as an indication of a good faith effort to attempt to resolve the controversy), and if a mediator was involved. The only exceptions to this are a few cases in which a documented settlement was reached among parties who never met face-to-face but participated in a kind of "shuttle diplomacy" by the mediator.

Even this relatively simple, observational approach is not without limitations, however. Several important forms of dispute resolution are left out in the interest of defining a study that is both manageable and clear. For example, by using the criterion that at least one joint meeting took place as a way to define a case, the study omits hundreds of instances when mediators assisted parties simply by a series of telephone calls or separate meetings, which may have enabled the parties to clarify the issues or to agree on a procedure for resolving their dispute without involving the mediator further. Unfortunately, although such assistance is a valuable part of the service mediators provide, these cases are extremely difficult to document.

Further, because this study is limited to those cases in which a mediator was involved, it excludes cases in which the parties negotiated a resolution of the issues on their own—including, for example, the vast majority of civil suits that are settled out of court by the parties, by their attorneys, or at the direction of the judge hearing the case. Many examples of valuable, creative negotiation without the assistance of a mediator can be found, but including them would have made this study unmanageable and would have deemphasized what is truly new in the repertoire of techniques for resolving environmental disputes—the assistance of a professional mediator.

It is relatively easy to know whether a joint meeting took place, but defining who can be called a mediator is more difficult. There has been, and will continue to be, an interesting and thoughtful debate in this field over distinctions between external, independent mediators and "inside mediators" who work for one of the parties but are instrumental in the resolution of many disputes.[8] Although inside mediators do indeed play an important role in resolving environmental disputes, a mediator is considered in this study to be someone who either has an independent reputation for operating as a "professional neutral" or who works for an organization that explicitly states that it offers neutral dispute resolution services. This more limited definition is used principally because the innovation that has occurred in resolving disputes has been not the role played by inside mediators but the intervention of independent mediators. In addition, the external, independent mediators are easier to identify. There are relatively few of them, compared to the thousands of professionals in government, consulting firms, law firms, public interest groups, businesses, and elsewhere who work diligently to resolve the environmental controversies in which their agencies, organizations, and companies frequently are parties.

Nearly all of the professional mediation organizations or independent mediators involved in environmental dispute resolution were contacted in collecting data for this report. Although, inevitably, some cases were missed, this study represents the most complete list of mediated, environmental dispute resolution cases available at this time. It is assumed in analyzing these cases that they provide a sufficiently comprehensive information base to represent the track record of the field as a whole.

Several methods for identifying cases to include in this study were used. Literature in the field was examined for all cases cited. The *Resolve* newsletter, which is published by The Conservation Foundation and edited by the author of this report, was particularly useful with its "updates" on specific cases since December 1978. In addition, letters were sent to all organizations in the United States that publicly offer mediation services in environmental disputes. These letters were followed by personal interviews with about 25 environmental mediators, through which additional cases were identified. Finally, a second round of letters was sent, listing the cases identified for each organization or individual and asking whether the list was complete.

This process resulted in the identification of 161 cases that, as of May 1984, met all the above criteria (figure 1). Of these cases, 115 involved controversies over site-specific issues, and 46 involved issues of environmental policy. The objectives set by the parties in each case were identified, and three categories of objectives were observed. The cases were then evaluated on the basis of how well those objectives were met. In 68 of the cases, the parties' objective was to reach a formal decision that resolved the dispute. This implies that those with the authority to make decisions were parties to the negotiations. In 64 cases, the objective was to reach a recommendation to the appropriate decision-making body on a resolution of

Figure 1
Distribution of Environmental Dispute Resolution Cases, by Objective

| | | Objective | | |
	All cases	To reach a decision	To agree on recommendations	To improve communications
Site-specific cases	115	64	35	16
Policy cases	46	4	29	13
Total cases	161	68	64	29

the issues that all the other parties concerned could support. In the remaining 29 cases, the objective was to improve communications among the parties.

It is important to point out that, although useful for evaluation purposes, separating environmental dispute resolution cases by these three objectives can be misleading. For example, reaching decisions or recommendations deals with the substantive issues in dispute, whereas improving communications deals with the relationships between the parties. Separating these objectives is not meant to imply that substantive objectives alone were important in some cases examined for this report and that relationship objectives alone were important in others. In practice, many dimensions of a dispute are important to the parties. In cases where the primary objective of a process was to reach a decision, the parties probably also intended to improve communications since communications between the parties almost necessarily must be improved for a settlement to be reached. Indeed, in settlement-oriented cases in which no agreement was reached, the parties often reported satisfaction with the mediation process because of the improved communications that occurred.[9] Similarly, parties to communication-oriented mediation attempts may have hoped that improved communications would increase the likelihood of a subsequent decision-making process resulting in a formal agreement.

The objective of a dispute resolution process was categorized as a decision when the parties at the table had the power to implement any agreements reached. For example, the East Bay Regional

Park District, located in the San Francisco metropolitan area, was involved in a dispute with park users and the communities adjacent to the Briones Regional Park over a proposed access road and recreation area. With the assistance of mediator Verne Huser, the parties reached an agreement on the road alignment and design of the access area. The park district had power of eminent domain, and all parties who could have sued to stop the project were involved in the negotiations. Once an agreement was signed and ratified, no other approval was necessary, and the park district could proceed to acquire the land and construct the access road.

A recommendation is distinguished from a decision in situations where the final decision-making body was not represented directly in the dispute resolution process. For example, the New England Environmental Mediation Center has mediated several disputes involving permits for small-scale hydroelectric projects. The Federal Energy Regulatory Commission (FERC) is responsible for issuing or denying such permits. The parties at the table in these negotiations have been the permit applicant and various groups or communities concerned about the effects of changing water levels, loss of white-water recreation opportunities, or disruption during construction. FERC staff have referred such cases to mediation but have chosen not to be involved in the negotiations. Thus, the negotiated agreements between the parties have been in the form of recommendations to FERC.

There is room for ambiguity in the distinction between decisions and recommendations. For example, in a dispute between the owners of a raceway and neighboring landowners over alleged noise violations, representatives of the state regulatory agency and the raceway negotiated proposed conditions for the operation of the raceway. The board of the regulatory agency rejected the agreement, however. Was this a recommendation that was reached but not implemented, or was it a decision that was not reached because it was not ratified? For purposes of this study, cases of this kind are put into the "decision" category and are considered a failure to reach an agreement, because the staff and board are part of the same organization. In only three cases in this study, however, did this apparently occur.

Local zoning disputes also may be ambiguous. For the most part, the land-use negotiations included in this study involved a developer and neighboring residents, with the agreement serving as a recommendation to the local city or county council. However, in a dispute described in chapter 1—the Hethwood Shopping Center case—the negotiations involved the director of the planning department in addition to the shopping center owner and a neighboring housing association. Both the planning commission and the city council had to approve the agreement. Both did approve the agreement, and it was successfully implemented. However, was the agreement a recommendation or a decision? It could be argued that the planning director represented the city in the negotiations and, thus, the objective of the process was to reach a decision. To be consistent with the other local zoning disputes in this study, however, agreements of this type are classified as recommendations by the planning department and its commission to the city council.

In a small number of cases, the parties at the table did represent organizations with the power to make decisions, but the process was explicitly designed to be informal. One example, the Metropolitan Water Roundtable, is described in chapter 1. In that case, the parties considered the agreements they reached to be recommendations. The organizations represented in the roundtable then implemented those agreements through separate, formal procedures. For example, cost-sharing contracts for a systemwide environmental impact statement and for a large water-storage project, required to implement parts of the consensus reached by the roundtable, were negotiated separately by the parties. The agreements in such cases also are considered in this report to be recommendations, because that was the intention of those involved.

In addition to classifying environmental dispute resolution attempts by their objectives, this report divides them by whether the issues involved were site-specific in nature or whether they principally concerned matters of general policy. A case was considered to be site-specific if it concerned a specific natural resource such as a river, lake, or island or a site that was defined by its proposed use. A case was considered to be a policy dispute if the area affected was designated by political boundaries such as a city, county, state, or the nation as a whole or if it involved a type of natural resource that occurs in many locations, such as all rivers.

Finally, although every effort has been made to portray these cases accurately, inevitably the stories look different in retrospect than they did at the time the dispute was being resolved. A distortion that is particularly hard to avoid is the tendency to oversimplify how difficult it was to resolve the dispute or even how difficult it may have been for the parties to agree even to participate in a dispute resolution attempt. The solution to a problem may look obvious once it has been found, but persons interviewed for this study frequently reported that getting from the problem to the solution often seemed next to impossible at the time.

Chapter 1 of this report describes the history and growth of the environmental dispute resolution field—the initial experiments with mediation in the early 1970s, the growth of new cases and new organizations based on the earlier successes, and the diversity of issues resolved as case experience has grown.

There are different points of view and different expectations for what environmental dispute resolution options could and should achieve. In chapter 2, several criteria that can be used to evaluate the success of environmental dispute resolution alternatives are discussed, and some of these criteria are applied to assess the success of these approaches.

In chapter 3, factors that are presumed to affect the likelihood of reaching a successful agreement are explored. Chapter 4 examines the expectation that voluntary dispute resolution processes will be more efficient than litigation, and chapter 5 concludes with a discussion of important issues and questions raised by this first decade of experience with environmental dispute resolution alternatives. For those interested in the case examples that form the basis of this study, short descriptions of some cases are included in an appendix. Disputes in which the parties failed to reach an agreement are not named, out of consideration for the parties and the confidentiality that mediators promise.

REFERENCES

1. Gerald W. Cormick, "Mediating Environmental Controversies: Perspectives and First Experience," *Earth Law Journal* 2 (1976):215-24.

2. Mass. Gen. Laws Ann. ch. 21D (Lawyers Coop. Supp. 1984); R.I. Gen. Laws sections 23-19.7-1 to 23-19.7-15 (1983); Code of Va., tit. 10, ch. 17.1, sections 10-186.1 - 10-186.21 and misc.; Wis. Stat. Ann. section 144.445 (West Supp. 1983-84).

3. Code of Virginia, section 15.1-945.7.

4. Pennsylvania Senate Bill 876.

5. This book is not organized as a teaching tool on how to negotiate more effectively, although it is hoped that the reader will learn a number of lessons from the past experience of others about factors that may influence whether a dispute

resolution attempt is likely to be successful. For those who would like to learn more about the process of successfully negotiating settlements of environmental disputes, Lawrence Bacow and Michael Wheeler have written a particularly thoughtful and analytical book entitled *Environmental Dispute Resolution* (New York: Plenum, 1985).

6. Although this is not intended to be a book of case studies, examples are described in the text to illustrate certain points. For detailed, in-depth accounts of mediated environmental disputes, see Allan R. Talbot, *Settling Things: Six Case Studies of Environmental Mediation* (Washington, D.C.: The Conservation Foundation, 1983); or Lawrence Susskind, Lawrence Bacow, and Michael Wheeler, *Resolving Environmental Regulatory Disputes* (Cambridge, Mass.: Schenkman, 1983).

7. Examples of different ways to define and to organize environmental dispute resolution processes include: Howard Bellman et al., "Environmental Conflict Resolution: Practitioners Perspective of an Emerging Field," *Environmental Consensus*, Winter 1981 (now published as *Resolve*); Gerald W. Cormick, "The 'Theory' and Practice of Environmental Mediation," *Environmental Professional* 2 (1980):24-23; Susan L. Carpenter and W. John D. Kennedy, "Environmental Conflict Management," training materials developed for the U.S. Department of the Interior (1981); and Lawrence Susskind and Sebastian Persico, "Guide to Consensus Development and Dispute Resolution Techniques for Use in Government-Industry Conflicts," prepared for the American Law Institute-American Bar Association Conference on Environmental Law, February 23-25, 1984.

8. Howard Bellman and Bruce Dotson, "The Case For and Against the 'Inside' Mediator," *Resolve*, Spring 1982.

9. Leonard G. Buckle et al., "Evaluation of the New England Environmental Mediation Center," January 1984, unpublished.

Chapter 1

The Growth of the Environmental Dispute Resolution Field

As with most social innovations, the emergence of alternative approaches to resolving environmental disputes can be traced to several independent sources—several concepts, several people, several locations. Although this study begins with the first mediated environmental dispute reported in this country, the roots of environmental dispute resolution approaches go back to dispute resolution concepts in other fields. Lawsuits are concluded more often by settlement negotiations than by trial. Planners have built their profession on public involvement techniques as well as on data analysis and design principles, and the role of the mediator has been well established in international affairs and labor management disputes. In the 1960s, mediators began adapting their practices to community disputes, which contained some of the problems of multiple parties and unequal power that many mediators would later encounter in many environmental disputes.

BEGINNING EFFORTS

Early environmental mediators individually pioneered new ways of resolving controversial environmental issues, often without knowing of each other's work until their practices had been under way for some time. Some mediators began their efforts by concentrating on certain kinds of issues, such as energy questions, toxic chemicals, or water policy. Others specialized in specific geographic regions. Either way, the mediators first had to create an awareness about dispute resolution alternatives among those who were involved in environmental disputes in their topical or geographic area and then establish a track record on which to build a mediation practice. Although a few of the earliest cases are described below, other pioneers in the environmental dispute resolution field are acknowledged in subsequent sections of this report.

Mediated Negotiations

In the early 1970s, the Ford Foundation was actively supporting the work of mediation groups trying to help neighborhoods and communities resolve local disputes, particularly those involving public interest law, civil rights, and minority issues. Among the mediators being supported by the foundation was Gerald W. Cormick. In 1972, Cormick wrote a memo to Stanley Brezenoff, the foundation's program officer in charge of community mediation grants, commenting that environmental disputes appeared to be on the increase and asking whether mediation's potential in resolving environmental disputes might be worth exploring. Eventually, the memo reached Jane McCarthy, a consultant to Ford's environment program, who recalls, "I was ecstatic about the idea." For the next six months, she and Cormick talked with government officials, environmental leaders, and corporate executives about whether mediation might be useful in the disputes they were encountering. The reaction was so positive that the foundation asked Cormick and McCarthy to try the process out.

In 1973, after talking with parties in a number of disputes around the country, without getting a mediation process started, they went to the state of Washington and talked to officials about environmental controversies there. Following the mediators' initially favorable explorations, Governor Daniel J. Evans invited them to help settle a long-standing dispute over a proposed flood-control dam on the Snoqualmie River. The controversy contained two elements essential to mediation attempts—the issues were seemingly intractable, and the parties were willing to try something new. There were few, if any, precedents to follow, either for the mediators or the parties. By December 1974, however, an agreement was signed in which the dam was moved from the middle fork of the river to the north fork, additional flood-control measures were suggested, new land-use controls were recommended, and a basinwide coordinating council was proposed.[2]

Much has been made of that first mediated dispute, more perhaps than anyone involved would have liked. The agreed-upon dam has never been constructed. But many of the land-use recommendations have been implemented, and the recently disbanded coordinating council existed for about ten years. Perhaps most important, the mere fact of the agreement was enough to inspire individuals from across the United States with the idea that controversial environmental disputes could be settled through mediation.

Soon after the Snoqualmie agreement was reached, Leah Patton joined Cormick to found the Office of Environmental Mediation at the University of Washington (now The Mediation Institute). In February 1976, Governor Evans turned to the mediators again for assistance in a tough, 12-year-old dispute.[3] Interstate 90 (I-90) was being widened and improved across the state, but it looked as though the new highway would simply stop at the suburban community of Bellevue, on the east side of Lake Washington, rather than continue into Seattle. Because heavy commuter traffic on the existing four-lane bridge and highway between Seattle and Bellevue was already congested, Bellevue strongly supported the construction of a new bridge and much wider bridge to extend the I-90 improvements into Seattle. The number of new lanes advocated changed over time as the dispute dragged on, but original proposals were to construct an additional, ten-lane bridge parallel to the existing four-lane bridge. Residents of Mercer Island, a relatively small town on an island of the same name, were torn between the problems of the current bottleneck and the impacts of widening the highway, which crossed the north end of their community. And neighborhood and environmental groups in Seattle—concerned about the impacts of the expanded highway on the neighborhoods through which it would pass, the increased car traffic in the downtown, and the absence of mass-transit alternatives in the overall project design as proposed by the state highway department—opposed the project vigorously.

With the governor's sanction, Cormick and Patton met with all the parties during February and March 1976. Out of those meetings, there emerged an agreement that Seattle, Bellevue, Mercer Island, King County (in which all three cities are located), the Washington

State Department of Transportation, and METRO, the regional sewer and transportation authority, would attempt to negotiate a resolution of the issues. Neighborhood and environmental groups in Seattle decided to participate indirectly through the Seattle City Council.

Resolving the issues was not easy. The Seattle City Council was firm that it wanted no more than six lanes of automobile traffic, three going each way, with two additional lanes set aside for mass transit. Bellevue was equally firm that it needed eight lanes for automobile traffic. A clever compromise emerged in September: Ten lanes would be built from Bellevue to Mercer Island, with two of them reserved for mass transit. On the island, two of the automobile lanes would disappear. In addition, residents of Mercer Island, who in the earliest proposals would have had the old four-lane bridge to Seattle for themselves, would get free access onto the mass-transit lanes during rush hour. Thus, in theory, Seattle would get the desired eight-lane highway, with six automobile and two mass-transit lanes. The Seattle City Council, however, rejected the proposal, pointing out that they would still be getting the equivalent of four lanes of traffic coming into the city, since automobiles from Mercer Island would be traveling on the transit lanes.

Negotiations through October were difficult. Mercer Island officials appealed to Governor Evans for assistance, but he refused to impose a solution. Instead, he suggested that, if the three jurisdictions could not agree, he might recommend that the available federal funds be transferred to a project in another part of the state. This raised the stakes for the involved communities, and, on November 1, Seattle offered a compromise—Mercer Island drivers could use the transit lanes, so long as traffic didn't slow to less than 45 miles per hour. This could be ensured by using a gate-controlled on-ramp. Bellevue concurred, and a meeting scheduled for November 3, 1976, at which the parties had expected to end the negotiations without a solution, became a drafting session for the details of an agreement.

By December 1976, the five parties had signed an agreement on a modified highway improvement plan that included mass-transit proposals and recommendations for solving related, regionwide transportation problems. Implementation of the agreement was slowed for six years, however, first by an unsuccessful lawsuit filed by neighborhood and environmental groups on the grounds that the environmental impact statement was inadequate and then by a freeze on federal highway funds. Nevertheless, most parts of the agreement had been implemented by mid-1985. Construction of the I-90 improvements, begun in late 1983, was scheduled to be completed by 1993.

Policy Dialogues

Although in the mid-1970s environmental policy debates in Washington, D.C., were extremely polarized, two individuals, Francis X. Murray and Sam Gusman, each thought that something constructive could be done by bringing environmental and business leaders together to discuss issues that appeared to divide them.

Murray, then conducting energy policy seminars at Georgetown University's Center for Strategic and International Studies (CSIS), was approached by Gerald Decker, then director of energy programs at Dow Chemical Company, and Lawrence Moss, past president of the Sierra Club.[4] Decker, concerned about the rising cost of oil and gas, was looking to coal for his company's long-term energy needs, but it was clear that a major increase in the use of coal in the United States would cause controversies with environmental groups. Rather than assuming that congressional battles or litigation were inevitable, however, he suggested to Moss that they at least make an effort to resolve the differences both knew they had. In 1976, after exploring the idea with their various colleagues, Decker and Moss turned to CSIS to provide an institutional home for a consensus-building forum on coal policy.

Out of these initial discussions grew the five-year National Coal Policy Project—one of the most visible early efforts at reaching consensus among business and environmental leaders on a major environmental policy issue.[5] During its course, the project involved 105 participants, either in plenary sessions or in task-force meetings. Working through nine task-force groups, the participants addressed more than 200 specific issues.

The participants were able to reach agreement on nearly 90 percent of those issues, but, since then, few of the project results have been implemented successfully.[6] In addition, some environmental leaders who did not participate in the process have strongly criticized the outcome.[7] Nevertheless, as in the Snoqualmie case, the most significant contribution of the National Coal Policy Project may have been the precedent it set, demonstrating that there might be less confrontational and more cooperative ways to deal with controversial environmental issues. According to Murray, "The most frequently cited accomplishment of the National Coal Policy Project was that it demonstrated a new process whereby individuals of opposing viewpoints could rationally discuss the issues until some agreement was reached."[8]

Independently, during 1976, Gusman, who had worked in research and management with the Rohm & Haas Corporation and had headed that company's Washington, D.C., governmental affairs office, began to contact leaders in both the chemical industry and the environmental community whom he had met during the often bitter debate over passage of the Toxic Substances Control Act (TSCA). Gusman recognized that the regulatory policies needed at that time to implement TSCA were likely to be as controversial as the passage of the act itself had been, when environmentalists and chemical industry leaders met only in hearing rooms and, even then, only listened to each other's separate testimony. Gusman saw an opportunity to do things differently during the development of regulations under TSCA. His idea was to create opportunities for dialogue on specific regulatory policy issues, through which leaders from both sides could develop clearer understandings of what the other side hoped to achieve, discover hidden areas of agreement, clarify disagreements, and perhaps, with time, work out new policy options that both sides could support.

In calling a preliminary meeting of about 10 chemical industry and environmental group leaders, Gusman encountered the same reaction from everyone—strong skepticism that anyone else would come to such a meeting, but "if you do get a meeting together, let me know." So, he let everyone know, and they all came. Their first advice was to find an existing organization that had credibility with business leaders, environmental advocates, and public officials to provide an institutional home for the activity, rather than to begin a new organization. William K. Reilly, president of The Conservation Foundation, had been an early advocate of the need to find common ground in the development of national environmental policy. Under his leadership, The Conservation Foundation, which in 1975 had launched a program on business and the environment, agreed to sponsor these dialogues.

Beginning in early 1977, under the Foundation's auspices, Gusman began facilitating regular meetings between representatives from environmental groups and chemical manufacturers. Initially, the original group of individuals saw itself as a policy dialogue group. Later, it became a steering committee to identify promising issues for dialogue, and participants for each dialogue group were identified separately. In contrast with the breadth of the National Coal Policy Project, participants in these dialogues discussed specific regulatory policy issues that arose under TSCA. "The participants wanted to identify a series of issues," Gusman remembers. "At the beginning, they decided to pick an issue that was not unduly divisive, so that a pattern of learning to work together would emerge."[9] The first issue the original dialogue group addressed was the extent of the need to train toxicologists and the creation of an appropriate civil service classification for them. Agreement was reached quickly; and, with the favorable response received from the National Research Council Commission on Human Resources and from the American Chemical Society, the participants became more confident in the possibilities of cooperation.

The second issue with which the dialogue group dealt was far more complicated and controversial—guidelines for testing new chemicals. The objective was to agree on an approach for testing the potential effects of chemical substances on health and the environment. The dialogue group invited a separate group of individuals from the chemical industry and environmental community to participate in a technical subcommittee. Dr. A. Karim Ahmed of the Natural Resources Defense Council and Dr. George Dominguez of CIBA-GEIGY were selected as cochairmen of the subcommittee, with Gusman as facilitator.

The 18-member subcommittee met twice in late 1977 and early 1978, with most of the work done in small group meetings and through correspondence. The result was a preliminary report in February 1978 in which the subcommittee proposed a concept of "tier-testing"—minimizing expensive tests on chemicals that were shown to be relatively benign in basic tests but encouraging much more sophisticated and detailed testing of other chemicals if preliminary tests so indicated.

This preliminary draft was discussed at two general meetings, one in March and the other in April 1978, to which a much larger group of individuals concerned about public policy for testing chemicals was invited. Although comments were generally favorable, unanimous agreement among all participants was not reached at these meetings. The dialogue group invited individuals with a broad range of perspectives to write letters commenting on the draft, which it then included in the final report it submitted to the U.S. Environmental Protection Agency (EPA) in July 1978. EPA did not immediately adopt the tier-testing concept, however, preferring to develop its own policies. The tier-testing concept did appear in EPA guidelines in late 1980, but with the change of administrations in 1981, the concept was dropped.*

The National Coal Policy Project and The Conservation Foundation's policy dialogues were not the only early experiments with policy dialogues. In 1976, the Center for Energy Policy (now the Center for Negotiation and Public Policy) in Boston convened a group of power-company officials and regulators from the New England states to discuss converting power plants from oil to coal. This led to the mediation of a site-specific dispute over conversion of the New England Power Company's Brayton Point power plant.[10] The Keystone Center in Colorado, founded in the mid-1970s with the specific intent to encourage dialogue on national policy issues, convened their first major policy dialogue on options for high-level radioactive waste disposal in 1979.[11]

Participants in most early policy dialogues served as individuals, not as official representatives of their organizations. The members' organizations were not expected to lobby on behalf of the consensus, although the participants were selected in part because they represented key points of view. The assumption was that, if a consensus emerged among a group of respected individuals representing a broad range of views, it would indicate where a broader consensus among others holding those views might lie. Representatives of government agencies were not invited, because it was felt that their absence would encourage business and environmental leaders to speak more freely to each other. At that time, everyone involved assumed that, because a regulatory agency would be looking for policy options that had a broad basis of support, implementing an agreement would not present insurmountable obstacles even though the agency was not directly involved in the discussion. Implemen-

---

*During this period, tier-testing also became a key element in Organization for Economic Cooperation and Development policy, but whether this could be credited to the dialogue group is unclear.

tation turned out to be more difficult than expected, however, leading the mediators and participants to work more closely with government officials during all phases of policy dialogues. The extension of this relationship—incorporation of negotiation into the administrative rule-making process—was proposed as early as 1980.[12]

Information Exchanges and Joint Problem Solving

At about the same time, the Rocky Mountain Center on the Environment (now ACCORD Associates[13]), in Colorado, then primarily a public policy research institute, began serving as a facilitator for the exchange of information among diverse interests in environmental and natural resources controversies.[14] The organization had been founded in 1968 by three individuals who were highly regarded in both industry and the environmental community[15] and who had seen a need for a forum for objective research and a broad exchange of views on environmental issues in the Rocky Mountain states.

Led by W. John D. Kennedy, who became executive director in 1974, and Susan Carpenter, who arrived as assistant director in 1976, ACCORD added another dimension to environmental dispute resolution, which was to bring individuals and groups together early in a planning or decision-making process to exchange information and improve their ability to anticipate and resolve potential conflicts before a polarized dispute occurred. Kennedy, for example, put together a meeting between Conoco's senior management and environmental leaders in Colorado, which, he says, oil-industry executives "still recall . . . as a turning point in establishing that communication between industry and environmentalists was possible."[16] That meeting was the first of several information exchanges that ACCORD staff facilitated in the mid-1970s to encourage more open and constructive discussion of environmental issues among individuals, organizations, and corporations that previously had been unable to talk directly with each other. At a meeting in Denver, the Colowyo Coal Company shared its plans for a new mine with Colorado environmental leaders. In Salt Lake City at another meeting, Plateau Resources provided information to concerned Utah residents about a proposed uranium mine.[17]

Particularly noteworthy among ACCORD's early efforts to improve the ability of individuals and groups with potentially conflicting interests or views to work together in solving problems was the Delta County Quality of Life Project.[18] In the mid-1970s, Delta County, Colorado, stood on the verge of rapid economic and population growth. When as many as 10 mining companies announced plans to open new coal mines or expand existing mines in the area, some residents became concerned about the effects that rapid growth might have on the county's resources and agricultural economy.

The Delta County League of Women Voters contacted ACCORD in January 1977, to explore how the county might prepare in advance for the problems of rapid growth. Of particular concern to league members were the lack of cohesiveness among residents of the county and the absence of a strong county government to manage problems. The county's population of approximately 19,000 was distributed between six relatively isolated towns and rural areas, and the county had no professional administrator or planner and only a volunteer planning commission. In addition, league members felt that there was growing polarization between county residents who favored growth and those who opposed it, and they were concerned that this would only make planning more difficult.

After preliminary meetings with community leaders, ACCORD and the Delta County League of Women Voters decided to cosponsor a one-day workshop to encourage a dialogue on the issues and to develop a joint vision of how the county should grow. To encourage the broadest perspective in planning the workshop, ACCORD and the league established a steering committee that met regularly and was open to any county resident interested in participating. The fact that local people took the lead in establishing the committee probably was a key factor in its ultimate success. Committee members began by identifying their goals and the issues they wanted to stress. After agreeing that one of their primary goals was to bring the people of the county together, they planned a meeting of leaders from all interests in the community to discuss preliminary plans for what became known as the "Quality of Life" workshop. Only 20 people showed up at that meeting, apparently in part because several organizations held meetings on the same night. Nevertheless, the steering committee and ACCORD decided to continue their plans for the workshop. Although early difficulties were encountered in attracting interest and in convincing local businesses, public interest groups, town governments, and the county to lend their public support to the project, it is the contrast between these obstacles and the subsequent results of the workshop that perhaps best illustrates how successful the slow process of building community cohesiveness actually was.

To get outside funding for the project, the steering committee needed local endorsements. One county resident, Edwina Eastman, recalls spending "hours on the phone, because there was such distrust in the county that a lot of people wouldn't have anything to do with it. . . . They wouldn't trust us, and in no way would they let their name be used as a sponsor."[19] Eventually, however, Eastman and the steering committee were successful in obtaining endorsements from 29 organizations, including the Delta County Commissioners.

Workshop planning and publicity were done by the steering committee members themselves, with ACCORD's assistance. According to a 1981 follow-up study of this effort:

> The publicity campaign before the workshop was especially interesting and probably contributed substantially to the workshop's success. In addition to the standard advertisements for the workshop in newspapers, radio, and television, the steering committee researched and wrote a number of informative articles about the issues to be discussed at the workshop and got them published in several local newspapers weekly for about three months before the workshop itself. . . .
>
> In addition to the articles, a local high school student worked with the steering committee to develop a slide show on the quality of life topic, illustrating the diverse character of Delta county and its residents, and showing what changes could be coming to Delta county in the future. The slide show was shown to local clubs and other organizations . . . thus further encouraging interest.[20]

In addition, as support grew, local organizations such as the chamber of commerce, service clubs, and banks began to take responsibility for the specific needs of such a program (for example, registration, coffee, and photocopying). By March 4, 1978, when the workshop was actually held, support for the process had expanded throughout the county, and about 270 people attended. A wide variety of ideas for future action emerged from the workshop. The three most popular ideas for dealing with the anticipated problems of rapid growth were to begin a county planning process, to improve education in the county, and to increase citizen involvement in decisions.

After the workshop had concluded, the steering committee continued to meet for about a year to implement the suggestions that had come out of the workshop. Subcommittees were formed on the various topics that had received the most support, including education, economy, planning, and community. The education subcommittee, recognizing that the county was facing an important school bond issue that had been defeated once before, sent a questionnaire to other communities that had successfully passed school bonds after earlier attempts had failed. The subcommittee and the school board worked together to implement some of the ideas suggested by those who responded to the survey, and in March 1979 the school bond issue passed. The economy and planning subcommittees studied how to attract industry other than mining to the county and worked to support the development of the first county-wide land-use plan. The community subcommittee hoped to publish a booklet on local organizations for new residents but was not able to find the necessary money to do so.

The steering committee itself sponsored public meetings on several controversial issues, including the siting of a new transmission line. The group was unsuccessful, however, in raising the money needed to expand its role as a facilitator of efforts to resolve local conflicts and has not been active in recent years. Although it is difficult to evaluate what influence the workshop had on long-term changes in the county, several changes have occurred that are consistent with recommendations made at the workshop and that improve the county's ability to deal with future problems. Most notably, the county now has a professional county manager and a county attorney, as well as a new zoning ordinance.

EXPANSION

Foundations played a significant role in the history of the environmental dispute resolution field.[21] The Ford and William A. and Flora Hewlett foundations, in particular, took the initiative in finding and supporting organizations interested in developing innovative environmental dispute resolution processes. These and other major foundations not only provided the principal support for environmental dispute resolution organizations, but the foundations' programmatic choices also influenced some of the directions in which the field has grown.[22]

Under the direction of Sanford M. Jaffe, the Ford Foundation's earliest ventures into mediation in general, before the grants to Cormick and McCarthy, were offshoots of its interests in public interest law, civil rights, and in the problems of racial minorities.[23] Early grantees were the American Arbitration Association's National Center for Dispute Settlement and the Institute for Mediation and Conflict Resolution in New York City,[24] both of which mediated disputes involving ethnic and racial groups, community organizations, government agencies, and other institutions. As the Ford Foundation's interest in mediation grew, other grants were made for research, training, and experiments in such diverse areas as grievance procedures for prison inmates, mediation by local residents in community or neighborhood disputes, and mediation of environmental disputes.[25]

The William A. and Flora Hewlett Foundation developed a somewhat different approach in 1978 and 1979 to encourage exploration of environmental dispute resolution alternatives. The foundation's Anne Firth Murray explains that

> We were trying to encourage processes that were not already clearly describable and circumscribed such as mediation and arbitration. We were interested in supporting practice, in order to expand acceptance of these processes, but our principal interest was in learning more about different processes and in building theory. Mediation and arbitration were fairly well understood, and the implications were fairly clear that the way to institutionalize them would be to set up centers offering the services of professional mediators. We were more interested in processes that mediators used *before* formal mediation begins, processes that could be used before a dispute crystallized, and processes that didn't necessarily need professionals to implement them but that lent themselves to implementation by ordinary people.[26]

The effect of these two funding strategies is evident in the different approaches to dispute resolution that are offered today. The organizations first funded by the Ford Foundation tended to be pioneers in environmental dispute resolution efforts oriented to formal dispute settlement processes, while those funded by the Hewlett Foundation tended to be innovators in less formal processes focused on helping parties to exchange information, clarify issues, or generate new alternatives so that they could better deal with their differences in subsequent decision-making processes (see chapter 2). Today, however, most environmental dispute resolution organizations use a range of approaches, depending on the parties' needs in an individual dispute. For example, the Hewlett Foundation now funds research and practice in the broad spectrum of environmental dispute resolution alternatives.[27] Following its sponsorship of the National Institute for Dispute Resolution, the Ford Foundation discontinued its program in this area.

As efforts to resolve environmental disputes became increasingly successful, and as the number of environmental mediators grew, mediators began defining environmental dispute resolution as a profession. In 1980, William Pendleton of the Ford Foundation sponsored a two-day meeting of about 20 representatives from each of the then-existing environmental dispute resolution organizations to explore how the work of those diverse organizations might constitute a "field" of professional practice.[28] As a result of that meeting, six mediators, whose work emphasized different approaches to resolving environmental disputes, met at The Keystone Center to draft a short paper describing the similarities and differences that characterized the practice of environmental dispute resolution as a whole.[29] A subsequent meeting of environmental dispute resolution professionals in 1982, sponsored by the Hewlett Foundation and hosted by ACCORD, brought about 50 practitioners together;[30] and, in 1983, the Society of Professionals in Dispute Resolution established an environmental mediation committee for the first time.[31]

Questions still remain about how a profession called environmental mediation or dispute resolution or conflict management should be defined, however. How should different processes be distinguished? Which processes should be included? What is the difference between planning and mediation? Who can or should be called a mediator? If a person who works for a public or private organization that has a role in making a controversial decision brings the rest of the parties to a dispute together to negotiate a voluntary agreement, can that person be called a mediator? Such questions, which are characteristic of emerging social innovations and new professions, are likely to remain unanswered, or answered in different ways, for some time.

A second part of the growth of any new field is the development of innovative university programs that train students in new professional skills. Several colleges and universities across the United States now offer courses that include information about environmental dispute resolution alternatives, and four major programs also give students the opportunity to *specialize* in environmental dispute resolution. The Massachusetts Institute of Technology and Harvard University are the center of a cooperative arrangement in which students from any of five colleges and universities in the Boston area can take courses in dispute resolution offered at all five of the participating campuses. The Program on Negotiation at the Harvard Law School also provides a special focus for research and practice. The School of Natural Resources at the University of Michigan supports a Project for the Study of Environmental and Natural Resource Conflict, and the University of Virginia has an Institute for Environmental Negotiation. Because these centers offer services, as well as courses, in mediation, consulting, and training, students have the opportunity to be involved in applied projects.

A body of literature on environmental dispute resolution and on alternative dispute resolution techniques in general also is emerging.[32] Included in these publications are books of case studies,[33] academic textbooks,[34] practical observations by experienced mediators,[35] and analyses of the potential merits of using dispute resolution alternatives in particular kinds of disputes.[36] One book on general negotiation principles and practice appeared on the *New York Times* best-seller list,[37] and another presents ways in which the tools of analysis can improve negotiations.[38] Two periodicals are available that contain papers on selected environmental dispute resolution topics as well as current information on environmental dispute practice nationally,[39] and a new journal broadly discussing the theory and practice of negotiation began publication in 1985.[40]

Finally, the number of environmental dispute resolution organizations has grown dramatically. Probably the most important factor in the number of cases being mediated at any one time has been the number of dispute resolution organizations and mediators. Five organizations offered mediation services for environmental disputes in the mid-1970s—the previously mentioned ACCORD Associates, Center for Negotiation and Public Policy, The Conservation Foundation, The Keystone Center, and The Mediation Institute. By 1978 and 1979, several new organizations had been founded. These included the Center for Collaborative Problem Solving in the San Francisco area; Clark McGlennon Associates in Boston (now ERM-McGlennon); Environmental Mediation International in Washington, D.C., and Ottawa, Ontario; the Environmental Mediation Project at Old Dominion University in Virginia (which has had two offshoots: the Institute for Environmental Negotiation at the University of Virginia and Public Mediation Services in Falls Church, Virginia); the Environmental Mediation Project at the Wisconsin Center for Public Policy in Madison (which became part of The Mediation Institute in 1981); Forum, On Community and Environment in the San Francisco area; the New England Environmental Mediation Center in Boston; and RESOLVE, Center for Environmental Conflict Resolution (which became part of The Conservation Foundation in 1981). In 1979, the Kettering Foundation in Ohio also began supporting and managing several experiments with intergovernmental negotiation, which it calls the Negotiated Investment Strategy.

Between 1980 and 1984, additional organizations began offering environmental dispute resolution services. Western Network, located in New Mexico, was founded in 1982 to conduct research on natural resource conflicts in the West, and later it began to mediate policy disputes. The Illinois Environmental Consensus Forum was established in 1981 by a consortium of business and environmental groups that wanted to formalize among themselves a continuing dialogue that was originally convened in 1979 and to expand dispute resolution activities in Illinois. Also in the early 1980s, the Neighborhood Justice Center in Honolulu expanded its work to include environmental issues, and in 1984 and 1985 the National Institute for Dispute Resolution provided funds to help establish statewide offices of mediation in Hawaii, Massachusetts, Minnesota, New Jersey, and Wisconsin.

Most environmental mediators in these organizations report that they are increasingly busy, and the data available on the cases that these mediators have undertaken provide graphic support for their observations (figure 2).[41] The large increase in the number of cases resolved between 1978 and 1980 may reflect the increase in environmental dispute resolution organizations at that time. A larger supply of environmental mediators means not just that a larger capacity exists for responding to requests for mediation assistance but, more significantly, that more individuals are doing the kind of outreach that is necessary if potential clients are to be informed that new dispute resolution options are available. Environmental mediators have spent, and continue to spend, a great deal of time giving

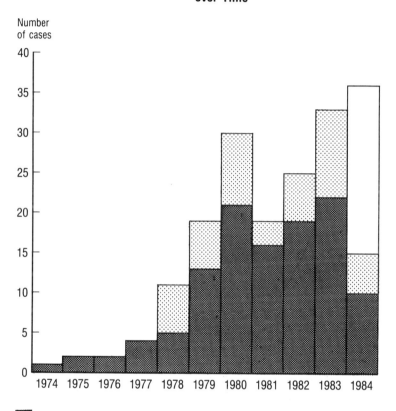

Figure 2
**Growth of Environmental Dispute Resolution Cases
over Time**

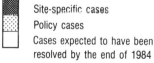

Site-specific cases
Policy cases
Cases expected to have been
resolved by the end of 1984

*Cases in which parties were not able to reach agreement are included, as are efforts to improve com-
munications among the parties. Cases are recorded by the year in which either an agreement was
reached or the dispute resolution effort was terminated. Not included in this table are the many dispute
resolution efforts that were still under way as of June 19, 1984, unless they were expected to be resolved
by the end of 1984. That expectation was based on the assumption that the number of cases resolved
per month in 1984 would continue at the same rate as number of the cases resolved per month in
the first five months of the year.*

speeches, organizing workshops, conducting training courses, writing articles, and otherwise attempting to create a market for environmental dispute resolution alternatives.

Environmental dispute resolution organizations also offer services in addition to mediation of specific cases. All provide consultation and technical assistance to parties that wish to explore the feasibility of alternative approaches to settling a particular controversy. Many conduct training courses in the use of environmental dispute resolution techniques. Some publish newsletters, sponsor conferences, and provide consultants to various organizations, particularly government agencies, that wish to develop their own organizational capabilities for more effective dispute resolution.

WHAT KINDS OF DISPUTES HAVE BEEN MEDIATED?

Environmental dispute resolution techniques have been used to settle, or attempt to settle, a diverse assortment of conflicts (figure 3). In general, however, the primary issues involved in these cases can be divided into six broad categories: land use, natural resource management and use of public lands, water resources, energy, air quality, and toxics. These categories also can be subdivided into site-specific and general policy categories.

Land Use

In about 70 site-specific and 16 policy-level cases, parties have attempted to resolve land-use issues with the assistance of a mediator. These have included disputes over solid waste landfills, port developments and dredging, highway extensions and transit terminals, housing construction and other neighborhood issues, commercial developments, and parks. Some of them have concerned projects with regional impacts, often involving state or federal agencies and public interest groups. Others have been local disputes, which usually have not involved regional or national parties.

One dispute that may be typical of local land-use disputes in communities throughout the United States occurred in Blacksburg, Virginia, where, in 1981, the Lester Development Corporation acquired the partially completed Hethwood Shopping Center.[42] The shopping center was experiencing financial problems, but the company hoped that it could attract more customers by constructing a gas station, car wash, and convenience store on one of the re-

maining vacant parcels. The company also felt that it was important to obtain the necessary permits and complete construction
quickly.

Local reaction was generally negative, however. Blacksburg city
planners were concerned that the proposal dealt only with one parcel,
leaving it unclear what future development proposals might include.
The planners wanted to see a more comprehensive plan. Strong complaints also came from the residents of a nearby townhouse development, Haymarket Square. They objected to the hours of operation,
increased traffic, and other impacts that commonly are associated
with that type of commercial activity. The final party involved was
the Hethwood Foundation, which represented approximately 6,000
residents of the planned unit development (PUD) of which the shopping center was a part, as well as the developer of the overall PUD.
Deed restrictions on the vacant parcels owned by the Lester Corporation gave the foundation board the authority to approve or
reject any design proposals.

When the foundation voted to deny approval of the preliminary
designs, it seemed that the case was headed for the courts whether
the town approved the permit or not. Blacksburg's planning director invited mediators Bruce Dotson and Douglas Frame from the
Institute for Environmental Negotiation to intervene.

Five negotiation sessions were held in February and March 1983,
after the corporation, city officials, Haymarket Square residents,
and the foundation all agreed on ground rules. A key issue that
had been a long-standing problem between the shopping center and
its neighbors was the shopping center's hours of operation. As
agreements were reached on other key issues, such as site design
and traffic patterns, hours of operation remained unresolved. Finally, the parties were able to make a classic breakthrough when they
began to discuss *why* the shopping center wanted to open earlier
on Sundays—the restaurant wanted to serve Sunday brunch. The
neighbors saw this as a desirable activity, and all parties agreed to
the hours used by other restaurants in the town.

In April, after a close review by the Blacksburg planning commission, the town council unanimously approved a negotiated
development plan that incorporated specified hours of operation
so that the area would remain quiet at night, designation of where
cars could enter the shopping center to avoid traffic problems, and

Figure 3

Distribution of Environmental Dispute Resolution Cases, by Primary Issues

Issue	Site-specific	Policy
Land use	**70**	**16**
Housing and neighborhood impacts	18	–
Parks, recreation, trails, open space	11	1
Annexation	9	–
Sewage treatment and sludge disposal	9	–
Commercial development, impacts on commercial areas and larger community development planning issues	7	3
Port development and dredging	5	–
Highway and mass transit	5	–
Noise (airports and raceways)	4	–
Solid waste and landfills	3	1
Agricultural land preservation, growth control, and other long-range regional planning	2	4
Historic preservation	2	–
Wetlands protection (excluding coastal wetlands)	2	1
Sand and gravel operation	2	–
Division of private property	2	–
Sale of publicly owned land	3	–
Hazardous waste siting	1	7
Industrial siting	1	–
Natural resource management and use of public lands	**29**	**4**
Fishing rights and resource management	7	–
Coastal marine resources, coastal wetlands	6	–
Mining and mine reclamation	5	1
Timber management	3	1
White-water recreation	3	1
Offshore oil and gas exploration (OCS)	3	–
Other public land management issues	3	1
Wilderness	1	2
Wildlife habitat (excluding coastal wetlands)	1	–
Watershed management	1	–

Water resources	**16**	**1**
Water quality	4	–
Water supply	5	1
Flood protection	4	–
Thermal effects	3	–
Energy	**9**	**4**
Low-lead hydropower	3	–
Coal conversions	3	–
Large-scale hydropower	1	–
Geothermal energy	1	–
Nuclear energy	1	–
Other energy policy issues (e.g., alternative energy, energy emergency preparedness, regional energy policy)	–	4
Air quality	**6**	**7**
Odor	3	–
Stationary source emissions control	3	6
Acid rain	–	1
Toxics	**5**	**11**
Asbestos	2	–
Pesticides and herbicides	1	1
Hazardous materials cleanup	2	2
Regulation of chemicals under TSCA	–	6
Hazardous waste reduction	–	1
Chemicals in the workplace	–	1
Miscellaneous	**2**	**4**

Each case is classified here according to the principal issue or issues in dispute.

---

an outline of future site revisions so that the neighbors would know what to expect. The developer obtained the building permits he needed, within the same time that the permits would have taken to obtain if there had been no dispute. Construction began in the summer of that year.

A second conflict illustrates how voluntary dispute resolution techniques also can be used to help settle disagreements over broader land-use policy issues. Proposals to site hazardous waste facilities are among the most hotly disputed environmental issues of the 1980s. Many state legislatures have attempted to break the impasse by establishing more stringent siting criteria, by appointing citizens to state siting boards, or by preempting local ordinances. These approaches, however, generally have been inadequate to resolve hazardous waste siting controversies.

The Gulf Coast Waste Disposal Authority (GCA), facing substantial public opposition to its attempts to find sites for hazardous waste facilities in Texas, turned to The Keystone Center to develop a consensus-building process through which concerned citizens would have a greater opportunity for early and substantive input in the siting process.[43] GCA officials' experience with public opposition led them to believe that, to be effective in building a consensus on a particular site, the key players in disputes first had to agree on *how* decisions would be made.

In 1982, The Keystone Center facilitated two meetings of a policy dialogue group that involved decision makers from Texas industry and public interest groups and from local, state, and federal government. One goal of the group was to agree on a process that would encourage negotiation between citizens and developers and give whatever regulatory agencies were involved in a siting decision the opportunity to consider citizen comments early in their permit-review process. The dialogue group continued its work in 1983 and developed two documents for use by municipalities, citizens, legislators, and regulatory agencies. In these documents, it recommended that, when a site is proposed, an appropriate regional government body and the local mayor or county judge jointly appoint a citizen review committee consisting of four members who live within five miles of the proposed site and eight regional members. Such a committee would work with the applicant in the preapplication stage in an effort to deal directly with citizen concerns. A "citizens' report" would then be submitted along with the permit application to the relevant permitting agency.

This approach was written into the regulations of the Texas Department of Water Resources and the Texas Department of Health in 1984 and was tried by the Texas Low-Level Radioactive Waste Disposal Authority in attempting to site its first facility. Also in 1984, the participants in The Keystone Center's dialogue group worked with the League of Women Voters of Texas and The Keystone Center itself to conduct regional workshops at which this siting process was introduced as part of an effort to educate the public on the waste disposal issue. In June 1985, the governor signed new solid and hazardous waste legislation that also incorporated this process.

Resource Management

Natural resource issues, particularly those involving public land management, concern many environmental organizations. Of the 29 site-specific and 4 policy-level natural resource disputes that have been mediated, 7 have involved fisheries resources; 6, coastal resources; and 5, mining. Others have involved timber management, white-water recreation, wilderness areas, and other public land management issues. The Homestake Pitch Mine case described below is a good site-specific example.[44] A policy dialogue on monitoring the effects of offshore oil exploration on Georges Bank is described in chapter 2.

The Homestake Mining Company owned the rights to a rich deposit of uranium ore in the Gunnison National Forest in Saguache County, Colorado. The company proposed to dig a mine, at a site at an elevation above 10,000 feet, that eventually would be one mile long, one-third of a mile wide, and up to 700 feet deep. Although the company was committed to what it felt was a sound reclamation plan, environmental groups were concerned about the magnitude of the reclamation they felt was necessary, the lack of scientific information about mine reclamation in high altitude, semi-arid environments, and the risks associated with potentially contaminated runoff from the site. To make matters more difficult, antinuclear individuals and groups, who wanted to prevent the mine from being opened at all, joined the opposition. Clearly, the stakes for all concerned were very high.

By 1980, when mediators Orville Tice and Gerald W. Cormick from the Mediation Institute were called in, the dispute had been dragging on for more than four years, Homestake had succeeded in obtaining all its permits except an approval of the mine reclamation plan, and the mine itself had opened. The coalition of Colorado environmental groups had not given up, however, and both sides saw that the coalition could keep the company and, perhaps, several government agencies tied up in time-consuming administrative hearings and court appeals for several more years. A mediated solution seemed attractive to Homestake officials, who thought they could win the case eventually but questioned whether it would be worth the cost. In addition, the attorney for the environmental coalition thought mediation would provide a better forum for discussing the substantive changes that the environmentalists wanted in the reclamation plan than would have been offered by a legal challenge based on the adequacy of an environmental impact statement.

Preliminary meetings with the mediators and the initial joint session between the parties revealed that both the company and the coalition were willing to discuss how best to reclaim the land—not whether to reclaim it, as the environmental groups had feared. It also became evident that the settlement of mine reclamation issues could not address the additional, antinuclear issues. Therefore, after considerable discussion among the coalition members, several individuals and one organization decided to temporarily drop out of the coalition for this negotiation. The remaining coalition members and the company agreed to negotiate with the knowledge that the others might continue legal action.

In April 1981, nearly a year after the mediators were first contacted, a three-part agreement was signed. The first part included agreements specifying standards for mine-site water quality, desired levels of backfilling after the uranium was extracted, and measures of success at revegetation, which would be submitted to permitting agencies. In part two, the company expressed its commitment to make certain data publicly available and to conduct research on how revegetation could best be accomplished at high altitudes. The final part contained the coalition's commitment to refrain from legal action on reclamation matters as long as the other agreements were kept. Thus, a seemingly intractible dispute, potentially headed for years of litigation, was resolved in a matter of months.

Water Resources

Few issues are more controversial than those concerning water resources, whether the specific debate is over water quality, water supply, or flood protection. Over 15 environmental dispute resolution cases have involved water resources. Dispute resolution efforts such as the Metropolitan Water Roundtable in Colorado described below have the potential for making an enormous impact on water allocation and development decisions.[45]

Water policy and planning issues have long been subjects of significant controversy throughout the West. Particularly intense in Colorado have been disputes, including protracted litigation, over proposals for meeting the future water needs of metropolitan Denver.

More than 80 percent of the residents of Colorado live east of the Rocky Mountains, and the majority of those live in the Denver metropolitan area. Although projected levels of population growth and demand for water for this area are themselves disputed, it is generally recognized that action of some form is necessary if Denver's future water needs are to be met. In contrast to population centers, almost 70 percent of the precipitation that falls in Colorado annually occurs west of the Continental Divide, in the Colorado River system. As a result, major new storage and diversion projects have been proposed for the west slope of the mountains. However, the pressure on these resources for additional water supplies for metropolitan Denver is increasingly controversial because of the environmental impacts of water projects on the west slope and because other east and west slope users' demands for water are also growing.

Facing this problem, 31 policy makers, both elected officials and private citizens, from both sides of the Continental Divide began meeting in October 1981 in a group known as the Metropolitan Water Roundtable in an innovative attempt to build consensus on how metropolitan Denver should meet its future water needs. The roundtable was designed and managed by ACCORD Associates and was convened by Colorado Governor Richard D. Lamm, who serves as its chairman.

The initiative for the roundtable came from the Boettcher Foundation, located in Denver, and from the Governor's office. Boettcher Foundation staff approached ACCORD Associates in 1981, originally asking whether mediation might be possible in an emerging dispute over an 860,000-acre-foot-capacity reservoir proposed for the Two Forks site at the confluence of the north fork and main stem of the South Platte River in the foothills of the Rockies southwest of Denver. After interviewing numerous key business, environmental, and governmental leaders about the feasibility of a dispute settlement process for the construction of the proposed Two Forks dam, ACCORD staff informed the foundation that, while an agreement on that proposal alone was unlikely, a process enabling all the parties to take a more comprehensive look at how to meet Denver's future water needs was promising.

From the beginning, the difficulties that the roundtable faced were similar to those in many other natural resource controversies across the nation. Many individuals and groups had competing interests in the allocation of the state's water resources. No mechanisms or planning procedures for bringing these groups together existed previously, and the issues themselves were quite complex.

For example, there was significant disparity in the estimates of how much additional water would be needed by Denver and its suburbs. It was unclear how much additional water could be made accessible by adopting measures to improve efficiency, and the consequences of increased groundwater use were not well understood. Disagreements about those factors only exacerbated the disputes over specific proposals to develop various water resources that could serve the metropolitan area.

Roundtable participants recognized that, before significant progress could be made in the mediation attempt, the parties would first have to agree on several assumptions that would affect the scope of the roundtable's deliberations. To reach this first level of consensus, they formed a Continuing Committee to agree on what communities should be considered as part of metropolitan Denver, what year and population size should be used as a basis for estimating the area's future water needs, and how much water to estimate would be used per person in making these calculations. The committee decided to focus, with some modifications, on communities that the Denver Regional Council of Governments (DRCOG) defined as its primary service area. The committee also recommended that the roundtable select 2010 as the target year for planning purposes and that it use the DRCOG's projected 2010 population for metropolitan Denver—2.76 million.

The committee could not agree, however, on the total amount of water that would be needed in 2010 for metropolitan Denver. Because roundtable participants disagreed about what role conservation measures could or would play in the future, they favored different estimates of the gallons of water that would be used per person per day in 2010. The Continuing Committee recommended that this question be given further study, but it was able to sufficiently narrow its estimates of additional water supply needed by the target year for the roundtable's discussions to proceed.

A Water Use Efficiency and Recycling Task Group examined the potential for making additional water available through efficiency measures, and a Groundwater Task Group was charged with studying the potential for, and impacts of, additional groundwater use in the Denver basin. In addition, a Water Development Task Group considered all other options for increasing the supply of water to metropolitan Denver; in the process, it estimated the amount of water obtainable from each source and the cost, impacts, and feasibility of each project.

Based on the work done by these task groups, the roundtable began the difficult task of building consensus on what actions should be taken to meet Denver's water needs. At a June 1982 meeting, participants reached a series of agreements in principle about east-slope storage projects, water-use efficiency, groundwater use, and other, general considerations that should be taken into account in water resource planning.

Included in these general considerations was the agreement that metropolitan Denver would face a genuine water shortage in coming years if measures were not taken to increase the supply of water and to use it more efficiently. Participants agreed that options should be selected that would maximize cost effectiveness and engineering efficiency while minimizing adverse social and environmental impacts. They also agreed that decisions regarding water development and supply should not be used as a means to control population growth in the metropolitan area and that many new water development projects should be cooperatively financed.

In addition, roundtable members agreed in principle both on ways to manage existing east-slope storage projects so that the necessity, or magnitude, of any future construction of east-slope storage facilities could be minimized and on planning considerations for any future west-slope water storage projects designed to supply water east across the Continental Divide. Finally, roundtable members agreed to recommend that a water conservation education program be established, that any water use efficiency recommendations include a commitment to thorough planning and implementation of water conservation techniques and measures, and that groundwater use issues required further immediate study.

By April 1983, these agreements were revised, expanded, and adopted by the roundtable to include specific action items as a "blueprint" for cooperative water resource planning for the Denver metropolitan area.[46]

Although the result of nearly two years of effort, this blueprint was only the beginning. The agreements still had to be implemented. An opportunity to take the next step emerged in the fall of 1983, when the U.S. Army Corps of Engineers conducted a mid-course evaluation of its "systemwide" environmental impact statement (EIS). Settlement of an earlier dispute over the Foothills water treatment plant[47] had included a stipulation that Denver complete an EIS on its entire water supply system before developing any major new water supply projects. The Corps had been designated lead agency for the systemwide EIS, and work on it had begun at about the same time that the roundtable was convened.

In the early stages of the roundtable, a task force had been set up to make suggestions on the scope of the EIS and then to monitor its preparation. Based on its fall 1983 re-evaluation, which included comments from this task force, the Corps decided to rescope the EIS and turned to the task force for advice. Two decisions were made. First, it was agreed that the EIS should contain adequate site-specific information for the document to be used both for systemwide evaluation and for obtaining federal permits for specific projects. Second, the Corps agreed to set up a coordinating committee to review EIS documents while they still were in draft form. This committee was made up of the key interests represented in the roundtable—the Denver Water Board, the other water providers in the metropolitan area, the environmental caucus, and the west slope.

This coordinating committee has met with the Corps on a weekly or biweekly basis since early 1984. It has provided direction about the alternatives being considered in the EIS and the information needed for an assessment to be seen as adequate by all parties and has reviewed the quality of the information gathered while the EIS is in draft form. Staff to the roundtable describe the results as unprecedented in the openness of the process, the access to information, the opportunity to develop consensus on the alternatives to be considered, and the resulting agreement on the validity of the information in the EIS. The systemwide portion of the EIS was released in 1985, and the remainder is expected to be completed in 1986.

The roundtable itself also continued to meet to work on implementation of its agreements, meeting perhaps eight times between April 1983 and fall 1985. Among the accomplishments during this period were the completion of a report by the roundtable's conservation committee and the formation of a new entity, Metropolitan Water Conservation, Inc., comprised of most of the water providers in the Denver metropolitan area. As was encouraged in the April 1983 agreement, negotiations continued between the city of Denver and Summit County in the Rockies west of Denver, and an agreement was signed in which issues concerning the stabilization of the level of the Dillon reservoir and its eutrophication were resolved. Also as urged in the 1983 agreements, the Colorado Water Resources and Power Development Authority funded a $2 million study of projects involving both east and west slope interests, such as the Green Mountain Exchange and a joint use facility. Such a study was an essential step, if these newer ideas were to receive equal consideration to the more traditional water projects that had been proposed and opposed in the past.

The major question before the roundtable has always been what is going to get built. In the spring of 1985, the roundtable began to discuss forming a new negotiation team made up of more technical people to negotiate what will be built, and when, on the basis of the alternatives and information to be released in spring 1986 in the systemwide, site-specific EIS. The "negotiating team," made up of representatives of the Denver Water Board, the other water providers in the metropolitan area, the Northern Colorado Water Conservancy District, west slope communities, the environmental caucus, and the Metropolitan Home Builders Association, met in July and August 1985 to carry this complex effort at consensus building one step further. In their meetings, they were guided by the cooperatively developed EIS and used the basic concepts in the roundtable's April 1983 agreements—that some new storage is needed on the east slope, that a significant conservation program should be established, and that some sort of joint use facility should be developed on the west slope.

Energy and Air Quality

Energy and air quality disputes constitute two more elements of the environmental dispute resolution track record. Among these disputes have been conflicts over small-scale hydroelectric projects, a geothermal facility, the thermal effects of a nuclear power plant on a reservoir, complaints about odor from sewage treatment facilities and meat processing plants, and stationary-source emission regulations. The dispute described below over the conversion of the Schiller Station power plant in New Hampshire from oil to coal encompassed both energy and air quality issues.[48]

In March 1980, the New Hampshire Public Utilities Commission ordered the Public Service Company of New Hampshire to convert three generating units at its Schiller Station plant from oil to coal. By early 1982, the utility company was making inadequate progress in the commission's view. The company argued that the conversion would be expensive, especially if additional air pollution control equipment were required, and that it needed a special rate mechanism to facilitate financing the conversion. Facing a controversy involving itself, the company, the New Hampshire Air Resources Agency (the state air pollution control agency), and consumer representatives, the commission invited the New England Environmental Mediation Center to set up a mediation process to resolve the dispute.[49]

The first joint session occurred March 1, 1982. At that meeting were representatives of the commission, the company, the New Hampshire Air Resources Agency, the New Hampshire Consumer Advocate, and the New Hampshire Community Action Programs. The major issues to be negotiated were the timetable for conversion and the design of a rate mechanism that would give the company access to nontraditional and lower-cost financing. Also on the table were some unresolved questions about the desired level of particulate emissions and coal-handling procedures.

Between March and October 1982, 14 joint meetings were held. One unanticipated obstacle arose near the end of the negotiation process. The U.S. Department of Energy announced that a full environmental impact statement (EIS) on the coal conversion might be necessary because the state of Maine, which had not been represented in the joint negotiations, was unhappy with an earlier decision made by the New Hampshire Air Resources Agency on particulate emission levels. Maine's particulate emission standards are stricter than New Hampshire's, and the Schiller Station plant is located near the Maine border. In classic shuttle-diplomacy style, mediators William Humm and David O'Connor helped the utility company and Maine officials work out voluntary emission reductions that satisfied the

Maine officials and avoided the necessity of an EIS. The issue of whether the New Hampshire Public Utilities Commission would allow reimbursement of the additional costs for meeting Maine's standards also was resolved. On October 22, 1982, the commission approved the agreement among the parties.

Toxics

The manufacture, transport, use, disposal, and cleanup of toxic chemicals has been the subject of intense controversy for years. Mediators have been called in on a variety of issues, including plans for removing asbestos from schools in New Jersey, application of herbicides along railroad rights-of-way and transmission lines, and regulatory policies under the Toxics Substances Control Act.

In a particularly dramatic example, a mediator helped resolve several disputes following the explosion of a hazardous waste treatment and storage facility operated by Rollins Environmental Services, Inc., in Logan Township, New Jersey.[50] The Rollins plant was a relatively large facility, able to treat hazardous wastes in three ways—through incineration, biological treatment processes (that is, algal lagoons), and chemical treatment processes. It was the only facility in the area licensed to handle hazardous wastes, and over 300 companies had contracted with Rollins to dispose of or treat their industrial wastes.

On December 8, 1977, an explosion apparently caused by an accident in a construction area at the plant crushed 10 to 15 10,000-gallon tanks, killed six people, and injured others. The resulting fire was difficult for the local fire department to put out, in part because they lacked information about what chemicals were in the plant. Toxic compounds contaminated the site, and unknown amounts of these materials were discharged into the air and water.

Not surprisingly, there were a large number of affected parties in addition to the company itself. EPA, the U.S. Centers for Disease Control, the U.S. Occupational Safety and Health Administration (OSHA), and the New Jersey Department of Environmental Protection each had responsibilities to help solve the problem. Logan Township, three neighboring townships, and Gloucester County, in which the four townships were located, also were involved. Families of the injured workers, individuals concerned about any exposure they might have had, and a citizens group, Residents Against Rollins, each had an immediate, personal stake in the problem.

Residents Against Rollins, which had formed prior to the explosion, wanted the plant shut down and approached the New Jersey Office of the Public Advocate to file a lawsuit against the state Department of Environmental Protection in an attempt to force the agency not to reopen the plant. The Office of the Public Advocate encouraged the group to consider mediation and turned to Ed Hartfield, then a mediator with the New Jersey Office of Dispute Settlement.

Between January and June 1978, while litigation on some issues proceeded, Hartfield helped different combinations of the parties to reach a series of negotiated agreements. One agreement was principally between Rollins and the Department of Environmental Protection concerning the cleanup itself, testing at the site, conditions under which the plant would reopen, and procedures each would follow if the Rollins plant was permitted to reopen. The Mutual Aid Fire Chiefs of the surrounding communities met with Rollins and the New Jersey Department of Environmental Protection to discuss coordination of information and emergency procedures. An agreement was reached in which the company agreed to provide information to the fire chiefs, hold joint safety drills, and take firefighters on a tour of the facility. A third agreement was between Rollins and Residents Against Rollins concerning Rollins's commitment to protect the environment. It included, among other things, increased use of on-site air and water monitoring equipment and increased involvement in the community on the company's part.

The Rollins plant reopened in June 1978, and Residents Against Rollins eventually disbanded.

WHO HAVE THE PARTIES BEEN?

When people think of environmental disputes, they commonly think of cases like the Homestake Pitch Mine case above, in which environmental groups challenge proposals made by private industry. Most environmental dispute resolution cases do not fit that model, however (figure 4). Environmental groups were at the negotiating table in only 35 percent of the site-specific cases documented in this study. Private corporations were at the table in only 34 percent of site-specific cases, and, in an additional 10 percent of such cases, business leaders participated in the resolution of controversies that affected commercial interests. More surprising, in no more than 21 percent of the site-specific cases studied were environmental

Figure 4
Distribution of Environmental Dispute Resolution Cases, by Parties Involved
(site-specific cases only)

Parties involved	Number of cases
Intergovernmental	19
Government agencies and local citizens/property owners	18
Governmental agencies and multiple interest groups (e.g., business, environmental, labor, fishing, commerical recreation)	13
Government agencies, private companies, and local citizens/property owners	11
Private companies and local citizens/property owners	9
Government agencies, environmental groups, and local citizens/property owners	9
Government agencies and private companies	7
Government agencies and Indian tribes	6
Government agencies and environmental groups	6
Private companies and environmental groups	4
Government agencies, private companies, and environmental groups	4
Private companies, environmental groups, and local citizens/property owners	3
Two or more private landowners	3
Government agencies, Indian tribes, and private landowners	1
Two or more Indian tribes	1
Two or more environmental groups	1
Total cases	115

groups and private companies involved in negotiations with each other. Federal and state agencies and units of local government were involved in 82 percent of the site-specific cases, and local citizens' groups were involved in 43 percent of the cases.

The stereotype that environmental disputes are principally between environmental groups and private industry may be due, in part, to the lack of distinction between groups that are organized to protect the environment and local citizens' groups that are formed to protect themselves against adverse environmental impacts. Although both kinds of groups are concerned about the environment, local citizens' groups and public interest groups sometimes have different concerns and may behave differently in a dispute resolution process. Combining the two, however, one still finds that private companies or business interests were involved in negotiations with either environmental groups or local citizens in only 34 percent of the site-specific cases studied.

When private companies were directly involved in dispute resolution cases, they generally were not among the nation's largest corporations. This does not mean, however, that large companies are not involved in site-specific environmental disputes. Rather, it means that the companies that have taken advantage of environmental dispute resolution alternatives for site-specific disputes have, with only a few exceptions, been either small companies such as housing and shopping center developers, sand and gravel operations, fishing businesses, and outdoor recreation outfitters or medium-sized companies such as utilities, hazardous waste facility operators, mining companies, and timber companies. Representatives of medium-sized and large corporations have participated more frequently in policy dialogues, although generally not as official company representatives but as individuals representing particular points of view.

Intergovernmental Disputes

The largest number of mediated environmental disputes in this study involved only public agencies. For example, in one dispute in the Pacific Northwest, 12 public agencies were able to reach an agreement on regional port development issues that were holding up state approval of land-use plans for two towns and a county on the Oregon side of the Columbia River estuary.[51]

The Columbia River Estuary Study Taskforce (CREST) had been formed by local officials from both the Oregon and Washington sides of the river in 1974 to prepare a regional management plan for the lower reaches of the river's estuary and its shorelands west of Portland on both banks. For five years, the members of the bistate task force had worked with each other and, informally, with state and federal agencies to resolve many controversial issues. In June 1979, the task force adopted a plan. No state or federal agencies had been formally a part of the task force, however. Largely as a result, the adopted plan essentially reflected local development interests on those issues that could not be resolved between the local governments and some Oregon state and federal agencies.

The principle unresolved issues that remained concerned the environmental impacts of development plans at five potential port-development sites along the river's Oregon side. Under the Oregon Land Use Act of 1973, however, one state agency, the Oregon Land Conservation and Development Commission (LCDC), had to approve all local comprehensive plans before they could be put into effect.[52] LCDC rejected the CREST plan and returned it to the task force for revisions. It seemed obvious to the CREST staff that agreement among local, state, and federal interests would be necessary to get the plan approved in Oregon, and in January 1981 the CREST staff contacted The Mediation Institute, with which they had been in informal contact in previous years, for assistance.

During early 1981, Verne Huser of the institute and Sam Gusman (on leave from The Conservation Foundation) began exploring the possibilities for mediation. During initial contacts with public officials, landowners, business executives, local and national environmental leaders, harbor pilots, port commissioners, fishermen, and others, a general consensus on who needed to be involved in the negotiations emerged. All of the private parties felt that their interests could be represented adequately by one or more of the public agencies. Huser and Gusman later reported,

> The essential problem, as most of the parties saw it, was that the local [public] entities were in agreement on what kind of development could occur and at which specific sites, but the state and federal agencies were telling them they couldn't do what they wanted to do where they wanted to do it. Ultimately the local jurisdictions suggested that the state and federal officials had to be involved because the differences between what locals wanted to do and what state and federal laws would allow them to do had to be reconciled.[53]

After five two-day negotiating sessions in May and June 1981, representatives of 12 federal, state, and local agencies initialed a 36-page agreement detailing kinds and locations of development that could occur at each site; maximum permissible dredge and fill; navigation channel depths and widths; mitigation policies; and locations at which no development could occur. Representing the federal government in the negotiations were the U.S. Army Corps of Engineers, EPA, U.S. Fish and Wildlife Service, and National Marine Fisheries Service. The Oregon government was represented by the state's Division of State Lands, Department of Land Conservation and Development, Department of Economic Development, and Department of Fish and Wildlife. The four units of local government involved were those of Clatsop County, City of Astoria, City of Warrenton, and Port of Astoria—all located in Oregon. By the end of summer 1981, each agency had approved the agreement, and the terms of the agreement had been incorporated into the comprehensive plans for Astoria, Warrenton, and Clatsop County. By the summer of 1983, LCDC had approved these plans.

Citizens and Local Government

In many cases, citizens' groups have been engaged in disputes with their local governments. In one example, residents of Montgomery County, Maryland, challenged their county government in court over a proposal to open a municipal landfill near their homes.[54] Many of those residents drew their water from wells and were worried that the landfill would pollute the groundwater. In addition, they did not want the increased truck traffic and noise of operation that the landfill would bring to their semirural area, and they worried that the facility would be an eyesore.

Rather than continue what appeared to be a protracted battle with county residents, which would have been costly not only in tax dollars but also in community relationships, a member of the Montgomery County Council invited Howard Bellman—then director of the Madison, Wisconsin, office of The Mediation Institute and now secretary of the Wisconsin Department of Industry, Labor, and Human Relations—to mediate an out-of-court settlement. The parties directly involved in the discussions were the county government and the Greater Laytonsville Civic Association, a local citizens' group coordinating the lawsuit, although each individual resident taking part in the suit would eventually have to sign the agreement for it to settle the dispute. The Maryland Attorney General's Office also would have to concur in the settlement.

After nearly a year of negotiation, the citizens and the county reached an agreement covering the operations of the facility, truck traffic, groundwater monitoring, closure and post-closure responsibilities, and the formation of a local council to discuss issues that could come up during the period the landfill would be in operation. The landfill opened in 1982 only a few months after the agreement was reached.

Multiple Government Agencies and Interest Groups

Many environmental disputes involve several government agencies at the federal, state, and local levels along with a variety of interest groups. A controversy over water pollution problems in the Patuxent River in Maryland is an example of one such dispute.[55]

At the heart of that dispute was a disagreement over whether the pollution control strategy for the river should emphasize the reduction of phosphorus or nitrogen loading in the river. The dispute pitted upstream counties against downstream counties and scientists against scientists; in addition, it involved fishermen, farmers, environmental groups, and other civic organizations. Also concerned were the seven counties through which the river flows, three Maryland state agencies, and one federal agency, each of which has overlapping jurisdictions over the Patuxent and numerous private parties interested in the river itself or the uses of adjacent lands that affect water quality.

In June 1981, the Maryland Office of Environmental Programs issued a draft "nutrient control strategy" for the Patuxent as a first step in preparing a regional water quality management plan for submission to EPA. The state's strategy emphasized removal of phosphorus at large sewage treatment plants in the four upstream counties that make up part of the rapidly urbanizing area around Washington, D.C.

In response, the Tri-County Council of Southern Maryland, which represented the interests of people in the largely rural downstream counties closer to the Chesapeake Bay, challenged the state's plan in court. Many of the residents of those counties make their living from recreational and fishing activities directly dependent on the Patuxent's water quality. They viewed the draft plan as unsatisfactory because it would not have removed enough phosphorus from the sewage treatment plants and because it would have done nothing to reduce nitrogen loadings both from treatment plants and from nonpoint sources along the river. The northern, upstream counties disagreed, in part because stricter controls on nutrient levels discharged into the river might have limited the growth of their communities.

Failure to agree could have caused the state government to lose $29 million in EPA water and sewer construction grant funds. Under section 208 of the 1977 Clean Water Act Amendments to the Federal Water Pollution Control Act of 1972, EPA had to approve a regional water quality management plan before it could release federal funds for construction of sewage treatment plant projects in the Patuxent watershed, and the nutrient control strategy was the first step in developing the regional plan. Previous delays in completing the plan had resulted in a consent decree with the U.S. Department of Justice in which the state agreed to follow a court-ordered schedule for completing the two documents. The deadline for getting EPA's approval on a publicly acceptable plan was January 15, 1982.

After meeting separately with both the northern and southern counties, William Eichbaum, assistant secretary for environmental programs at the Maryland Department of Health and Mental Hygiene, felt that a solution was possible but that any decision would be more stable if the parties could find and agree to it themselves. Under his auspices, mediators from the Boston-based ERM-McGlennon Associates met with each of the parties to explore whether they would be willing to participate in a mediation effort and how the process should be designed. The mediators' assessment indicated that there actually were two parallel disputes—one over the nature and causes of the water quality problem in the river and the other over what should be done about it and by whom.

Two meetings were convened in late 1981, only a few months before the January 1982 deadline. In the first, 18 scientists and engineers, whose differing studies had been used as evidence by both sides in the controversy, met. This was the first time that some of these technical experts had had the opportunity to share their data and views with one another in an attempt to compile a single set of data on what was and was not known about water quality problems in the river. The mediators then brought approximately 40 people representing all interests together for three days in early December 1981 to develop a consensus on a nutrient control strategy for the river. On the basis of the information that came out of the technical group, the participants developed a list of goals for the river's use and began to discuss alternate methods for achieving as many of those goals as possible. Among the recommendations in the plan that emerged were agreements to reduce the amount of both phosphorus and nitrogen loading from sewage treatment facilities to specified levels, to develop a plan for controlling non-point sources of pollution, and to begin a major experiment with land disposal of sewage.

EMERGING INFLUENCE ON GOVERNMENTAL PROCEDURES

For the most part, environmental dispute resolution processes have been used on an ad hoc, case-by-case basis. Recently, however, some efforts to institutionalize the practice have been made in statutes, administrative procedures, agency mandates, and the judicial system. Negotiation, mediation, and arbitration procedures have been written into state laws governing specific kinds of issues.[56] The Administrative Conference of the United States, a federal agency responsible for reviewing administrative procedures and making recommendations for improvements, adopted a resolution in 1982 recommending that federal regulatory agencies incorporate negotiation into the rule-making process under certain circumstances.[57] In New Jersey and Hawaii, the state supreme courts are now sponsoring experimental efforts to explore ways in which the courts can encourage the voluntary resolution of disputes concerning various issues, including environmental questions, that frequently come before them.[58] Finally, as noted earlier in this chapter, the National Institute for Dispute Resolution has helped establish and fund statewide offices of dispute resolution in five pilot states.[59]

Statutes

Institutionalizing negotiation, mediation, and arbitration procedures by statute offers two major advantages: (a) statutorily defined procedures may make environmental dispute resolution processes more predictable; and (b) depending on how a statute is written, clearer mechanisms may be available for enforcing agreements reached and for providing other protections to the parties electing to use these procedures. As a result, under certain circumstances, statutory authorization may increase the frequency with which environmental dispute resolution alternatives are used. Authorization statutes also may limit the use of voluntary dispute resolution processes, however, if the procedures are not thought through carefully.

In recent years, five states—Massachusetts,[60] Rhode Island,[61] Texas,[62] Virginia,[63] and Wisconsin,[64]—have enacted solid or hazardous waste statutes that require an applicant for a solid or hazardous waste facility permit to negotiate a siting agreement with the host community or communities, in addition to obtaining state regulatory permits. The procedures established by these laws for working out such a siting agreement differ somewhat in each state with respect to who or what triggers the negotiation process, the selection and composition of the negotiating committee that represents the host community, issues that can be negotiated, ratification of the agreement, and the rules of arbitration if the parties fail to reach an agreement.[65]

Although the experience thus far is too meager for any definite conclusions to be drawn about which of these statutorily mandated environmental dispute resolution procedures is most effective, there does seem to be reason for optimism that direct negotiations between a developer and a host community can be an effective way to site well-designed solid and hazardous waste facilities and to solve some of the problems faced by communities asked to host these facilities. In Wisconsin, 50 solid waste siting cases had begun to go through the process by mid-1985. Eight of those had been settled, 4 applications had been withdrawn or the community had decided to waive negotiations, 37 were in negotiation, and 1 was in mediation.[66] In Providence, Rhode Island, a siting agreement on a proposed hazardous waste treatment and storage facility had been reached by the city and the facility's developer, the Antonelli Company.[67]*

A state law allowing negotiated resolution of a different type of public sector dispute provides further evidence of the potential that statutorily authorized environmental dispute resolution procedures might offer. In Virginia, cities and counties have the option under a 1979 statute of using a mediator to help them settle the complex, intergovernmental disputes that arise when a city moves to annex part of the adjoining county.[68] By early 1985, of 21 major annexation-related petitions filed with the state, 18 had been settled through negotiation. In comparison, in the 60 years prior to the 1979 statute, only 2 or 3 annexations were resolved through negotiation. The rest were litigated. Of the 18 negotiated settlements achieved in the past

---

*In Massachusetts, Texas, and Virginia, no proposed facility had reached the negotiation stage. The Virginia statute had just been passed by the state legislature in 1984, the Texas statute passed in 1985, and in Massachusetts several hazardous waste facility developers had withdrawn their applications for reasons not clearly related to the provisions for negotiation.

six years, 7 were settled through direct bilateral negotiation. In 4 cases, a state agency provided technical assistance and conciliation services. In 10 additional cases, the parties solicited mediation. Agreements were reached in 7 of the 10 mediation cases; in the remaining 3, the parties resumed litigation.[69] An analysis of this experience concludes that the role of the mediator and the addition of broader issues such as joint water and sewer sharing arrangements were significant factors in the success of these negotiations.[70]

Still, much remains to be learned about how to draft statutes that specify general procedures for negotiation, mediation, or arbitration of environmental disputes.[71] One of the characteristics, and probably one of the principal strengths, of environmental dispute resolution attempts thus far has been flexibility. The mediators and parties to a dispute have had to design a process and ground rules to fit the specific circumstances of their particular case. It is difficult to draft general procedures because, for example, it is not yet known with any certainty whether environmental dispute resolution processes should always be voluntary or whether circumstances exist when they should be required. Moreover, it is questionable whether it is advisable, or even possible, given the variation among individual disputes, to specify in a law who the parties at a negotiation table will be or what issues will be negotiable. It also is not clear what effect establishing specific rules has on parties' incentives to negotiate in good faith or at all.

Each of the statutes mentioned above handles these questions somewhat differently. For example, in the Virginia annexation law, negotiation and mediation are completely voluntary options. In Wisconsin, the potential host and neighboring communities can choose whether to negotiate a siting agreement with a solid or hazardous waste facility's developer, but strong incentives for agreeing to participate in negotiations are written into the statute. If the community chooses not to negotiate, all local permitting authority over the proposed facility is preempted. The developer is required to negotiate, if the community wishes to do so. In Massachusetts and Rhode Island, both the developer and the community are required to negotiate with each other. In the Massachusetts, Rhode Island, and Wisconsin siting statutes, the issues go to some form of binding arbitration if the parties are unable to reach an agreement.

Representation issues also are addressed in these statutes. Under the Virginia annexation law, elected officials from the city and county negotiate directly with each other, with no provision for direct participation by separate interests within the community. Under all five hazardous waste siting statutes, officials of the host community appoint a committee to negotiate with the permit applicant. Each statute specifies in different detail who within the community should be on that committee, however. In addition, in Rhode Island and Massachusetts, neighboring communities can petition the state for status to negotiate with the developer as a host community; whereas in Wisconsin, neighboring communities within a certain distance of a proposed facility participate on a single negotiating team with the host community, if they choose to negotiate with the developer. No provision for neighboring communities is made in the Virginia law. It is not yet clear whether, in practice, all the affected interests in the cases that arise under these statutes are being adequately represented. Lawsuits have been filed at the conclusion of one hazardous waste siting and one annexation negotiation by citizen groups that had not participated in the negotiations, but these suits dealt with issues other than the negotiation process itself.

The scope of the issues that can be negotiated is left very broad in all cases. In Wisconsin, the only restrictions are that the parties cannot negotiate over whether the facility is needed and cannot agree to any terms less strict than those set in the separate state permit-review process. The Massachusetts and Rhode Island statutes require that certain issues be resolved in a siting agreement but do not limit the scope of negotiations. In Virginia, the language defining the issues to be negotiated is very broad and only specifies that agreements shall not conflict with state or federal law.

The Pennsylvania state legislature is considering a bill that would revise the state's land-use and zoning enabling act, which includes a mediation section.[72] That bill approaches the problem of writing general mediation procedures in a way much different from those in the laws described above. It authorizes the resolution of local land-use disputes through mediation, but, because land-use and zoning disputes vary considerably, it does not tell municipalities which parties or issues should be included in a case or exactly how mediation must be conducted. Instead, it describes seven ground rules that must be agreed on by the parties themselves before any mediation can proceed. This approach allows the procedures for mediation to differ not only by municipality but also by the circumstances in individual cases.[73]

Administrative Procedures

In 1982, the Administrative Conference of the United States (ACUS) recommended that representatives of the major interests affected by a proposed regulation meet jointly with senior officials of the appropriate government agency in a structured attempt to reach agreement on the language of the proposed rule.[74] If agreement were reached, the agency would be expected to publish it in the *Federal Register* as a notice of proposed rule making, unless there were good cause for not doing so. The proposed rule would then go through normal notice and comment procedures. In each of the negotiated rule-making efforts so far at the federal level, the regulatory agency asked an independent mediator to convene the negotiations by identifying potential parties, key issues, and concerns that might affect the ground rules under which the negotiations would take place. Except in the OSHA rulemaking on benzene, an announcement of the negotiations was published in the *Federal Register*, comments were solicited about the process and about whether all interests were represented satisfactorily, and senior agency officials participated directly in the negotiations. Although the agency asked mediators to convene the negotiations, OSHA regarded the process as a private sector effort.

As of mid-1985, three federal agencies—the U.S. Department of Transportation, EPA, and OSHA—had used this approach,[75] and the Federal Trade Commission was in the process of starting its first negotiated rule-making effort. On the basis of the mediated agreements that resulted from its first two attempts, EPA issued a notice of proposed rulemaking on nonconformance penalties (NCP) under the Clean Air Act on March 6, 1985,[76] and one on exemptions under Section 18 of the Federal Insecticide, Fungicide and Rodenticide Act was issued on April 8, 1985.[77] Chris Kirtz, director of the Regulatory Negotiation Project at EPA, reports that only 13 comments were received on the NCP rule and 19 comments were received on the Section 18 rule; no major objections to either rule were raised. Most comments were from participants, and six endorsed future negotiated rulemaking efforts.[78] A final rule on nonconformance penalties was issued on September 30, 1985,[79] and the final rule on the pesticide exemption policy was expected to be out in early 1986. EPA officials are now exploring the potential for a negotiated rule making on additional rules, among them farmworker protection standards under the Federal Insecticide, Fungicide and Rodenticide Act.[80] The Department of Transportation issued a final rule on flight and duty time for crews on commercial aircraft on July 18, 1985.[81] A tentative agreement among industry and labor negotiators on OSHA's benzene regulation ultimately was not ratified, however. Although interest and experience is growing, it is too soon to tell whether negotiated rule making will become a regular option at the federal or state levels.

In 1984, ACUS again recommended the increased use of negotiation in administrative procedures—this time in the implementation of the Comprehensive Environmental Response, Compensation and Liability Act (CERCLA), or Superfund. Implementation of Superfund, designed to clean up toxic waste sites, had been very slow, but public concern about exposure to toxic chemicals remained high. Numerous suggestions for improving the implementation of the cleanup law had been made; among the ideas were enlarging both the fund and EPA program offices, setting deadlines, creating provisions for citizens to sue, and encouraging voluntary cleanup by private parties identified under CERCLA as responsible for taking care of problems at toxic waste sites. Endorsing this final suggestion, ACUS urged EPA to "place greater emphasis on the negotiation of voluntary cleanups at hazardous waste dump sites before resorting to litigation."[82] At the same time, ACUS recommended that EPA use professional mediators in resolving disputes and involve the public in whatever negotiations took place. Agency officials were exploring several ways to use voluntary dispute resolution techniques in Superfund disputes as this book went to press.

A separate, private-sector action in 1984 also encouraged the use of mediation to aid in the cleanup of hazardous waste sites.[83] Clean Sites, Inc. (CSI), was formed by a group of leaders from the chemical industry and the environmental community, which had met for 10 months under the auspices of The Conservation Foundation to explore problems arising in implementing Superfund and to find ways to encourage voluntary cleanups at Superfund sites. The concept was that an independent, nonprofit organization might be useful in bringing together potentially responsible parties to resolve disputes and allocate the costs of cleanup, in working with EPA and concerned parties to develop approved cleanup plans under the provisions of Superfund, and in managing site cleanup projects. By late 1985, CSI staff had examined more than 100 waste sites and were actively working at or intensively reviewing 45 sites on the Superfund National Priorities List.

Judicial Encouragement

Voluntary dispute resolution approaches are frequently described as alternatives to litigation. Some judicial officials in the United States, however, are looking for ways that the courts themselves can develop and sponsor alternative dispute resolution programs. In one example, the administrative director of the Courts of the State of New Jersey and the New Jersey Supreme Court recently commissioned a study that presents a long-range plan for developing such alternatives.[84] As a result of the interest generated by the study, the state's chief justice, Robert N. Wilentz, appointed a Supreme Court Committee on Complementary Dispute Resolution Programs to study existing dispute resolution programs across the United States and to make recommendations for incorporating specific programs into the New Jersey court system. A pilot project is now under way to implement the committee's recommendations.

In June 1985, the New Jersey Supreme Court issued an authorization order to establish a Comprehensive Justice Center in Burlington County. All civil suits filed in the county first will be evaluated by an officer of the court, who will make a recommendation to the presiding judge as to how each case might best be handled. Options will include factfinding, arbitration, mediation, summary jury trials, and other techniques for speeding the process and resolving the dispute most effectively. Based on its experience with this demonstration project, the New Jersey Supreme Court will consider wider application of this approach.

The state of Hawaii also has established a Judiciary Program on Alternative Dispute Resolution. Administered under the chief justice and the state court administrator, the program has begun to set up comprehensive judicial and nonjudicial dispute resolution programs including mediation of public policy conflicts.

Agency Mandates

In May 1984, the National Institute for Dispute Resolution (NIDR) announced grants to four states—Alaska, Massachusetts, New Jersey, and Wisconsin—to help them fund statewide offices whose function it will be to provide mediation services for resolving public policy disputes. NIDR announced support for two additional states—Hawaii and Minnesota—in January 1985. Each of these states also committed state funds to these projects. Implementation of these programs is underway in five states; Alaska has decided not to proceed with its plans.

The institutional approaches for these statewide offices of mediation vary from state to state. In Hawaii, the Judicial Program on Alternative Dispute Resolution has been established in the administrative office of the state supreme court. The new Massachusetts Mediation Service is in the Executive Office of Administration and Finance, with a 12-member advisory board drawn from both the public and private sector. Minnesota has established a dispute resolution program within the State Planning Agency. The Office of Dispute Settlement, now called the Center for Public Dispute Resolution, in the New Jersey Office of the Public Advocate, which has offered mediation services in that state since 1974, has been expanded. In Wisconsin, a cabinet committee appointed by the governor refers cases to a pool of qualified mediators whose fees will be paid out of the fund.

If these experiments are successful, the National Institute for Dispute Resolution hopes that the programs in each state will continue to operate using support from sources within the state and that other states will launch similar programs.

REFERENCES

1. Personal communication with Sanford M. Jaffe, Institute for Judicial Administration, June 1984; Jane McCarthy, New York Municipal Arts Society, February 1984; and Gerald W. Cormick, The Mediation Institute, on several occasions.

2. Gerald W. Cormick, "Mediating Environmental Controversies: Perspectives and First Experience," *Earth Law Journal* 2 (1976):215-24.

3. Allan R. Talbot, *Settling Things: Six Case Studies in Environmental Mediation* (Washington, D.C.: The Conservation Foundation, 1983); personal communications with Gerald Cormick, Gary Zimmerman, and others; and project documents.

4. Personal communications with Francis X. Murray, on several occasions.

5. Francis X. Murray, ed., *Where We Agree*, report of the National Coal Policy Project (Boulder, Colo.: Westview Press, 1978).

6. Francis X. Murray and Charles Curran, *Why They Agreed* (Washington, D.C.: Center for Strategic and International Studies, Georgetown University, 1983).

7. Tom Alexander, "A Promising Try at Environmental Detente for Coal," *Fortune*, February 13, 1978, pp. 94-102.

8. Murray and Curran, *Why They Agreed*, p.31.

9. Personal communication with Sam Gusman, The Conservation Foundation, February 1984.

10. David O'Connor. "EPA Announces Approval of Mediated Conversion of Power Plant to Coal." *Environmental Consensus*, July 1979 (now published as *Resolve* by The Conservation Foundation.). See also "Conversion to Coal at Brayton Point Power Plant for Somerset, Massachusetts," Final Report to the New England Energy Task Force (1978).

11. Personal communication with John Ehrmann, The Keystone Center, on several occasions.

12. This idea was raise in several articles at the time and in testimony before Congress on Senate Bill 1291; see testimony of Sam Gusman and others on regulatory negotiation before the Senate Select Committee on Small Business and the Committee on Governmental Affairs, 96th Cong., July 29, 1980.

13. In 1978, the organization became known as ROMCOE, Center for Environmental Problem Solving, reflecting the organization's increasing emphasis on consensus building; and in 1983, the name was changed again to ACCORD Associates.

14. Personal communication with W. John D. Kennedy, ACCORD Associates, March 1984.

15. Edward Hillyard, president of the Colorado Wilderness Society and managing director of the Redfield Gunsight Corporation; Stanley Dempsey, then with the AMAX Corporation and now a partner at Arnold and Porter in Denver; and Ralph Sargeant, ornithologist and vice-president of the Public Service Company of Colorado.

16. Personal communication with W. John D. Kennedy, ACCORD Associates, March 1984.

17. Personal communication with Susan Carpenter and W. John D. Kennedy, ACCORD Associates, on several occasions.

18. A. Heidi Burgess, "The Delta County Quality of Life Project: Conflict Anticipation at its Best?," prepared for the Institute of Environmental Studies at the University of Washington, unpublished manuscript (1981). Also personal communication with Susan Carpenter, ACCORD Associates, May 1983.

19. Interview with Edwina Eastman in Burgess, p. 7.

20. Burgess, "The Delta County Quality of Life Project," p.9.

21. The Ford Foundation, the William A. and Flora Hewlett Foundation, the Rockefeller Foundation, and the Andrew W. Mellon Foundation each supported several environmental dispute resolution groups during the middle to late 1970s. In addition, a number of other foundations played key roles in supporting the initial growth of the environmental dispute resolution field. These included the Atlantic Richfield Foundation, the Donner Foundation, the Joyce Foundation, the Richard King Mellon Foundation, the Charles Stewart Mott Foundation, the J.N. Pew Jr. Charitable Trust, and the Virginia Environmental Endowment. More recently, the National Institute for Dispute Resolution (NIDR) was founded with contributions from the Ford Foundation, the William A. and Flora Hewlett Foundation, the John D. and Catherine T. MacArthur Foundation, the American Telephone and Telegraph Company, and the Prudential Foundation. NIDR also provides support for the environmental dispute resolution field.

22. Personal communication with Anne Murray, William A. and Flora Hewlett Foundation, June 1984.

23. Personal communication with Sanford M. Jaffe, Institute for Judicial Administration, June 1984.

24. The Ford Foundation, *New Approaches to Conflict Resolution* (New York: The Ford Foundation, 1978).

25. Among the grantees were Linda Singer at the Center for Community Justice, in Washington, D.C.; James Laue at the Center for Metropolitan Studies at the University of Missouri at St. Louis; and Gerald Cormick at the Office of Environmental Mediation in Seattle.

26. Personal communication with Anne Murray, William A. and Flora Hewlett Foundation, June 1984.

27. Personal communication with Robert Barrett, William A. and Flora Hewlett Foundation, January 1985.

28. This meeting was held at the Seven Springs conference center in Mt. Kisco, New York.

29. Howard Bellman et al., "Environmental Conflict Resolution: A Practitioner's Perspective of An Emerging Field," *Environmental Consensus*, Winter 1981 (now published as *Resolve* by The Conservation Foundation).

30. "Workshop Summary," from Environmental Conflict Management Practitioner's Workshop, October 27-29, 1982, available from ACCORD Associates.

31. The author serves as the environmental mediation committee's first chair.

32. See The Conservation Foundation's "Environmental Conflict Resolution Selected Bibliography" (unpublished manuscript); Michael Lesnick and James Crowfoot, "Bibliography for the Study of Natural Resource and Environmental Conflict," *Council of Planning Librarians Bibliography No. 64* (1981); and John Ehrmann and Patricia Bidol, "A Bibliography on Natural Resources and Environmental Conflict: Management Strategies and Processes," *Council of Planning Librarians Bibliography No. 84* (1982).

33. Talbot, *Settling Things*; and Lawrence Susskind, Lawrence Bacow, and Michael Wheeler, *Resolving Environmental Regulatory Disputes* (Cambridge, Mass.: Schenkman, 1984).

34. Lawrence Bacow and Michael Wheeler, *Environmental Dispute Resolution* (New York: Plenum Publishers, 1984)

35. Jane McCarthy with Alice Shorett, *Negotiating Settlements: A Guide to Environmental Mediation* (New York: American Arbitration Association, 1984).

36. Lawrence S. Bacow, Michael O'Hare, and Debra Sanderson, *Facility Siting and Public Opposition* (New York: Van Nostrand Reinhold, 1983); and Timothy J. Sullivan, *Resolving Development Disputes through Negotiations* (New York: Plenum Press, 1984).

37. Roger Fisher and William Ury, *Getting to Yes* (Boston: Houghton Mifflin, 1981)

38. Howard Raiffa, *The Art and Science of Negotiation* (Cambridge, Mass: Harvard University Press, 1982)

39. *Resolve*, published by The Conservation Foundation, and the *EIA Review*, published by Plenum Press.

40. *The Negotiation Journal: On the Process of Dispute Settlement* (Plenum Press, published in cooperation with the Program on Negotiation, Harvard Law School.)

41. Cases concluded after May 1984 are not included.

42. A. Bruce Dotson, "Who and How? Participation in Environmental Negotiation," in Nancy A. Huelsberg and William F. Lincoln, eds., *Successful Negotiating in Local Government* (Washington, D.C.: International City Management Association, 1985).

43. Personal communication with John Ehrmann, The Keystone Center, on several occasions.

44. Luke Danielson and John Watson, "Environmental Mediation," *Natural Resources Lawyer* 15 (1983):687-723; Orville Tice, "What Does a Mediator Really Do?" unpublished manuscript; personal communications with Orville Tice, The Mediation Institute, and Luke Danielson, Danielson and Euser; and project documents.

45. Gail Bingham, "Metropolitan Water Roundtable Formed to Build Consensus on Meeting Denver's Long-term Water Needs," *Resolve*, Summer 1982; personal communication with Susan Carpenter and W. John D. Kennedy, ACCORD Associates, on several occasions; and John Huyler, Huyler and Associates, September 1985; and project documents.

46. Personal communication, W. John D. Kennedy, ACCORD Associates, May 1983; and Draft Metropolitan Water Roundtable Agreement, June 27, 1983, revisions.

47. Heidi Burgess, "Environmental Mediation (The Foothills Case)," in Susskind, Bacow, and Wheeler, eds., *Resolving Environmental Regulatory Disputes*.

48. Peter Ognibene, "Environmental Negotiation," *Electric Perspectives*, Fall 1983; and personal communication with William Humm, New England Environmental Mediation Center, December 1983.

49. New Hampshire Public Utility Commission order DE 79-141.

50. Personal communication with Edward Hartfield, Federal Mediation and Conciliation Service, March 1984; and John Busterud and Barbara Vaughn, "Mediation or Litigation?" *Solid Wastes Management*, February 1979, pp.24-31.

51. Sam Gusman and Verne Huser, "Mediation in the Estuary" *Coastal Zone Management Journal* 11 (1984):273-95; Verne C. Huser, "The CREST Dispute: A Mediation Success" *Environment* 24 (Summer 1982):18-20, 36; personal communications with Sam Gusman, Verne Huser, George Blomberg, Stan Hamilton, Burt Paynter, and Jackie Wyland; and "Mediation Panel Agreement," June 30, 1981.

52. H. Jeffrey Leonard, *Managing Oregon's Growth: The Politics of Development Planning* (Washington, D.C.: The Conservation Foundation, 1983).

53. Gusman and Huser, "Mediation in the Estuary," p.281.

54. Personal communications with Howard Bellman, on several occasions.

55. Peter Schneider and Andy Sachs, "The Patuxent River Clean-up Agreement," *The Environmental Forum*, May 1983, pp. 39-43; personal communications with John McGlennon, Peter Schneider, and William Eichbaum; and project documents.

56. Mass. Gen. Laws Ann. ch. 21D (Lawyers Coop. Supp. 1984); R.I. Gen. Laws sections 23-19.7-1 to 23-19.7-15 (1983); Code of Va., tit. 10, ch. 17.1, sections 10-186.1 - 10-186.21 and misc.; Wis. Stat. Ann. section 144.445 (West Supp. 1983-84); Code of Virginia, section 15.1-945.7; and the Texas "Comprehensive Hazardous Waste Management Act," House Bill 2358, June 1985.

57. *Federal Register*, vol. 47, no. 136, July 15, 1982, pp. 30708-30710; and Philip J. Harter, "Negotiated Rulemaking: A Cure for Malaise" *Georgetown Law Journal* 71, no. 1 (1982):1-118.

58. Sanford M. Jaffe and Linda L. Stamato, "Dispute Resolution: Complementary Programs and the Courts," prepared for the New Jersey Supreme Court and the Administrative Office of the Courts, 1983.

59. National Institute for Dispute Resolution, "Statewide Offices of Mediation—Fact Sheet," October 1985.

60. Mass. Gen. Laws Ann. ch. 21D (Lawyers Coop. Supp. 1984).

61. R.I. Gen. Laws sections 23-19.7-1 to 23-19.7-15 (1983).

62. Texas "Comprehensive Hazardous Waste Management Act," House Bill 2358, June 1985.

63. Virginia Hazardous Waste Facilities Siting Act, Chapter 17.1 Section 10-186.1 - 10-186.21 and misc.

64. Wis. Stat. Ann. section 144.445 (West Supp. 1983-84)

65. Gail Bingham and Daniel S. Miller, "Prospects for Resolving Hazardous Waste Facility Siting Disputes through Negotiation," *Natural Resources Lawyer* 17, no. 3 (1984):473-489.

66. Annual Report of Wisconsin Waste Facility Siting Board, 1984-85.

67. Bingham and Miller, "Prospects for Resolving Hazardous Waste Siting Disputes."

68. Code of Va., tit. 10, ch. 17.1, sections 10-186.1 - 10-186.21 and misc.

69. Roger Richman, "Structuring Interjurisdictional Negotiation: Virginia's Use of Mediation in Annexation Disputes," *Resolve*, Summer 1983; and personal communication, Roger Richman, February 1985.

70. Roger Richman, Orion White, and Michaux Wilkinson, *Intergovernmental Mediation: Negotiation in Local Government Disputes* (Boulder, Colo.: Westview Press, 1986).

71. Jonathan Brock, "Developing Systems for the Settlement of Recurring Disputes," unpublished manuscript prepared for the National Institute for Dispute Resolution by The Mediation Institute.

72. "Mediation Provisions Included in Proposed Revisions of Pennsylvania Planning Code," *Resolve*, Summer 1983.

73. The bill states that:
   Participation in mediation shall be wholly voluntary. The appropriateness of mediation shall be determined by the particulars of each case and the willingness of the parties to negotiate. Any municipality offering the mediation option shall assure that in each case, the mediating parties, assisted by the mediator as appropriate, develop terms and conditions for:
      1. Funding mediation.

2. Selecting a mediator who, at a minimum, shall have a working knowledge of municipal zoning and subdivision procedures and demonstrated skills in mediation.

3. Completing mediation, including time limits for such completion.

4. Suspending time limits otherwise authorized in this Act, provided there is written consent by the mediating parties, and by an applicant or municipal decision-making body if either is not a party to the mediation.

5. Identifying any additional important parties and affording them the opportunity to participate.

6. Subject to legal restraints, determining whether some or all of the mediation sessions shall be open or closed to the public.

7. Assuring that mediated solutions are in writing and signed by the parties, and become subject to review and approval by the appropriate decision-making body pursuant to the authorized procedures set forth in the other sections of this Act.

74. *Federal Register*, July 15, 1982; and Harter, "Negotiated Rulemaking."

75. Philip J. Harter, "Regulatory Negotiation: The Experience So Far," *Resolve*, Winter 1984.

76. Jaffe and Stamato, "Dispute Resolution."

Chapter 2

How Successful Have Environmental Dispute Resolution Processes Been?

A common question asked about environmental dispute resolution is "How successful has it been?" People hold many and varied views, however, about what success means. In this chapter, some of the successes and failures of environmental dispute resolution approaches are described by using relatively simple, observable measures. The actual result of each dispute resolution attempt studied here is compared with what the people involved had hoped would occur. An alternative approach would have been to measure each result against what mediation theory or theories of social conflict say should have happened.[1] Currently, however, such theories are not sufficiently predictive, nor is there sufficient agreement about what theory says should occur to permit rigorous theoretical analysis.

DEFINING AND MEASURING SUCCESS

People differ in their views and assumptions about social conflict. Because these assumptions about disputes influence people's views about dispute resolution processes, what is important to achieve, and how to go about accomplishing those objectives, they also affect the kinds of questions people raise about success and failure. Three different perspectives about social conflict and how it should be resolved have a bearing on environmental dispute resolution approaches.[2] In practice, however, people's views do not fit neatly into one perspective or another. Also, each perspective may be useful in understanding different aspects of environmental disputes. Therefore, no attempt to choose among these views is made here in evaluating the track record of the environmental dispute resolution field. Rather, the distinctions are drawn to help the reader clarify his or her own perspective about conflict and about the assessment of environmental dispute resolution practice, which is presented in this report.

In one view, the dynamics of social interactions arise from a fundamental conflict over the distribution of power between those who have power and those who do not. Disputes over specific projects, programs, or policies are simply particular instances of this deeper conflict. Depending on whether one represents the interests of the powerful or of those who lack power, what is most important in any conflict is either to protect or to gain power. Little credence is given to the notion that all parties may gain something from a negotiated agreement. Those who represent minority or less powerful interests may see little value in a negotiated solution to a dispute because they believe that the only possible outcome will be an appeasement that could blunt attempts to raise more fundamental issues, more pervasive problems, or new principles. For some parties in some instances, the public awareness created by continued conflict may have greater value than the benefits to be gained by resolving a particular dispute. Thus, resolving that specific dispute without achieving a more sweeping change in precedent or policy may be viewed not as a success but as a failure.

From a second perspective, conflict between different interests also is seen as a natural consequence of how society is organized, but for a different reason. Social systems are viewed as pluralistic—composed of multiple, diverse, and interdependent interest groups that form around specific issues. Conflict among these groups can be productive if the political pressure that disputing parties exert improves the final outcome by increasing the number of interests or breadth of views that are considered. The likelihood of this improvement in the outcome increases if disputing parties are directly involved in the decision-making process. Thus, desirable dispute resolution strategies are those that offer opportunities for these coalitions to organize effectively to clarify their interests and to influence public decisions. The success of a dispute resolution process is measured by each party according to how well its interests are achieved by the outcome. Outside observers may measure the success by considering how well the agreement increased the joint gains by all parties.[3] Reaching and implementing agreements are seen in this perspective as important mechanisms for ensuring that the satisfaction of interests is actually achieved.

The timing of negotiations may also be a factor in whether a process is perceived to be a success according to this second view. As an interest group begins to form, it also begins to mobilize power. The more power it has to influence the decision-making process, the more the group is able to ensure an outcome that satisfies its interests. Therefore, an accurate assessment of the future distribution of power may be critical for any party deciding whether or when to negotiate the resolution of a conflict. Negotiating too soon or too late may result in fewer gains for that party and, thus, a less successful outcome from its point of view.

The third perspective is that society can best be explained not by conflict between groups but by a broad consensus about shared goals and values. From this perspective, it is important in a successful conflict resolution approach for the parties to identify their common interests and to work together in solving problems. Clarifying values, sharing information, and building trust are particularly important in reestablishing the consensus on which public decisions can be based. At least as important as, and perhaps more important than, reaching specific agreements during a dispute resolution process is for the parties to develop an improved ability to work together in managing this and future controversies.

As in the second view, maximizing the joint gains of all parties is an important goal in this final perspective, but the question of timing may be viewed differently. Attempts to deal with conflicts in their early stages are almost always viewed under the third theory as desirable, because the dispute resolution process itself is seen as a way to empower individuals and groups to work together, not against each other, in solving common problems. Prolonging conflict is seen as having little value, since conflict increases the polarization between groups, impairs their ability to communicate with each other effectively, and reduces their ability to solve problems cooperatively.

No one of these views is necessarily the sole correct perspective. Most persons hold all three views in some measure, in part because disputes differ and in part because each perspective is useful in revealing different facets of any given environmental dispute. In some controversial situations, the parties also may share values and goals to a greater degree than in other situations. In addition, the different parties to, and observers of, disputes almost always will view the same situation from different perspectives. Because of these differences, there can be no simple correlation between the parties' (and the mediator's) views of conflict in general, of the degree of conflict in a specific situation, of a conflict resolution process's design, and of an appropriate means to measure success.

Despite these differences, individuals and groups still care about similar factors. They care about the outcome of a dispute resolution attempt and the extent to which it satisfies both their interests and what they perceive to be the public interest. They care about the process—its fairness and legitimacy, its efficiency, and the extent to which they will be able to influence the decision. And, to the degree that the parties have or wish to have a continuing relationship, they care about the quality of that relationship and their ability to communicate with each other.

The interest in alternative approaches for resolving environmental disputes seems to come largely from dissatisfaction with more traditional decision-making processes. Specific complaints about traditional processes are legion, but most are related to the same problem—the frequent inability of those processes to deal satisfactorily with the real issues in dispute. When a dispute is not adequately resolved, dissatisfied parties may attempt to prolong it, hoping to change the outcome, and may use whatever means are available to them. In an environmental dispute, the parties often have many such opportunities—through administrative appeals, perhaps in several different regulatory agencies; through litigation; and through political action. The result, however, may only be stalemate—leaving the parties with inefficient procedures and unsatisfactory outcomes.

Site-specific decisions that affect the environment and environmental policy decisions do not often lend themselves to easy solutions. Not only do the parties have different, and perhaps competing, interests in the outcome, but available scientific and technical information may be in dispute or insufficient. For example, regulatory policy decisions on toxic chemicals are made more difficult by the lack of certainty about the nature and extent of the risks from exposure. The possible effects of chronic exposure are debated particularly strongly. The controversy over the facts on which to base regulatory policies extends even to the validity of different testing methods. Because traditional decision-making processes such as litigation and administrative hearings encourage polarization and discourage attempts to find creative solutions to difficult problems, these adversarial proceedings frequently force parties to use information as a tool of combat, even though what may be needed is a search for new information.

It is reasonable to assume that the problems parties experience with existing decision-making processes become criteria against which they measure the success of innovative dispute resolution processes. This study raises several questions that are commonly raised in analyzing how successful the environmental dispute resolution field has been. Were the parties able to agree on a resolution of the issues in dispute? How stable was the agreement? How long did it take? How much did it cost in dollars and in staff time? Other common questions are more difficult to answer objectively and, therefore, are not considered in this report: How well did the agreement satisfy the interests of the parties in dispute? Did the agreement maximize joint gains? How equitable were both the process and the outcome? Did the process leave the parties better able to resolve future disagreements with each other?

In most dispute resolution attempts, the results are mixed, with success achieved in some ways and not in others. In this chapter and the next, the focus is on whether the parties have been able to resolve the issues in a dispute, as they defined them, and on how stable their agreements have been. The problems of delay and questions about the relative efficiency of environmental dispute resolution alternatives are taken up in chapter four.

If the dissatisfaction with traditional dispute resolution processes comes, in part, from the frequent inability of those processes to deal satisfactorily with the real issues in dispute, do environmental dispute resolution alternatives do a better job? This is not easy to measure. How can one determine (a) precisely what those issues were and (b) the best way to measure whether and how well they were resolved? Two assumptions inherent in environmental dispute resolution alternatives provide guidelines. One is that the parties to disputes are themselves good judges of what the real issues are and whether they are resolved adequately. Another is that the voluntary nature of dispute resolution processes, in deciding both whether to participate and whether to concur in an agreement, allows the parties to exercise that judgment freely.* In theory, therefore, environmental dispute resolution approaches allow broader attention to the real issues as defined by the parties themselves because the parties set the agenda and they decide what the terms of the agreement will be. Thus, the first and simplest measure of how successful a dispute resolution process has been in resolving disputes' real issues is the frequency with which it has resulted in agreements being reached, at least for those cases when reaching an agreement was the parties' objective.†

The logical extension of these assumptions is not, however, that an agreement per se necessarily constitutes a success, but that reaching an agreement is a success when the parties themselves judge that the outcome is better than the most likely outcome using some other strategy. A negotiated agreement may not be perceived as a success when one side or another achieves less through negotiation than through another strategy.

Although it is significant, in evaluating the success of environmental dispute resolution cases to date, the voluntary nature of environmental dispute resolution processes is not a perfect guarantee that a decision to participate was completely a matter of free choice. Problems could have arisen, particularly if one or more parties had significantly more power or authority than others. In such cases, it is possible that, even if some parties were reluctant to participate (perhaps because issues of concern to them were not on the agenda), they might nevertheless have felt compelled to participate because the proposed dispute resolution process was their only realistic opportunity to affect the decision.‡

---

*A decision not to participate in a dispute resolution process often is an important protection for a party when the process either does not include the issues of importance to that party or when the way the process is designed is not in its best interests.

†For those cases in which the objective of the process was to exchange information, clarify issues, generate new alternatives, or build a better working relationship—but not necessarily to reach an agreement—it was potentially more difficult to measure how well the process helped the parties resolve the real issues in dispute. These cases are discussed separately later in this chapter.

‡The issue of whether or not a negotiation process should be convened in such circumstances is taken up in the discussion of mediator accountability and ethics in chapter 5.

Moreover, this voluntary nature of the dispute resolution processes studied is no guarantee that, if an agreement was reached, all the issues were resolved to the complete satisfaction of all the parties. Although, presumably, parties would have approved only those agreements that they calculated would make them better off than they might have been without any agreement, sometimes they might have signed an agreement only because they were convinced that it was the best deal they could get—not because they achieved everything they wanted. Since the conclusions about the quality of an agreement in any dispute resolution attempt depend heavily on the values of each individual party, it is hard to determine when or how *well* agreements resolved the issues.[4]

A second test of how successful a dispute resolution process has been at resolving the real issues in a dispute is how stable the agreement is, or the extent to which the parties have implemented agreements after reaching them. Presumably, the less satisfied parties are with the terms of an agreement, the less likely they will be to implement it. It is also during implementation that other problems with a process may emerge. For example, if all the parties with a stake in an issue have not been involved in a resolution attempt, the agreement reached may not address the issues of concern to the unrepresented parties. As a result, they may take action to block the agreement's implementation. Similarly, because environmental issues tend to be public issues, if an agreement or the process fails to satisfy community norms of fairness, the community may exert public pressure to reconsider the decision. In addition, it may be discovered during implementation that an agreement is not technically sound because the parties were not well informed during the dispute resolution process. Or, if no mechanism was established for dealing with unanticipated events (including subsequent disputes over interpretations of the agreement) after the agreement was reached and the negotiations terminated, success in implementing agreements may be more difficult.

Other intangible factors also are likely to have been important to parties in dispute. Sometimes as part of reaching an agreement, and sometimes in spite of *not* reaching one, the participants have reported that the process itself was valuable. They have felt that they gained valuable insights into their opposition's point of view on the issues and created more open lines of communication with each other. For example, in one dialogue sponsored by The Conservation Foundation, the Agricultural Chemicals Dialogue Group (ACDG), the parties reported more than a dozen instances in which one or another of them contacted others on issues outside the scope of the dialogue group's discussions.[5] They had not done so in the past, although many had been involved in these issues for many years. There have been several reciprocal invitations for one party in the dialogue group to give a presentation at another organization's meeting, as well as two or three occasions when one group has approached another on other toxic chemical policy issues. Moreover, in the fall of 1985, leaders representing the U.S. pesticide industry and a coalition of environmental and other public interest groups announced agreements in principle on the reauthorization of the Federal Insecticide, Fungicide, and Rodenticide Act (FIFRA), and members of this FIFRA negotiation credit the ACDG experience as a breakthough in their relationships that made the subsequent negotiations possible.[6]

Even in many cases when parties decided after discussion with a mediator not to participate in mediated negotiations, those parties believed that the contacts by the mediator helped them to clarify the issues and to better understand the dynamics of the dispute, thus helping them to deal with each other more effectively through more traditional decision-making processes.[7]

SUCCESS AT RESOLVING DISPUTES

Most environmental dispute resolution processes as defined in this study share four characteristics: (*a*) they are voluntary, (*b*) the parties meet face to face, (*c*) the parties are assisted in their meetings by a mediator, and (*d*) the goal is to reach a mutually acceptable resolution of the issues in dispute. The processes employed to reach these agreements vary, but they each offer the hope that the parties in a dispute can mutually agree on solutions to problems. Is this hope valid? What has experience shown about whether parties to environmental disputes can resolve the issues more successfully by dealing directly with each other?

In 132 of the 161 cases documented in this study, the parties objective was to reach an agreement with one another (figure 1; see introduction). In 68 of the agreement-oriented cases, the parties at the table had the authority to make and implement the decisions; in the other 64, the participants hoped to agree on recommendations to a decision-making authority that did not participate directly in the negotiations.

Overall, agreements were reached in 103, or 78 percent, of these cases (figure 5). Whether an environmental dispute is site-specific or concerned with general policy seems to make little difference in whether an agreement is reached. The parties were successful in reaching agreement in 79 percent of the site-specific cases studied here and in 76 percent of the policy dialogues or negotiations. However, because the objectives of attempts to resolve site-specific and general policy disputes often differ, the definitions of success can also vary substantially.

Reaching agreement can mean several things. For this study, it means either that the negotiations resulted in a signed, written agreement or that the parties reported verbally that they had reached an agreement and could describe its terms. Because environmental disputes usually are between organizations and groups, not individuals, reaching agreement usually means more than an agreement among the individuals who participate in an actual mediation discussion. Those persons, as representatives of particular interests or organizations, often choose, or are required, to obtain ratification of any agreement by the groups that they represent.

Figure 5
Success in Reaching Agreements, by Objectives

	All cases	Site-specific cases			Policy cases		
		All	To reach a decision	To agree on a recommendation	All	To reach a decision	To agree on a recommendation
Agreement	78% (103)	79% (78)	81% (52)	74% (26)	76% (25)	100% (4)	72% (21)
No agreement	22% (29)	21% (21)	19% (12)	26% (9)	24% (8)	0% (0)	28% (8)
Total cases	100% (132)	100% (99)	100% (64)	100% (35)	100% (33)	100% (4)	100% (29)

Numerals in parentheses represent actual number of cases.

Again, for this study, the ratification step is considered part of reaching an agreement. If failure to ratify an initial agreement led to the termination of a negotiation effort rather than the successful renegotiation of an agreement, that dispute resolution attempt is here considered a failure to agree. Finally, agreement in environmental dispute resolution processes almost always means unanimous agreement. If there were six parties in a mediation effort examined for this report and just one party did not agree, the parties themselves described that as a failure to reach agreement.

These high success rates are consistent with interviews with mediators who report that, although in many disputes about which they are contacted the parties are not yet ready to work out a voluntary settlement of the dispute, once the parties do agree to negotiate they usually do reach an agreement.

Parties to environmental disputes are not always successful at resolving the issues that divide them, however. The parties in 29, or 22 percent, of the environmental dispute resolution attempts documented for this report, failed to reach agreement (figure 5). In some cases, the parties' underlying interests were mutually exclusive, or they were unwilling to compromise sufficiently to reach an agreement. In other cases, parties were unable to reach agreement because of the actions or personalities of individuals.

Failure to agree may be the best outcome, however. For example, in one case two parties invited mediators to help them resolve disputed claims over a fisheries issue. During the negotiations, representatives of both sides realized that one had a much stronger case than the other and that, as a result, they were only going to be able to reach an agreement that heavily favored that side. Both realized that, if the losing representatives tried to sell such an agreement to their constituency, they would face serious political consequences. As a result, they decided to let the court make the anticipated, though unpopular, decision.

Examples of cases in which parties have failed to agree are included in chapter 3.

SUCCESS AT IMPLEMENTING AGREEMENTS

Reaching an agreement does not mean that it sticks. In theory, this should be less a problem with alternative dispute resolution techniques than with more traditional approaches. The problem with litigation and administrative proceedings usually is not that decisions are not reached but that those decisions frequently are appealed. If the parties themselves have voluntarily agreed to a decision, they should be more likely to be satisfied with it and more likely to implement it. How well is this claim borne out in practice?

Analyzing whether and how well public policies and decisions are implemented is complicated, whether the decisions were reached by administrative action, judicial order, or a voluntary dispute resolution process. In this chapter, such analysis is focused principally on the extent to which the terms of agreements were implemented and not on why.* Although the latter is important, understanding why agreements are or are not implemented is more easily accomplished using more detailed case study analysis. Some factors that appear to increase the likelihood that agreements will be implemented are discussed in chapter 3.

To measure how successful the environmental dispute resolution field has been in implementing agreements that have been reached, individual dispute resolution cases are divided here into four categories:

- The parties reached an agreement and fully implemented it.
- The parties reached an agreement but only partially implemented it.
- The parties reached an agreement but failed to implement it.
- The parties failed to reach an agreement.

Cases in which parties reached agreement but it was too soon to judge the implementation results are not considered.

One practical problem in reporting on the implementation of agreements is determining how long to wait before deciding that

---

*Nevertheless, the implementation of mediated agreements raises several important questions. The simplest is whether the expectation that parties to an agreement will not oppose it during implementation is true—sometimes lack of opposition is all that the parties want from each other. In less than a half dozen cases documented in this study have one or more parties alleged that another actively opposed the implementation of a decision to which they had agreed. Whether or not such allegations are true is difficult to prove. Assuming that perceptions are important, however, this is still a small number of cases. More difficult questions are whether the parties have fulfilled their part of a bargain when it required effort on their part to do so and, further, whether they have made an effort to save an agreement threatened by unanticipated events.

an agreement is not going to be implemented. The construction of Interstate 90 (I-90) into Seattle, described briefly in chapter 1, is a good example both of the possibility for error in analyzing the track record of this field and of the positive momentum that can build as a result of successfully mediated disputes.

In 1982—six years after the I-90 agreement had been signed by the Washington State Department of Transportation, King County, the regional sewer and transportation authority (METRO), and the cities of Seattle, Mercer Island, and Bellevue—it had not yet been implemented. That failure was in no way due to the signators to the agreement, however: shortly after the agreement was signed, President Carter froze highway construction funds nationwide.[8] Although it appeared on the surface that the agreement would not be implemented, the momentum behind the agreement was still working. Building on the relationships established during the negotiation process, key public leaders in all three communities had organized an ad hoc committee that was active both in encouraging local governments to implement elements to the agreement that did not depend on federal funds and in urging the state legislature to allocate state funds to the I-90 project in phases.[9] In the intervening years, participants in the mediation process had been appointed to METRO and to positions in state government and thus were in a position to further the agreement's implementation. By the time Congress passed a five-cent gasoline tax in 1983, thus making federal dollars available for construction of the I-90 expansion, a small segment of the new highway had already been constructed over the east channel of Lake Washington using state funds, and the state had allocated additional funds for the next phase of the project. With the new federal funds, full-scale construction of the complete project was under way by late summer 1983.

Because similar uncertainties and unanticipated events have occurred in other cases, the implementation status of each case considered in this report was assessed very carefully. In all of the cases classified as not implemented or partially implemented, the parties themselves report that the situation is unlikely to change.*

Of the 103 cases studied here in which agreements were reached,

---

*Nevertheless, change must always be considered a possibility, even if only a remote one.

implementation results could be determined for 71 (figure 6). Of these cases, approximately 70 percent had been fully implemented. Fourteen percent had been partially implemented, and about 15 percent were unlikely ever to be implemented. It was too soon to judge whether the remaining 32 agreements would be implemented.

Parties have been much more successful at implementing their agreements in site-specific cases than in controversies over policy issues. Fifty-four of the 71 cases for which implementation results are known were site-specific. In 80 percent of those site-specific cases, the agreements had been fully implemented. Thirteen percent of the agreements had been partially implemented, and 7 percent had not been implemented at all. Seventeen of the 71 cases for which implementation results are known involved policy issues. Agreements had been fully implemented in 41 percent of these cases, partially implemented in 18 percent, and not implemented in 41 percent.

Comparative data are not available to evaluate how these results compare with other processes that are used to settle environmental disputes, but, on their own, these results themselves are promising.

SPECIAL CHARACTERISTICS OF POLICY DISPUTES

The resolution of policy disputes is sufficiently different from the resolution of site-specific disputes that the objectives of policy dialogues and the implementation of the results must be given separate attention. In site-specific disputes, identifying the affected parties, discovering the key issues that must be resolved to satisfy all of those parties, and determining how and by whom an agreement might be implemented are not always simple tasks—but they are relatively straightforward when compared with policy issues. Controversies over policy issues generally do not begin as disputes between specific sets of parties over clearly definable issues. Instead, they are shaped gradually as public concern brings issues to the attention of policy makers or scientists or as policy makers and scientists themselves raise issues.[10] Public debate and additional research help define the issues further, and clarification of the issues attracts the attention of more interested parties. Almost inevitably, the status and definition of policy issues change as the information available and the number of individuals and groups concerned grows.

In the early stages of a controversial policy issue, there frequently is disagreement not only about the nature and magnitude of the problem but also about whether the problem exists at all. When

Figure 6
Success in Implementing Agreements, by Objective

	All cases	Site-specific cases			Policy cases		
		All	Decision	Recommendation	All	Decision	Recommendation
Agreement fully implemented	70% (50)	80% (43)	85% (34)	64% (9)	41% (7)	0% (0)	50% (7)
Agreement partially implemented	14% (10)	13% (7)	7.5% (3)	29% (4)	18% (3)	100% (3)	0% (0)
Agreement unimplemented	15% (11)	7% (4)	7.5% (3)	7% (1)	41% (7)	0% (0)	50% (7)
Subtotal— Cases with known implementation results	100% (71)	100% (54)	100% (40)	100% (14)	100% (17)	100% (3)	100% (14)
Cases with unknown implementation results	(32)	(24)	(12)	(12)	(8)	(1)	(7)
Total—Cases in which agreements were reached	(103)	(78)	(52)	(26)	(25)	(4)	(21)

Numerals in parentheses represent actual number of cases.

the issue is first raised, parties that do not believe that the problem warrants public action may be reluctant to participate in a dialogue if the objective is to reach agreement on new policy options. Moreover, those who *do* believe that public action is necessary also may not wish to participate in a dialogue. They are likely to prefer putting their effort into raising the issue to public attention and into prodding public officials to take action. For parties on both sides of an issue, a policy dialogue may not be appropriate until the issue is clearly on the public agenda. Even then, depending on the timing, such a dialogue is almost as likely to merely shape the debate on an issue as it is to lead to a specific decision. Thus, implementation of consensus documents that emerge from policy dialogues may be more difficult to accomplish and to measure than implementation of agreements that settle site-specific disputes.

Environmental policy issues often affect larger proportions of the population than do site-specific disputes, and the key parties active at either the national or regional level are likely to change as the issues are redefined and as coalitions are built. Thus, it can be very difficult to determine who the interested parties are or who can represent these interests in a policy dialogue. As a result, in most of the policy dialogues included in this study, participants were representative *of* the diverse interests concerned about the issues but were not representatives *for* specific companies, public interest groups, or other interested parties. Because of this characteristic, policy dialogues are much less likely to produce formal decisions and are more apt to result in recommendations for action or simply to discuss the issues. Less than 9 percent of the policy cases studied for this report had as their objective reaching a formal decision, compared with 56 percent of the site-specific dispute resolution attempts (figure 1; see introduction). While just over 30 percent of site-specific dialogues sought only to agree on recommendations to policy makers, a full 63 percent of the policy dialogues set that as their original goal—and those dialogues often became more open-ended and communication-oriented. Moreover, in 28 percent of the cases involving policy issues, the objective from the start was to improve communication and to clarify issues, without the intention of coming to a concrete agreement, compared to 14 percent of the site-specific disputes.

Because of the differences between the evolution of the debate on a controversial policy issue and a dispute over a site-specific proposal, an assessment that participants in a policy dialogue actually were successful in reaching an agreement does not always mean quite the same thing as it does in a site-specific dispute, because an observer cannot as easily measure how completely the issues in dispute were resolved. Participants in policy dialogues usually report that, in some sense, any identification of areas of agreement constituted a success. In practice, the participants in some cases indeed did reach specific agreements, but in many cases they were more likely to have agreed on general principles than on specifics or to have reached agreements on some issues but not others. Because participants often are justifiably proud of reaching any agreement at all, it can be difficult to separate cases into relative levels of success.

Further complicating the structuring of policy dialogues is the fact that environmental policies are rarely the result of a single decision. Rather, several bodies in the various branches, agencies, and levels of government may be participants in environmental policy making. As a result, parties to a dispute whether they choose to act separately or attempt to build a consensus and act together must think through what forum or forums for action will achieve their purposes most effectively and then often must coordinate several strategies at once. A key issue in many policy dialogues is how to implement potential agreements. Some parties may favor legislative change and choose to lobby elected officials; others may try to work with regulatory agencies because they prefer administrative decisions within the framework of existing laws. If a party believes that a government agency is not fully implementing legislative mandates, that party may file a lawsuit in an attempt to force change. In addition, there may be a question whether solutions should be implemented at the federal, state, or local level. Finally, some parties may propose solutions that could be implemented by private actions or may want no action to be taken at all.

Once agreement has been reached in a policy dialogue, implementation can be particularly difficult. In early policy dialogues, it was assumed that a broad consensus among private parties at interest would be sufficient to persuade public officials to adopt suggested policy options. Except in a few cases, the complexity of the policy-making process has proved this assumption wrong. A policy dialogue convened to discuss plans for monitoring off-shore oil and gas exploration on Georges Bank off the coast of New England is a good example of the complexities that can affect policy dialogues and the implementation of dialogue-produced agreements.[11]

The controversy over oil and gas exploration on Georges Bank involved federal and state agencies, the oil industry, fishermen, and environmental groups. The issues were complex, but, basically, one side wanted to develop domestic energy resources on Georges Bank, while the other side felt that oil and gas exploration was not worth the possible damage to valuable fishing resources there. The interested parties took advantage of nearly every available legal, administrative, and political opportunity to influence the Georges Bank lease sale.

Some of the issues in the dispute were resolved when Congress passed the Outer Continental Shelf Lands Act Amendments in 1978, creating compensation funds for environmental damage, economic losses, and the loss of fishing gear caused by oil and gas exploration. The amendments also authorized the federal government to cancel leases where serious environmental damage appeared likely and provided compensation to leaseholders whose leases were revoked.

However, many controversial issues remained, both inside and outside the government. In the fall of 1979, the U.S. Department of the Interior (DOI), the U.S. Environmental Protection Agency (EPA), and the National Oceanographic and Atmospheric Administration (NOAA) signed a memorandum of understanding that, among other things, established an interagency Biological Task Force to identify sensitive areas, make recommendations for conducting baseline and monitoring studies, and propose mitigating measures. At about the same time, Tom Scott, president of the Boston-based Center for Negotiation and Public Policy, and Virginia Tippie, director of the Center for Ocean Management Studies at the University of Rhode Island (URI), convened a two-day policy dialogue attended by government officials and leaders from the scientific community, the oil industry, the fishing industry, environmental groups, and local communities. The focus of the meeting was to examine what was known about the potential effects of oil and gas exploration on Georges Bank and the extent of agreement about the validity of this information, to agree on what problems existed, and to explore alternative solutions to those problems. The conveners made a particular effort to involve scientists in the discussion, because a critical element of the controversy was uncertainty about what the potential environmental impacts might be.

Out of that meeting came a clearer definition of a problem that all participants agreed was important to solve—and important to solve cooperatively. Scott recalls, "The group made it clear that the most important issue to them was the impact of oil, drilling muds, and cuttings on the marine ecosystem . . . The fear [was] that there was no effective mechanism both to monitor changes in the ecosystem that might be due to oil exploration and then to use that data in managing the resource."[12]

In February 1980, Scott and Tippie convened an ad hoc committee made up of representatives of the three private-sector interest groups (oil, fishing, and environmental) and three scientists trusted by each of these interests. Although the level of distrust and disagreement was high, members of the committee all were concerned about whether government agencies were going to draw on the best scientific information available. Their goal, therefore, was to reach a consensus first among themselves and then to collaborate with the Biological Task Force to agree on a monitoring plan that would be acceptable both to the public agencies represented on the task force and to the private interests on the committee.

Expecting that drilling would begin in June 1980, the ad hoc committee was under considerable time pressure. Its members met in March of that year and within the month were able to agree on a draft plan. The scientists on the committee invited a group of their colleagues to an April 1980 meeting at the Woods Hole Oceanographic Institute in Woods Hole, Massachusetts, to review the plan. Meanwhile, the Biological Task Force had been meeting to develop its own monitoring plan. Representatives of the ad hoc committee attended each task force meeting, and the task force monitoring subcommittee was invited to hold its June meeting at URI. Drilling was postponed to 1981, easing the time pressure somewhat. When the Biological Task Force's draft was completed in July 1980, it contained most of the ad hoc committee's recommendations.

The story does not end there, however. The Biological Task Force's monitoring plan was only a recommendation to DOI. The members of the ad hoc committee were concerned about whether the monitoring plan would be implemented before drilling began and approached representatives of Secretary of the Interior Cecil D. Andrus and their congressional delegations. Andrus asked the

Fish and Wildlife Service, the Bureau of Land Management (BLM), and the U.S. Geological Survey (USGS) to review the monitoring plan being proposed by the Biological Task Force and to report back to him by October 1980. Comments also were solicited from the five New England coastal states and the advisory committees formed under the 1978 Outer Continental Shelf Lands Act Amendments. The criticisms of the proposed monitoring plan were more extensive than the ad hoc committee had anticipated. Indeed, when the recommendations made by the three agencies, the five states, and the advisory committees reached the secretary in mid-October, they would have substantially changed the monitoring plan and delayed its implementation. Part of the problem was the fact that different parts of DOI had overlapping responsibilities and disagreements among themselves that had not been resolved.

Initially, the prospects for implementing a monitoring plan that each of the major stakeholders could support seemed grim. The ad hoc committee persevered, however, and, according to Scott, the situation turned around at a December 1980 meeting attended by key people from BLM, USGS, the Massachusetts Office of Coastal Zone Management, and three scientists representing the environmental, oil, and fishing interests from the ad hoc committee. The participants at that meeting agreed on the duration of the monitoring program, the number of sampling locations, and joint BLM and USGS funding and implementation. The monitoring plan was formally approved in March 1981.

Scott attributes the earlier problems in implementing the proposed monitoring plan in part to misunderstandings and in part to the selection of the agency representatives on the Biological Task Force. "The problem was essentially solved," he says, "when the responsibility for the final design and funding of the monitoring plan was assumed by the Washington, D.C., office of BLM and the field scientists at USGS. These same people then became the agency representatives on the Biological Task Force."[13]

Given the complexity of the policy-making process, as illustrated by the Georges Bank case, it is remarkable how many policy dialogues have resulted in consensus statements that have then been implemented, even though (as was noted earlier) the track record for implementing agreements reached in policy dialogues is not as good as that for site-specific disputes. Some factors in successful implementation are discussed in chapter 3.

SUCCESS AT IMPROVING COMMUNICATION

Under some circumstances, it may be most appropriate to bring the parties in an environmental dispute together to facilitate improved communication rather than to reach a decision or agree on recommendations. Parties generally hope that such communication-oriented dialogues will increase the subsequent likelihood that a more traditional, public decision-making process leads to actions that are acceptable to all interested parties.* The specific objectives most frequently reported in efforts to improve communications in controversial issues seem to be conciliating among the parties, sharing information, clarifying issues, or generating alternatives to controversial proposals.

Of the 161 cases examined for this report, 29, or 18 percent, were communication-oriented (figure 1; see introduction). Of these cases, 16 concerned site-specific disputes, and 13 related to policy issues. This relative infrequency of communication-oriented attempts could mean that most parties prefer to set negotiating an agreement as their goal, or it could simply indicate that the method used to identify cases in this study simply was less effective at identifying efforts in which the objective was to improve communications without negotiating an agreement.

Parties to a dispute may want a mediator's assistance at improving communications for several reasons. Sometimes, the objective may be to help parties in a highly charged situation resume communications that have broken down. For example, in one case involving an Indian tribe and a state environmental agency, the relationship between the different parties had become so hostile that they found it virtually impossible to speak with each other.[14] The tribe, which for several years had fought step-by-step to gain control over the sewer system on its reservation, had long felt that the basic cause of the dispute was racism on the part of white officials.

*One such approach, "scoping," is now widely accepted as a part of environmental impact assessment processes, although no scoping meetings that required the assistance of a mediator were discovered in the research for this study. Scoping brings together interested parties at the beginning of a proposed project's impact assessment process to consider what issues should be examined in depth in that process and to discuss what alternatives to the proposal should be included in the environmental impact statement. The hope is that scoping meetings will help identify a project's problems early in the process and will encourage the design of mitigation measures that reduce the potential for controversy over the proposed project.

Eventually, the tribe appeared to have been successful: a court-ordered contract had been negotiated between the tribe and the environmental agency, the specific issues apparently had been resolved, and the state attorney general's office was drawing up the contract's final language. When tribal leaders received the final documents, however, they discovered that old language that had been eliminated earlier because the tribe considered it racist had reappeared in the contract. At this point, the tribal leaders were unwilling to talk to state officials about the same issues yet one more time. If there had not been a new acting agency director and if the tribe had not had an earlier positive experience with mediation, the dispute would have gone back to court. At the Indians' request, the mediator agreed to speak with the new acting agency director on behalf of the tribe in an effort to restore communications between the two parties. That official heard the mediator out and, over the objections of his staff, agreed to change the wording.

Poor communications don't always threaten to end in litigation, but they often make problems more difficult to solve. One such case involved Woolen Mills, Virginia, a neighborhood near Charlottesville that had been established as a "factory town" in the late 1800s by the Woolen Mills company.[15] In 1964, the mill was sold to Security Storage and Van Lines, with the mill's housing sold to its long-term tenants. From the time those sales were made, the relationship between the moving company and the residents was never as close as the relationship between the mill and its tenants had been; and, as communication between the two parties broke down, resentments grew. As vans traversed the community's small residential streets, noise, parking, and traffic circulation problems increased, and tolerances decreased. For its part, the company felt that illegal parking at the entrance to their property, which it blamed on the residents, was blocking its trucks from turning around and forcing the drivers into the manuevers that caused some of the residents' complaints. In addition, the county never accepted ownership of certain roads, firelanes, and utility lines previously owned and maintained by the mill. No side would accept responsibility for solving the traffic and maintenance problems that continued to deteriorate along with the relationships.

A small group of residents living nearest to Security Storage was seeking a lawyer's advice about the possibility of legal action against the company when a neighborhood leader contacted the Institute for Environmental Negotiation at the University of Virginia to see if mediation could help address the area's problems. The first meeting, facilitated by Elizabeth Waters of the institute, allowed people from Security Storage and the neighborhood, who in some instances had never met, to exchange information and to identify shared problems that would require cooperative solutions. Although the discussions at this first meeting were heated, a list of issues to be addressed was established. It included truck traffic, illegal parking, road maintenance, police protection, and abandoned buildings. By the end of the third meeting, participants had begun to understand each other's concerns and the constraints within which each operated. This enabled them to agree to work together in the future to solve a number of problems such as alleviation of circulation and parking problems near the moving company's gates, joint monitoring of parking problems in the area, and adoption of some roads into the county/state road system.

A third reason that a mediator may be desired is to help the parties to a dispute exchange information. Controversies can arise or be made more difficult simply because parties interested in an issue lack adequate access to information or have differing sets of information. In some site-specific cases, local citizens potentially affected by a project may not have adequate information about the project's potential impacts. In such cases, they or the project proponent may ask a neutral intervenor to organize and facilitate meetings that allow the different sides to communicate their concerns more effectively to each other, to answer questions about a proposed project, and to help the participants become sufficiently well acquainted with each other that they can continue to work together during subsequent planning and decision making about the project.

Access to information about a project does not make its impacts less severe. Sometimes, however, if the process is designed in a credible fashion, a company may help to diffuse misunderstandings about what it is proposing and to focus the debate on a project's real effects by providing citizens with more detailed information about the project and its environmental impacts. And, since project developers need good information just as much as citizen groups do, possessing accurate information about a community's concerns and learning about studies done by others may give a project proponent the opportunity to modify the proposal or to make additional offers that satisfy others' concerns more effectively. For example,

ACCORD Associates has conducted several meetings in the Rocky Mountain states to help parties interested in proposals to open new coal and uranium mines to exchange information before decisions were made prior to the permitting process on whether and how the projects actually should go forward.[16] The hope in those situations has been that such meetings might give communications between the project proponent and a concerned community a constructive beginning, so that they could continue to work together more effectively to identify and solve potential problems.

Thus, mediators may be able to augment traditional planning or permitting processes by providing a more informal process in which parties can identify possible conflicts and discuss alternatives. For example, in early 1984, with the assistance of Philip Marcus, executive director of the Illinois Environmental Consensus Forum, representatives of the Illinois Department of Transportation, the Illinois Tollway Authority, and the Morton Arboretum met to discuss plans for a new highway that was to be constructed next to the arboretum.[17] Arboretum officials were concerned about the effects that freeway lights might have on sensitive plants, about gasoline- and salt-polluted water that might run off the freeway, and about noise that might disrupt the peaceful atmosphere enjoyed by arboretum visitors. Although the parties did not meet formally to negotiate decisions on the design and construction of the new highway, the information exchange and clarification of issues allowed alternatives to be developed that later were incorporated into project planning decisions.

The obstacle to resolving a dispute may go beyond the problem of lack of access to information. In many environmental disputes, the consequences of an action are either unknown or uncertain. In one such case, the U.S. Army Corps of Engineers had proposed a dredging project in an inlet at the mouth of the White Oak River on the North Carolina coast.[18] The Izaak Walton League opposed the dredging, arguing that deepening the channel would cause scouring of the bottom of the inlet and would change currents in the mouth of the river in such a way that the estuary would silt up more rapidly. Others disagreed. A dispute between competing experts over the effects of the dredging was getting nowhere. In addition, the purpose of the dredging project was to open a channel for fishing boats, but, because local fishermen used boats made for shallow waters, they worried that a deeper channel would encourage competing fishermen from other harbors to come to their harbor.

The Izaak Walton League approached John Clark of The Conservation Foundation, who suggested that a mediation process be tried. Clark and mediator Roger Richman, then of the Environmental Mediation Project at Old Dominion University, visited the area, meeting with the local Izaak Walton leaders, Corps of Engineers representatives, and local officials to explore what could be done about the controversy. Richman continued separate meetings with the parties over the course of a week, getting an agreement on how to approach the mediation process. Richman then arranged a meeting of elected officials from the North Carolina counties and towns bordering the estuary, as well as representatives from the Izaak Walton League, the Corps of Engineers, the local fishing industry, the North Carolina Coastal Zone Management Program, and a staff representative of the area's U.S. representative. The objective of that meeting was simply to talk about the problem and exchange information. However, despite distrust that had been fueled by a lack of earlier communication among the parties, the persons at the meeting were able to agree quickly that the estuary was an important resource that needed protection. After realizing that everyone involved shared this basic assumption, the participants were able to move on to discuss the need for additional studies of the effects of dredging in the estuary. They agreed to form a White Oak River Advisory Council and to undertake joint studies that would be credible to all concerned. Funding for the joint study was subsequently obtained from the North Carolina Coastal Zone Management office.

Measuring success at meeting the objectives of parties in communication-oriented efforts is more difficult than measuring whether an agreement was reached. It is particularly hard to find any objective measure of whether the policy dialogues in this category succeeded in improving communications among the parties or in improving subsequent efforts to resolve controversies.

Clearly, there is anecdotal evidence in support of the success of attempts to improve communication in environmental disputes. Each of the cases described above was successful. Not only did they improve communication; they also resulted in agreements being reached by the parties even though that generally was not an original goal of the mediation. Interviews with the mediators and selected participants in the disputes indicated that, in slightly more than half of the site-specific cases, positive progress was made toward solving the controversy following a mediator's effort to help improve communications. In most of the remaining site-specific cases and all of the policy controversies, there is no clear evidence that the communications process either helped or hindered in the long run, but, of course, it is not possible to tell whether or to what degree the conflict would have escalated if there had been no effort to improve communications. In all 29 disputes, only one clear failure to improve communications and two cases in which the parties gave mixed reports of some improvement in communications and some continued animosity were discovered.

The clear failure involved an effort by an educational institution to consult with neighboring communities during the planning of a large housing development.[19] The mediation attempt broke down in part because the parties had different expectations for it. The developer thought that the intent was to discuss issues and generate alternatives, while the others thought that the developer had made a commitment to reaching an agreement with them as a condition for proceeding with the housing project.

In that case, the problem was that one of the important determinants of whether a mediation attempt is apt to be successful— clarity about the ground rules for the process—was violated. That factor and others affecting the likelihood of success in resolving disputes through mediation and in then implementing agreements that are reached are explored in chapter 3. However, because of the difficulty in measuring the success of efforts to improve communication, the discussion will be limited to cases in which the objective was to reach an agreement.

REFERENCES

1. Paul Wehr, *Conflict Regulation* (Boulder, Colo.: Westview Press, 1979).

2. The three perspectives described are taken from James E. Crowfoot, "Negotiations: An Effective Tool for Citizen Organizations?' *Northern Rockies Action Group Papers* 3, no. 4 (1980):24-44.

3. Lawrence Susskind, "Environmental Mediation and the Accountability Problem," *Vermont Law Review* 6, no. 1 (1982):1-47.

4. The best attempts have been made in Howard Raiffa, *The Art and Science of Negotiation* (Cambridge, Mass.: The Belknap Press of Harvard University Press, 1982).

5. Personal communications with ACDG participants by the author, who serves as one of the mediators.

6. "How They Pulled Off the FIFRA settlement," *Industrial Chemical News*, November 1985.

7. Leonard G. Buckle et al., "An Evaluation of the New England Environmental Mediation Center" (unpublished report, New England Environmental Mediation Center, Boston, January 1984); and Leonard G. Buckle and Suzann R. Thomas-Buckle, "Placing Environmental Mediation in Context: Lessons from 'Failed' Mediations," *Environmental Impact Assessment Review* (forthcoming).

8. Allan R. Talbot, *Settling Things: Six Case Studies in Environmental Mediation* (Washington D.C.: The Conservation Foundation, 1983).

9. Personal communication with Gary Zimmerman, Seattle University and former mayor of Bellevue, September 1983.

10. J. Clarence Davies III, "Setting the National Agenda," (unpublished manuscript, 1976).

11. Thomas J. Scott and Lisa Hirsh, "Managing Conflict in the Development of a Resource Management Process on George Bank," *Environmental Impact Assessment Review* 4, nos. 3 & 4 (1983):561-76.

12. Personal communication with Tom Scott, Center for Negotiation and Public Policy, December 1983.

13. Scott and Hirsh, "Managing Conflict," pp.573-4.

14. Personal communications with the mediator.

15. Personal communication with Elizabeth Waters, Institute for Environmental Negotiation, December 1983; and meeting minutes.

16. Susan L. Carpenter and W.J.D. Kennedy, "ROMCOE Case Studies," (unpublished manuscript, 1979), and personal communications with Carpenter and Kennedy on several occasions.

17. Personal communication with Philip Marcus, Illinois Environmental Consensus Forum, June 1984.

18. Personal communications with Roger Richman, Public Mediation Services, April 1984; and memorandum of agreement.

19. Personal communications with the mediator and selected parties.

Chapter 3

What Factors Affect the Likelihood of Success?

Deciding what approach to resolving a controversial environmental issue has the greatest likelihood of success can be complicated. Each party must decide whether it prefers to litigate, to lobby for legislative change, to turn to an administrative agency, to avoid the dispute, to exchange information and clarify the issues, to negotiate a voluntary resolution of the issues with the other parties, or to engage in some combination of these options. What choice a party makes in any given situation is affected by its experiences and resources, as well as by its calculation of the value of possible outcomes against the probability and cost of success in attaining those outcomes.

A party to an environmental dispute may find it difficult to evaluate the likelihood of success or failure in using a voluntary dispute resolution process for at least two reasons: (*a*) it may not have participated in a such a process before and, therefore, may not know which factors to look for, and (*b*) the dispute may involve many other parties, whose willingness to participate may be difficult for the initiating party to determine because communication with them is poor or nonexistent. As a result, the interested party may first contact a mediator or other neutral intervenor to learn more about different dispute resolution options and to receive assistance in evaluating whether, and under what conditions, a voluntary dispute resolution process might be successful.

After being contacted, the mediator generally will begin by conducting an assessment of the dispute to identify in advance the opportunities for resolving the issues and the problems that might occur during the dispute resolution process. As part of that assessment, the mediator usually will interview all the parties to the dispute (and others who may play a role in resolving it) to gain a clear understanding of the causes, characteristics, and complexities of the controversy. The mediator then will discuss the possibility of a voluntary dispute resolution process with each of the parties, consult with each about what their needs and concerns are, identify for the parties any conditions that may make it difficult to resolve the dispute, and help the parties decide how they wish to proceed.

Depending on the mediator's skill and on the circumstances of the dispute, the parties may be able either to modify many of the identified obstacles to resolution or to solve them in the design of the process to be used. Many factors in a dispute can be modified, and concerns about participating in a negotiation or mediation process can be resolved by the parties and the mediator before and during a dispute resolution attempt. If one side lacks sufficient incentives to negotiate, the others often can raise the ante either with assurances about implementation, mitigation, or compensation if an agreement is reached or with reminders of ways that the dispute might be escalated if an agreement is not reached. If a dispute concerns a particularly large number of parties, coalitions may be possible. If no externally imposed deadline exists (for example, one mandated by a government agency), the parties may be able to create one. If those with power to implement the agreement are not direct participants in the negotiation, the mediator may be able to provide an appropriate link between the other parties and the eventual decision maker.

With these and other possible obstacles in mind, the mediator will help the parties decide who should represent their interests at the negotiation table, who else should be invited to participate in the process, what the objectives of the process should be, what issues should be discussed, how a possible agreement might be implemented, and what additional ground rules for the negotiation will be needed (for example, to govern dealing with the media, obtaining technical information, setting a schedule for meetings, and adding new parties to the process if any emerge).

The dispute assessment and process design phases of a voluntary dispute resolution effort are closely linked, since agreement on *how* a dispute resolution process will be conducted frequently is a prerequisite to the decision by each party about *whether* to participate.

If concerns cannot be resolved in the way the process is designed, however, and a significant risk of not reaching an agreement remains, the parties may choose to deal with their differences in another way. They also may decide that an attempt to exchange information and clarify the issues still might be valuable despite the improbability of an agreement being reached at that time.

In assessing whether to use a negotiation or other consensus-building approach, it is useful to ask what factors to look for (or to create) to increase the likelihood of a successful outcome. The purpose of the analysis that follows is to explore the relevance of certain conditions on the likelihood of success. Environmental disputes and dispute resolution processes have many characteristics that one might study as factors potentially affecting the success of a dispute resolution process, however. The characteristics most frequently cited as significant by mediators and other observers of the field have been selected for study in this report.

There are several factors that mediators generally believe have significant influence on the likelihood of success—among them that the parties have sufficient incentives to reach an agreement, that all the parties are willing to participate in the dispute resolution process, that the parties can agree on the scope of issues to negotiate, and that a reasonable deadline exists.[1] Other factors often are mentioned when individuals and groups inquire about mediation: Does the number of parties make a difference? What kinds of issues are most likely to be resolved successfully? Can disputes be mediated after a lawsuit has been filed? Each of these factors is discussed below.*

A mediator's assumptions about what would increase or decrease the likelihood of success influence both the way that person analyzes a dispute and the way he or she helps the parties design a dispute resolution process to deal with the problems and opportunities identified. If current mediation practice is based on accurate assumptions, one of the reasons for the relatively high success rate of the cases in this study may be the mediators' having conducted such dispute assessments at the beginning of each case. For each of the 161 cases in this study, there were many others in which preliminary

---

*Some factors may be more likely to affect success in reaching agreements, while others may be more important for success in implementing those agreements. Both concerns are addressed in this discussion.

dispute assessments were conducted but which, for a variety of reasons, never reached the stage at which the parties could agree to negotiate with each other.[2]

To the extent that dispute assessments screen out efforts that are likely to fail, this is a valuable service to the parties. Using this sample of cases that have been mediated to test the different factors that are assumed to affect the likelihood of success creates a problem, however, because the cases included in this study all were analyzed and modifications were suggested by mediators to increase the chances of success. As a result, the analysis in this chapter is limited to a comparison between cases in which the parties were successful at reaching agreements and those in which they failed to agree.* Some consideration was given to the possibility of identifying a control group of cases that were negotiated but were not influenced by mediators, but the difficulty of finding comparable samples was too great.

POSSIBLE FACTORS IN REACHING AGREEMENTS

Few absolutes exist in predicting whether parties in any particular dispute will be successful in reaching an agreement or, if one is reached, in implementing it. No single factor necessarily makes success or failure certain. Rather, factors act interdependently with the combined positive effect of some factors offsetting potentially negative factors, or the reverse. Unfortunately, however, it is difficult to test rigorously how the many variables involved in an environmental dispute interact with each other. In this report, each variable's effect on a party's ability to resolve a dispute is examined separately, despite the distortion in findings that inevitably results.

Some of the basic characteristics of a dispute are sufficiently concrete that they can be measured fairly easily; other factors are more subjective (figure 7). For example, the number of parties in a mediation effort generally is simple to determine, as is the question whether a lawsuit has already been filed by one or more of the parties. Similarly, it is usually clear whether there is a deadline for the con-

---

*This analysis is further limited, though, because only 29 cases in which the parties failed to reach agreement were documented in this study. Unfortunately, that is too small a sample for drawing very definite conclusions. It is probably best, therefore, to use this analysis to raise questions about current assumptions, to suggest useful directions for future research, and not to generalize too much from the individual case examples that are given.

Figure 7

Factors that May Increase or Decrease
the Likelihood of Success

	Concrete	Subjective
Party-related factors		
Identification and involvement of all affected interests		X
Number of parties involved	X	
Types of parties involved	X	
Direct involvement of decision makers, including public agencies	X	
Process- and context-related factors		
Agreement on procedural issues*		X
Presence of a deadline	X	
Possession of sufficient incentives		X
Ability to satisfy each party's underlying interests		X
Whether the dispute was in litigation	X	
Maintenance of good representative/constituency relationships		X
Negotiation in good faith		X
Substance-related factors		
Issues in dispute	X	
Agreement on the scope of issues		X
Agreement on the facts		X

*Section includes whether agreements were put in writing, which can be measured concretely.

clusion of negotiations—a factor that some mediators consider quite helpful. The importance of such factors is tested in this chapter against the case-study data available. Other, more subjective variables (such as whether all the parties to a dispute have sufficient incentives to reach an agreement) are less easily measured. However, because such factors are widely believed by mediators or parties to significantly influence the likelihood of success, they are also discussed here.

Finally, most of the analysis comparing whether agreements were reached by the presence of specific factors is done with site-specific cases only. For the most part, the data on site-specific disputes has been more concrete than the data for policy dialogues or negotiations.

Party-Related Factors

During a dispute assessment, mediators attempt to identify all parties who have a stake in the controversy or the ability to influence the implementation of any agreement that a dispute resolution effort might produce. Who participates in a dispute resolution process can significantly affect the terms of an agreement. What satisfies the participating parties may not satisfy other parties that did not take part directly in reaching the agreement. Yet, if an agreement fails to address the interests of all who are affected, neither it nor the process is likely to be considered fair. Moreover, those who have been left out of a mediation process are likely to try to block an agreement's implementation. Other party-related factors in an environmental dispute resolution effort include the number of parties involved and who those parties are.

Identification and Involvement of All Affected Interests

It is not always easy to identify all the affected interests in a dispute or to determine how they can be represented most effectively. For one thing, the parties to an environmental dispute may get involved at different times. In hazardous waste siting disputes, for example, some organizations, groups, and government agencies get involved in policy decisions early, usually at the state level, when the issues in dispute involve determination of need, technology choices, and general site-selection criteria. Later, when the issues shift to siting a facility at a particular location, the local government and local citizens become concerned. A second difficulty in identifying and involving all affected interests is that some persons who would be affected by a decision may not be sufficiently organized or powerful to be called "parties." Local community interests, for example, may have no already-existing body that can effectively represent their interests against the proponents of a particular project or policy. Finally, a dispute may involve so many parties that it simply is not possible to identify and ensure the representation of all of them in a dispute resolution attempt. For example, this may be the case with some national environmental policy issues that affect entire industries and large portions of the population.

In practice, the question of who should participate in environmental dispute resolution attempts has been answered in a variety of ways. In some of the cases in this study, groups that had an interest in the outcome did not participate directly in the dispute resolution process.* For example, in the Columbia River Estuary Task Force case, private parties such as landowners, fishermen, or public interest groups could have been represented directly rather than by public agencies. In the Schiller Station coal conversion case, the local community or the state of Maine could have been represented directly in the joint negotiations. Although there were over 30 participants in the Metropolitan Water Roundtable, others asked to be invited as well. (See chapter 1 for discussions of all three cases.)

It is difficult to evaluate how much impact the selection of participants has had on the success or failure of the various mediation attempts examined for this report. Obviously, no one went back and mediated a case a second time to see whether the outcome would be different by adding or removing specific parties, and separating cases into two groups by whether all parties were represented would require retrospective judgments that would be difficult to justify. The cases, and the ways they were mediated, also are sufficiently different from each other that comparisons between them are risky. In the simplest terms, looking at the 29 cases in which the parties failed to agree, there appears to be no case in which the parties who were included in the negotiation failed to reach an agreement because other parties had been left out. Still, in some cases in which agreements were reached, there does seem to be evidence that special efforts had to be made to satisfy the concerns of groups not directly involved in the process, and, as is discussed later, there sometimes were problems during implementation because unrepresented parties objected after an agreement was reached.

Sometimes, citizens who are directly involved in a controversy are willing to be represented by others in the resolution of the

---

*This may not have been inappropriate, however. Decisions about who will participate in a dispute resolution process are made sometimes by the mediators but more often by the individuals and groups involved in the dispute.

dispute. In the site-specific cases in this study, if citizens' interests were not represented by citizen leaders, they were most likely to have been represented by a public agency. For example, in the three cases examined for this report involving odor problems, local citizens had made complaints to, and were represented by, a state regulatory agency. Agreements between the state agency and the company or town government that owned the facility causing the problem were reached and successfully implemented in all three cases.

Still, representation of citizens' interests by public agencies is not always successful. In a case involving noise from an auto raceway, nearby residents were represented by the state regulatory agency. The agreement between the raceway owners and agency staff was not ratified by the agency's appointed board, however, in part because of a change in decision makers in the agency during the process and in part because the attorney for the local residents, who was not satisfied with the agreement, had significant influence with the board. In this case, the case might have been resolved more successfully if that attorney had been involved directly in the negotiations, although citizens represented by their own leaders in similar cases have not always been successful, either.

In disputes over environmental policy issues, or in site-specific disputes with large potential environmental impacts, the interests of the public at large also have occasionally been represented by nonprofit public interest organizations. Different organizations have widely varied perspectives of what constitutes the public interest in environmental disputes, however. Some public interest groups represent the concerns of consumers; others, concerns for the maintenance of a good climate for economic growth; and others, concerns for environmental protection. There is no clear way to represent the public interest most effectively in policy negotiations, but the best approximation thus far has been to involve the widest diversity of public interest organizations that either have taken an active role on the issue in dispute or have shown obvious concern in other areas about aspects of the issue at hand.

Because the cases in this study are so varied, it is hard to draw conclusions from them about how citizens' interests can best be represented in environmental dispute resolution efforts. Nevertheless, it may be significant that in only two cases in this study have local citizens filed lawsuits to challenge the outcome of a mediated negotiation in which they did not participate directly.

Number of Parties Involved

Contrary to what is often assumed,* there is no evidence among the cases studied to indicate that a large number of parties in a dispute resolution process makes it more difficult to reach an agreement. The average number of parties in the cases examined in this study was just over 4, and the range was between 2 and over 40. In fact, the average number of parties for cases in which the parties failed to reach an agreement was lower than the average number of parties in cases in which agreements were reached (figure 8). It should be noted, however, that the preliminary assessments conducted by most mediators may have screened out many cases in which a large number of parties could have reduced the likelihood of success, thus affecting the sample of cases studied.

The number of parties in a dispute does seem to have some effect, however, on how a dispute resolution process is conducted. Mediators in disputes with many participants sometimes use a workshop format rather than more formal negotiations to facilitate group problem solving. Subcommittees also are used to break large groups into manageable proportions. Also, agreements on less controversial issues often can be reached more quickly in committees, with broader ratification done in the large group sessions. In this way, issues can be narrowed and large group sessions focused on the most important issues. Drafting proposals on key issues in committees also may help facilitate later discussion in large groups by giving the group something concrete for consideration.

For example, in the dispute over water pollution control measures for the Patuxent River (see chapter 1), mediators brought over 40 people together in a consensus-building process using both subcommittees and a workshop format. A steering committee met before the workshop to agree on such decisions as who should be involved, the scope of the issues, and the agenda. A technical committee of scientists who disagreed about which pollutants were the dominant cause of existing pollution problems also met before the workshop to share information on what was and was not known about pollution problems in the Patuxent. The results of the technical meeting were presented at the beginning of the larger workshop of represen-

---

*Some dispute resolution experts recommend limiting mediation attempts to cases involving 15 or fewer parties.

Figure 8
Success in Reaching Agreements,
by Number of Parties
(site-specific cases only)

	All site-specific cases*	Number of parties									Average number of parties per case
		2	3	4	5	6	7	8	9	10+	
Agreement reached	78% (74)	71% (25)	67% (8)	86% (12)	75% (3)	100% (4)	75% (3)	100% (4)	100% (1)	82% (14)	4.9
No agreement reached	22% (21)	29% (10)	33% (4)	14% (2)	25% (1)	0% (0)	25% (1)	0% (0)	0% (0)	18% (3)	3.9
Total cases	100% (95)	100% (35)	100% (12)	100% (14)	100% (4)	100% (4)	100% (4)	100% (4)	100% (1)	100% (17)	

Numerals in parentheses represent actual number of cases.

* Four successfully resolved site-specific cases are not included because either the number of parties changed during the course of the negotiation or, for some other reason, the number of parties is not easily determinable. As a result, the percentage figures for reaching agreement differ from figure 5 by 1 percent.

tatives from all the affected interests, who for the first time were able to look at the problem from a shared information base. At different times during the course of the meeting, the participants met in small groups of diverse interests, in caucuses of those with shared interests, and as a committee of the whole. Much of the work in developing alternatives was done in committees.

Types of Parties Involved

A remarkable diversity of parties has participated in environmental dispute resolution efforts (figure 9). Although the reasons are unclear, the success rates for reaching agreements, while consistently impressive, differ by the combination of types of parties.* In many combinations, parties have reached agreements between 86 and 100 percent of the time—among them, mediated negotiations between government agencies and local citizens or property owners; between government agencies, private companies, and local citizens; between government agencies, environmental groups, and local citizens; between government agencies and private corporations; and between government agencies and Indian tribes. Mediated negotiations between government agencies and multiple interest groups or between government agencies and environmental groups have been successful about 80 percent of the time. Intergovernmental mediation efforts without any private parties directly involved seem to have done less well than average—but still have reached an agreement in over 70 percent of such cases studied. The number of cases in other categories is too small to draw any conclusions.

*Direct Involvement of Decision Makers,
Including Public Agencies*

Although public agencies have participated in more environmental dispute resolution efforts than have any other organizations, both agency staff and private parties often question whether agency representatives should participate directly in dispute resolution attempts that also involve private parties. The reasons for concern differ. Sometimes private parties feel that they will be able to talk more freely with each other if government decision makers are not present. Agency staff may not want to express an opinion on the

---

*Whether these differences would hold with a larger number of cases in each of the categories is unclear.

Figure 9

Success in Reaching Agreements, by Parties Involved

(site-specific cases only)

Parties involved	Agreement	No agreement	Subtotal[1]	Total[2]
Intergovernmental	71% (12)	29% (5)	100% (17)	(19)
Government agencies and local citizens/property owners	88% (15)	12% (2)	100% (17)	(18)
Government agencies and multiple interest groups (e.g., business, environmental, labor, fishing, commerical, recreation)	80% (8)	20% (2)	100% (10)	(13)
Government agencies, private companies and local citizens/property owners	88% (7)	13% (1)	101% (8)	(11)
Private companies and local citizens/property owners	50% (4)	50% (4)	100% (8)	(9)
Government agencies, environmental groups, and local citizens/property owners	86% (6)	14% (1)	100% (7)	(9)
Government agencies and private companies	100% (7)	0% (0)	100% (7)	(7)
Government agencies and Indian tribes	100% (6)	0% (0)	100% (6)	(6)
Government agencies and environmental groups	83% (5)	17% (1)	100% (6)	(6)
Private companies and environmental groups	67% (2)	33% (1)	100% (3)	(4)
Government agencies, private companies, and environmental groups	75% (3)	25% (1)	100% (4)	(4)
Private companies, environmental groups, and local citizens/property owners	– (0)	– (0)	– (0)	(3)
Two or more private landowners	33% (1)	67% (2)	100% (3)	(3)
Government agencies, Indian tribes, and private landowners	–[3]	–[3]	(1)	(1)
Two or more Indian tribes	–[3]	–[3]	(1)	(1)
Two or more environmental groups	–[3]	–[3]	(1)	(1)
Total site-specific cases	79% (78)	21% (21)	100% (99)	(115)

[1] Cases in which the objective was to reach agreement.
[2] Includes cases in which the objective was to improve communications (see figure 4).
[3] Information on some cases is excluded to preserve confidentiality.

issues too soon, especially when the issues are very political or the agency does not have a large stake in the outcome. Agency staff also may feel that they should not participate in negotiations either because they believe that it would be an improper delegation of their responsibilities or because they think that their authority to make decisions would be threatened. Finally, agency staff may be willing to convene a negotiation process but unwilling to participate in a process convened by an independent mediator, because the agency sees itself as the appropriate mediator or feels that accepting the assistance of an independent mediator would be seen as a confession of failure. Depending on the circumstances, some of these concerns may be well founded; others may be less so.

Determining the appropriate role of public agencies in a voluntary dispute resolution process and how that role will affect the likelihood of success also is complicated by the agencies' various kinds of responsibilities in different situations. In some cases, an agency is responsible for constructing projects or preparing plans. In other cases, agencies serve as regulatory authorities, in promulgating regulations, in granting permits, or in enforcement. In still other cases, agencies are resource managers, land owners, or owners of public facilities. In addition, the role of local governments may be slightly different from the role played by state or federal agencies.

Regardless of a public agency's role, however, its representatives usually must participate directly in efforts to resolve a dispute when that agency is a party to a lawsuit or potential lawsuit. Similarly, in most of the cases in this study in which an agency was a project proponent or developer, representatives of the agency also have been at the table. For those cases in which a public agency proposed a project but preferred to be the recipient of a consensus reached by the affected private parties, evidence indicates that, although the parties at the table have reached agreements, they have had three times as many problems during implementation as agreements have had on average. Isolating the consequences of participation or the lack of participation by public agencies by correlating success to the many other roles that agencies play is more difficult because agencies play so many different roles and the nature of the role in each case may be difficult to define.

The various concerns to the contrary, however, the results of the overall experience to date shows that public officials can participate effectively in environmental dispute resolution processes. More important, however, experience also strongly indicates that the direct participation of all parties having the authority to make and to implement decisions, in particular the participation of the public agencies with decision-making authority in a dispute, is a factor that seems to have major importance in increasing the likelihood of success in both reaching and implementing agreements. Combining both site-specific cases and policy dialogues, when the parties at a negotiation table had the authority to make decisions, they were able to reach agreement in 82 percent of the cases (figure 10). By contrast, when the agreements took the form of recommendations to a decision-making body that did not participate directly in the negotiations, the parties reached agreement 73 percent of the time. A breakdown of these cases shows that, in the site-specific cases, agreement was reached in 81 percent of the cases in which the parties with decision-making power participated in the negotiations but in only 74 percent of the cases in which the parties attempted to agree on recommendations. The record of success for policy issues is similar. Agreements were reached in 100 percent of those policy-level cases in which the parties at the table had the power to make final decisions* and in 72 percent of the cases in which the agreement sought was a recommendation. (This factor seems to be even more important in influencing the likelihood of agreements being fully implemented, as is discussed later in this chapter.)

Why parties are more likely to reach agreements when all decision makers are at the table is unclear. One hypothesis is that the presence of decision makers lends the outcome of negotiations an extra measure of certainty: once these parties have concurred, there are no other decision points at which a change in the terms of the agreement is likely to be made. As a result, the participants in a negotiation attempt can be fairly confident that promises made will be kept. All of this is confused, however, by the inevitable blurring in practice of distinctions between reaching decisions and making recommendations (see introduction). When the parties at the table have the power to make decisions, representatives often still must go back to their organizations to get tentative agreements ratified. And, in some of the cases in which the objective was to

---

*The sample size here was only four cases, however.

Figure 10

Success in Reaching Agreements,
by Whether the Parties
Had the Authority to Make Decisions

	All cases	Authority to make decisions			Authority to make recommendations		
		All	Site-specific cases	Policy cases	All	Site-specific cases	Policy cases
Agreement reached	78% (103)	82% (56)	81% (52)	100% (4)	73% (47)	74% (26)	72% (21)
No agreement reached	22% (29)	18% (12)	19% (12)	0% (0)	27% (17)	26% (9)	28% (8)
Total cases	100% (132)	100% (68)	100% (64)	100% (4)	100% (64)	100% (35)	100% (29)

Numerals in parentheses represent actual number of cases.

agree on recommendations, representatives of the final decision makers may have participated, but their organizations specifically did not want to give the negotiations any official sanction as a decision-making process.

Process- and Context-Related Factors

Mediators emphasize the importance of the way a voluntary dispute resolution process is conducted in determining the success of a negotiation effort. Several different process- and context-related factors are commonly mentioned as significantly influencing negotiations. The importance of a few of these can be measured, although the importance of most of these factors is difficult, if not impossible, to quantify.

Agreement on Procedural Issues

An important task for a mediator early in a dispute resolution effort is to anticipate procedural questions that are likely to arise during the effort and to help the parties agree on how those questions will be handled. Not only can agreements on procedural issues allow a negotiation process to proceed more smoothly, but demonstrating to disputing parties that they can agree on how to negotiate with each other can increase their sense of optimism, as well. That, in turn, can increase the likelihood that the dispute resolution effort itself will be successful. Procedural issues can include deciding whether to allow the use of alternate representatives, selecting meeting sites, scheduling meetings, handling confidential information, using outside experts, deciding how to handle relations with the media, and determining whether agreements will be put in writing and, if so, in what form. Another procedural issue, deciding whether to set a deadline and what the deadline should be is discussed in a separate section below.

One important procedural question is whether or not the parties will choose to put their agreements in writing. In virtually all of the site-specific cases in this study, some written account of the agreement was prepared, but the variation in the forms written agreements have taken seems to reflect the diverse situations in which mediation has been applied. Sometimes a separate document of agreement was signed by the representatives of the various parties; sometimes an informal written record of agreements was created either by the parties or by the mediator but not signed. On other occasions, the terms of a verbal agreement were written directly into the conditions of a permit or an official planning document without a specific, written agreement being signed by the parties. The various forms that agreements have taken include, among others, consent decrees filed in court to terminate litigation, contracts, memorandums of understanding between public agencies, joint letters, reports, handbooks, voluntary guidelines, permits, water quality plans, land-use plans, U.S. Forest Service decision notices, rate-setting orders by public utility commissions, draft notices of proposed rule making, and draft legislation. Because such a high percentage of cases had written agreements of some kind, whether or not the simple existence of a written document affects the likelihood of success in reaching agreements is hard to determine. So much variation exists among cases in the form the agreement took, who drafted it, whether it was signed, and the nature of the dispute that valid comparisons of the effect these more detailed characteristics of written agreements have must wait until there is a larger sample of cases. The effect that other procedural issues have on the likelihood of success is even more difficult to measure.

Presence of a Deadline

It is commonly assumed that the presence of a reasonable deadline plays an important role in the likelihood of success in reaching agreements, both in allowing enough time to deal with the issues effectively and to create pressure for closure. Although mediators and parties consistently report that deadlines, as long as they are reasonable, do assist efforts to resolve disputes, it does not appear from the cases studied for this report that simply the presence of a deadline increases the likelihood of success in reaching an agreement. Indeed, while agreements were reached in 76 percent of the site-specific disputes in which clear deadlines existed, they were also reached in 81 percent of the cases known to have no deadline (figure 11). These results, however, are clouded somewhat because of the 14 cases in which the existence of a deadline is not known. It may be that the parties' sense of urgency, which can be created not only by deadlines but also by other factors, is more relevant than the presence of a deadline per se.

Several kinds of deadlines can exist, and other factors can create a sense of urgency. Some deadlines may be quite firm, but many are easily subject to change. Court dates are a common form of

Figure 11

Success in Reaching Agreements, with and without Deadlines
(site-specific cases only)

	All site-specific cases	Deadline	No deadline	Deadline unknown
Agreement reached	79% (78)	76% (32)	81% (35)	79% (11)
No agreement reached	21% (21)	24% (10)	19% (8)	21% (3)
Total cases	100% (99)	100% (42)	100% (43)	100% (14)

Numerals in parentheses represent actual number of cases.

deadline, but, if progress is being made in negotiations, these usually can be changed. Court-imposed deadlines for certain kinds of action may create a greater sense of urgency. Some deadlines are created by administrative hearings or decision schedules, while others are agreed to by the parties. In some of the cases in this study, a very real sense of urgency was created because an individual who had great influence was about to retire or leave office. Some of the most effective time pressures also have been created not by deadlines set by human institutions but by the urgency of the problem itself.

Possession of Sufficient Incentives

Experienced mediators emphasize that the parties to a voluntary dispute resolution process must have sufficient incentives to negotiate an agreement with each other. Parties will be unlikely to participate, let alone agree to a settlement, if they think they could achieve more of what they want in another way—sometimes even if that approach costs more. A simple illustration of the point is the I-90 case in Washington State (see chapters 1 and 2). In the early stages of the negotiation, the political pressures in each community for specific highway options were strong enough that it was difficult for community officials to compromise. The incentives to agree (or the costs of continuing the dispute) remained smaller than the costs of compromise until Governor Daniel J. Evans suggested that the available federal money might be spent elsewhere in Washington if Seattle and its suburbs couldn't reach an agreement.

In most cases, however, the incentives to agree are not as obvious as this choice between losing everything or gaining something. Sometimes, all that may be necessary to bring reluctant parties to a bargaining table is an assurance, by those responsible, that any agreement reached will be implemented. At other times, the incentives may come from opportunities for mutual gains that would be unavailable except through cooperation. For example, in a mediated negotiation between commercial fishermen and a consortium of petroleum companies over conflicts arising from their joint use of the Santa Barbara Channel, the parties were able to organize and fund a liaison office to help them coordinate their operations so that they could reduce their interference with each other's operations at sea. With the assistance of mediators Alana Knaster and Jim Arthur of The Mediation Institute, the oil companies, fishermen, and state and federal agency officials also designed and directed a jointly sponsored study of the effects of seismic testing techniques on fish behavior. A similar, joint committee is applying the same process to investigate the effects of seismic testing on fish eggs and larvae. The first program would not have been possible, and the others would have been less credible to all sides, without the cooperation of both the petroleum companies and the fishermen.

In practical terms, incentives are not easy to measure. The parties to environmental disputes inevitably face different stakes; different probabilities of achieving their goals using different strategies; different costs in time, money, and reputation associated with these strategies; and different risks associated with winning, losing, or compromising. Each of these factors affects the total calculation of gains versus losses that determines a party's decision about whether to participate in a voluntary dispute resolution process or to agree to the particular terms of a potential agreement.

Incentives are difficult to measure also because they are affected by perceptions that may or may not be accurate and because both the incentives and the parties' perceptions of their incentives are subject to change. As a matter of strategy, parties to a dispute frequently attempt to alter each other's perceptions of relative advantage. In addition, the discussions between parties and mediators sometimes can alter the parties' perceptions, particularly when the parties have unrealistic expectations about their chances of achieving their objectives. Moreover, mediators may point out unrecognized opportunities for mutual gain. (A mediator's perceptions of a situation, however, also may or may not be accurate. Questions of mediator accountability and ethics are discussed in chapter 5.)

Ability to Satisfy Each Party's Underlying Interests

Not surprisingly, any party's incentives to agree to a proposal depends largely on whether the proposal satisfies its principal interests. Mediators commonly stress the importance of using "interest-based negotiation" instead of "positional bargaining," believing that the various parties' ability and willingness to identify the interests that underlie each other's positions and to invent new alternatives that satisfy those interests helps enormously in resolving disputes.[3] Indeed, in most of the cases in this study in which negotiations failed to produce agreements, at least one of the reasons was the parties' failure to discover a solution that at least met the minimal needs of each involved party.

Mediators commonly ask the various parties, either in confidence or at the negotiating table, the reasons why they hold a particular position—that is, what their underlying objectives or interests in the dispute are. In doing this, the mediator hopes to discover that those interests are not as incompatible as the parties' positions on the issues appear to be—either because they can find some common ground or because their interests are sufficiently *different* that they are not necessarily mutually exclusive—thereby giving the parties a new opportunity to develop alternatives that may satisfy their real needs more effectively.

In some cases, however, the parties' underlying interests may be mutually exclusive, with the result that the parties are unwilling to compromise sufficiently to reach an agreement or are unable to invent any options that meet each other's needs. One such dispute was over whether an off-road vehicle (ORV) race would be allowed in the California Desert, managed by the U.S. Bureau of Land Management (BLM). The race's opponents were willing to propose alternative routes along existing roads or trails in the desert, but the ORV enthusiasts wanted the race so they could travel across overland terrain. No agreement between the two parties could be reached, and the necessary permit for the race was denied. A new federal statute governing management of public lands prohibited ORV activity outside designated areas, and the draft plan for the area involved in this dispute did not allow such activity. A permit might have been issued under an exception in time for the scheduled race to have been held, if the environmental groups would have agreed not to object to the exception.

Sometimes, when parties cannot agree, a ruling on key issues can enable negotiation on other issues or allow an unsuccessful negotiation to resume under new circumstances. The Homestake Pitch Mine case described in chapter 1 is an example. In that case, some of the parties in a coalition opposed the mine on antinuclear grounds. Their interests and the company's were mutually exclusive—the antinuclear forces wanted the uranium left in the ground, while the company was in business to mine the uranium—so they didn't even attempt to negotiate. At the time that mediation was suggested, however, the coalition had lost on all issues except the mine reclamation plan. Because the principal concern of other members of the coalition was mine reclamation, the antinuclear opponents agreed to leave the coalition temporarily, reserving their right to continue to oppose the mine. As a result, the other groups were able to negotiate an agreement resolving the mine reclamation issues.

A dispute involving leases on moorage sites,* provides an example of a case in which an unsuccessful negotiation resumed after a key issue was resolved by an outside decision maker. Because the state's shoreline management act restricted the number of moorage sites in that locale, the city council had put a cap on the rate at which moorage-rental fees could be raised, on the theory that moorage owners had an effective monopoly. The state supreme court, however, had ruled the rent-control provisions unconstitutional. The city council responded by urging the two sides to the dispute to jointly propose a new ordinance settling rent-control and other moorage-related disagreements. Also, because the moorage owners had evicted several tenants after the court decision, the city council passed a 120-day moratorium on evictions threatened by the owners, which allowed both sides time to negotiate. The city council also invited two mediators to assist the negotiations, but the parties were unable to reach an agreement resolving all their differences.

According to persons involved in the negotiations, the principal difficulty was that the parties shared no common ground about whether any rent control should be allowed at all, and both sides thought that they could prevail. The lessees, although willing to compromise on the amount that moorage fees could be raised, were unwilling to give up all rent-control protection and knew that the city council generally favored their cause. The moorage owners opposed any rent-control provisions and believed that there was a good chance that the courts would continue to back them up. When the negotiations failed to produce a mutually acceptable ordinance proposal, city attorneys stepped in and wrote a new ordinance that they believed could survive a legal challenge. The city council passed the new ordinance, settling the basic issue in the dispute. The owners still had the option of going back to court, but the lessees now had a stronger legal position. The two parties resumed negotiations, this

---

*Facts about this case, including the kind of moorages, parties, mediators, and location, have been kept confidential.

time without a mediator, on the lessees' offer to purchase the moorage sites using a condominium-type arrangement and were able to produce an agreement.

Cases such as the Homestake and moorage-rental disputes are reminders that reaching an agreement does not necessarily mean that all interests in a dispute are *well* satisfied. The parties to environmental disputes want to achieve certain objectives, not to reach an agreement for the sake of agreement. How well each parties' interests are satisfied depends in part on the assumptions that define the issues to be negotiated. Parties who do not look carefully at these assumptions and evaluate whether they are acceptable may find that they have agreed to participate in a process that is not in their best interests. In such cases, the dispute resolution process may be unsuccessful once people realize that they don't agree on basic assumptions about what is being negotiated, or the parties may find themselves backing into agreements that do not satisfy their interests as well as they might have under a different set of assumptions.

How well each party's interests are satisfied also depends on the balance of power in a situation and whether the parties make accurate assessments about their chances of winning more through another dispute resolution strategy. Voluntary agreement is assumed to be a measure of success in resolving disputes, not because each party gets everything it wants but because it reflects a judgment by the parties that the issues in dispute have been resolved more adequately than they would have been using other available means of dispute resolution. Parties who underestimate their relative advantage may agree to options that achieve too little, and those who overestimate their relative advantage may lose if their bet is called. Also, the balance of power in a situation may be so unequal that parties accept proposals that do not adequately satisfy their principal interests.*

In the moorage case, the parties could not agree on one of the basic assumptions that defined the issues—whether or not there would be rent control. Clearly, the moorage owners' interests would have been *better* satisfied if they had been able to defeat rent control outright, although the lessees interests would then have been

---

*This judgment must be regarded as speculative, however, since it assumes that an outsider can second-guess what was in someone else's best interests.

less well satisfied. Once that issue had been decided by an external force, the negotiations could proceed. Presumably, once they had lost the rent control issue, the moorage owners felt they would be better off selling than leasing with rent controls, because they agreed voluntarily to the sale of the moorage sites. Only those involved know whether any of the proposals that the moorage owners rejected would have made them better off with rent control than they now are with the sale of the moorage sites.

Fortunately, efforts to resolve environmental disputes are not always zero-sum games, in which a gain by one side means an equal loss for the other side. The skill of the parties to a dispute in inventing creative solutions also affects how well all parties' interests are satisfied. Although parties may fail to reach agreements when they are unable to invent solutions that satisfy each other's principal interests, it does not follow that agreements reached always satisfy the parties' interests as well as they could have. A few thoughtful observers of the use of voluntary dispute resolution processes have begun to evaluate how to improve the joint gains by all parties through better use of analytical techniques in negotiations.[4]

Whether the Dispute Was in Litigation

Potential parties to a dispute resolution effort commonly assume that once a lawsuit has been filed, all hopes are lost of resolving the dispute through mediation. This does not seem to be true, although the cases in this study in which a lawsuit had been filed were resolved less frequently than were those in which no lawsuit had been filed (figure 12). As is discussed in chapter 4, over 90 percent of all environmental lawsuits are settled before the case goes to trial, clearly demonstrating that parties in a lawsuit can negotiate with each other. Although a lawsuit can draw the battle lines and possibly increase the hostile feelings of those being sued, lawsuits also can clarify or focus the issues and raise the stakes sufficiently that parties who had been reluctant to negotiate previously may be more willing to take their opponents seriously.

In many of the cases studied for this report, litigation was not even a relevant option. In other cases, the parties could have taken each other to court, but had not yet done so. In still other cases,

---

*Whether or not the parties to the disputes examined here could have done a better job in maximizing their joint gains is beyond the scope of this report.

Figure 12

Success in Reaching Agreements,
by Whether a Lawsuit Had Been Filed
(site-specific cases only)

	All site-specific cases	Not in litigation	On the verge of litigation or administrative hearing	In administrative adjudicatory process	Lawsuit filed
Agreement reached	79% (78)	88% (43)	71% (12)	50% (5)	78% (18)
No agreement reached	21% (21)	12% (6)	29% (5)	50% (5)	22% (5)
Total cases	100% (99)	100% (49)	100% (17)	100% (10)	100% (23)

Numerals in parentheses represent actual number of cases.

parties were on the verge of litigation, were in adjudicatory proceedings within an administrative agency, or were in litigation. Parties who were not in litigation with each other, whether litigation was a relevant option or not, were able to reach agreement in 88 percent of the site-specific cases studied.* Parties who were in litigation were able to reach agreement in 78 percent of the site-specific cases studied, a figure noticeably lower than that for cases not in litigation but still nearly the same as the overall success rate for site-specific cases. Parties who were on the verge of litigation were still less successful, reaching agreements in 71 percent of the site-specific cases studied. The cases in which parties were involved in a formal, administrative dispute resolution proceeding were the least successful, reaching agreement in only 50 percent of the cases studied. The reasons for this are unclear, however.

Maintenance of Good Representative/ Constituency Relationships

Because environmental disputes usually are between organizations and groups, not between individuals, it is generally assumed that

---

*No significant difference was evident between those cases in which litigation was a relevant option and those cases in which it was not.

the likelihood of success in reaching stable agreements is increased when the representatives of each party are able to speak for their constituencies. Not only must the representatives of different parties work with each other to find a mutually acceptable resolution of the issues, but they also must maintain effective communication with their constituencies or organizations to ensure the eventual ratification of an agreement.

However, identifying who should represent the various groups, organizations, and agencies in a dispute resolution effort can be difficult. Large corporations, government agencies, public interest groups, and ad hoc citizens' organizations each have different internal decision-making processes that affect who the best representative or team of representatives might be, and the intraorganizational dynamics of any party can be complicated. Under some circumstances (particularly in policy dialogues), mediators invite particular individuals to participate in a dispute resolution effort, but, usually, mediators prefer to have the various parties select their own representatives because those persons are then more likely to have the support of their constituencies.

A general problem, particularly for public agencies and corporations, is that often the individuals with decision-making authority who can speak for the organization are not the same as those with specific technical expertise on the issues. Also, in large organizations, it is often not possible for the policy makers to spend the time to be present personally in all negotiations. Establishing clear and effective internal communications between meetings so that representatives can check with policy makers can be very helpful. In addition, the issues are often complex enough that organizations and groups nccd to draw on the expertise of technical staff, managers, legal counsel, and perhaps others to negotiate effectively. Teams of representatives can be used to solve this problem. Assessing whether the right representatives were at the table or how well they kept their organizations or groups informed is difficult to do objectively, however.

Representatives of ad hoc citizens' organizations may have particular difficulties maintaining effective communications between representatives and their constituencies because the internal decision-making process of a new group may not be well organized at first. A quantitative assessment of cases in which one or more of the parties was not well organized was not conducted because lack of organization requires making subjective judgments, but a party's lack of organization was never reported to be the cause of failure to agree in specific cases. Some observers of these processes worry, however, that, although agreements may be reached, parties that are not well organized may agree to terms that are not in their own best interests. This concern is even harder to evaluate objectively, however.

Finally, a significant problem arises in policy-level dialogues or negotiations when representatives are sought not just for specific organizations but for constituencies of interests. For example, a federal policy or regulation may affect all the states, an entire industry made up of hundreds of companies, thousands of workers, or some other set of interests itself comprised of many organizations. Finding ways for representatives to maintain communication with these constituencies presents a very difficult challenge.

Negotiation in Good Faith

Good faith also is commonly assumed to be an important factor in successfully resolving a dispute. Mediators generally will not become involved in a dispute if there is reason to believe that any party will not negotiate in good faith. During the dispute assessment and process-design phases of a voluntary dispute resolution process, mediators may ask the parties to make a public commitment to each other that they will make a good faith effort to reach agreement. Such public assurances (especially in cases where relationships between the parties have become particularly hostile), although not always completely accepted, often help ease some of the tension.

Understandably, it is hard to determine whether or not parties to a dispute resolution effort have acted in good faith. However, among the cases studied for this report, some of the failures to reach agreement do seem to have been due to actions by one party that caused the other to question the first's intentions. In one case, a recycling company had obtained local permits to construct a new plant. Citizen opposition emerged after the company had made a significant investment in the new site. The opponents threatened to take legal action to block the plant, if necessary. Both sides agreed to mediation, however, and were exploring alternatives when one member of the citizens' group acted unilaterally, initiating litigation without consulting anyone. The company's attorneys advised against further participation in the mediation process. In the end, the court authorized the company to proceed with the new plant site, and the local citizens lost the opportunity to resolve some of their concerns.

In another case, two local political leaders had been arch rivals for years. Each agreed during negotiations to a joint study of the intergovernmental taxation and service sharing issues in their area, but, instead of using the joint study as a vehicle for clarifying the issues and thinking through alternative strategies, they each used it to document their own positions. Not surprisingly, they were unable to reach an agreement. The case is now in legal proceedings estimated to cost each side at least $1 million.

On a very few occasions, one of the parties to an environmental dispute resolution process is reported to have participated cynically, hoping that an agreement would not be reached. In at least one such case, an agreement was reached anyway, to that party's surprise, For the most part, although the parties may be skeptical about the likelihood of reaching an agreement, mediators report that negotiations are entered into in good faith.

Substance-Related Factors

Those interested in voluntary dispute resolution processes often wish to know whether such approaches are likely to be more successful for some issues than others and whether parties need to agree on the facts in dispute before they can negotiate successfully. Mediators often add the hypothesis that parties need to agree at least on the scope of issues to be negotiated.

Issues in Dispute

Mediators are frequently asked whether the kind of issues involved in a dispute resolution effort makes a difference in how successful the process is likely to be. The results of this study indicate that, at least in site-specific disputes, there probably is little significant relationship between the general types of issues involved and the likelihood that a dispute will be resolved (figure 13). The parties successfully reached agreement in 79 percent of the 99 site-specific cases in which reaching agreement on a decision or recommendation was the objective. In land-use issues, the category with the largest number of cases, the parties successfully reached agreement 78 percent of the time. The results were somewhat higher for natural

Figure 13

Success in Reaching Agreements, by Issue
(site-specific cases only)

	All site-specific cases	Land use	Resource management	Water resources	Energy	Air quality	Toxics	Misc.
Agreement reached	79% (78)	78% (47)	83% (19)	87% (13)	78% (7)	100% (6)	60% (3)	50% (1)
No agreement reached	21% (21)	22% (13)	17% (4)	13% (2)	22% (2)	0% (–)	40% (2)	50% (1)
Total cases	100% (99)	100% (60)	100% (23)	100% (15)	100% (9)	100% (6)	100% (5)	100% (2)

Numerals in parentheses represent actual number of cases.

resource management and water resource issues, in which the parties reached agreement in 83 and 87 percent of the cases, respectively, but the sample sizes were smaller. The cases in the remaining issue areas were so few that the results are inconclusive. More study, done perhaps at a more detailed level, may show different results. The influence that the kind of issue has on the likelihood of success also may be linked to other factors, such as whether the particular dispute has precedent-setting implications.

Agreement on the Scope of Issues

Many mediators assume that the parties to a dispute must agree on the objective of a dispute resolution process and the scope of the issues to be addressed before successful negotiation efforts can commence; others believe that it may be useful to bring parties together to discuss what issues should be on the agenda as part of the face-to-face negotiations. Unfortunately, however, measuring the extent to which agreement on the scope of issues was a significant factor in the success of the cases in this study proved too difficult, in part because in some cases it may have been only a matter of timing, in others a matter of degree, and in others a matter of perception.

Reaching agreement on the scope of issues, particularly in highly polarized or controversial issues, usually requires private conversations between the mediator and the parties individually to discuss what each party's real concerns and goals are. In the Metropolitan Water Roundtable case (see chapter 1), for example, the mediators met with potential parties during a prenegotiation dispute assessment. These discussions focused initially on whether and how the anticipated controversy over the proposed Two Forks water supply project could be resolved. However, the parties and the mediators agreed during the dispute assessment process that, if the issue was the proposed Two Forks dam alone, resolving the dispute would not be possible, since satisfying the underlying interests of some of the parties required looking at water supply issues more broadly. Those parties, concerned about the depletion of the state's water resources that could be made available for other uses, had urged greater consideration of conservation measures as an alternative to new water projects. They were reluctant to discuss *how* the Two Forks dam would be built until the question of *whether* it needed to be built at all had been answered. Rather than limiting the scope of the negotiation only to the one project proposal, the parties agreed to consider the broader question of how the Denver area could obtain the water supplies it needed in the future. This change in the scope of the issues, or how the issues were defined, allowed the parties to discuss one of the underlying issues in dispute—how much water did Denver really need? This probably increased the chances of success in this effort because, in the parlance of the dispute resolution field, the parties had to agree on the problem before they could agree on a solution.

Agreement on the Facts

Environmental disputes often are further complicated by disputes over just what the facts are. People disagree about the effects of proposed projects, plans, or policies on the environment, and information about the potential impacts or risks of an action may be unavailable or uncertain. People have different attitudes toward risk, and disputes can result over what actions are appropriate in the face of uncertainty. There may be disagreements over the accuracy, completeness, or relevance of the facts presented; over what degree of detail is acceptable; and over the relative importance of different factors (that is, how the data should be weighed). Mediators look for such problems during the dispute assessment process and help the parties agree on how they want to handle disputes over data or risks. Opportunities for exchanging information, analyzing the information presented, agreeing on joint fact-finding, or jointly sponsoring new studies are all options that can be built into an agenda before negotiations begin.

For example, in Virginia, temperature levels in Lake Anna, which was created to cool several nuclear power plants, currently exceed permitted levels even though not all of the projected power plants have been built. With assistance from Richard Collins of the Institute for Environmental Negotiation at the University of Virginia, experts representing environmental groups, federal and state agencies, and the Virginia Electric Power Company reached an agreement in spring 1984 on the design for a study of the effects of temperature levels in the lake.[5] When that study is completed, the Virginia State Water Control Board will use it to help determine whether compliance actions are needed or whether the conditions of the permits should be modified.

One problem in deciding how to design a dispute resolution process to deal effectively with complex technical information and disputes over facts is that the parties often do not have equal resources for marshalling the data and analysis that they need to negotiate effectively. Mediators often express concern that, unless this obstacle is overcome, the chances of success are limited. In some cases, mediators have been able to help the parties obtain additional resources or to pool resources to engage in a joint fact-finding effort.

Of course, agreement on the facts and the complexity of the technical issues involved are matters of degree. As they are with the importance of reaching prior agreement on the scope of issues to be discussed, concrete measures of whether this factor increases or decreases the likelihood of success are not easily found.

POSSIBLE FACTORS IN IMPLEMENTING AGREEMENTS

Success in reaching an agreement is not usually the end of the process. In most cases, an agreement must lead to action if the parties are to feel that the process has been completely successful. In theory, one of the principal advantages of a voluntary dispute resolution process is that, if all the parties have agreed to the outcome, the likelihood of successful implementation of the decision should be increased. This does not mean, however, that implementation will be easy. Negotiated decisions face many of the same technical, financial, and administrative difficulties that public decisions reached in other ways face.

The analyses of site-specific disputes and policy dialogues are kept separate in this examination because important characteristics of these cases differ (see chapter 2). First, the objectives of the efforts had different overall emphases, with policy dialogues often being convened as much to improve communication between parties and shape the debate over policy issues as to lead to specific decisions. In addition, the participants in policy dialogues often are opinion leaders invited by the conveners of the dialogues more for their differing perspectives and leadership abilities than as formal representatives of their groups or organizations. Thus, implementation of agreements reached, if any, in a policy dialogue may be less straightforward and face more difficulties than the implementation of agreements in site-specific cases.

Site-Specific Disputes

As was noted in chapter 2, of the site-specific agreements for which implementation results could be determined, 80 percent had been fully implemented. Thirteen percent had been partially implemented, and only 7 percent were unlikely ever to be implemented.

From the data available, the most significant factor in the likelihood of success in implementing agreements in site-specific disputes is the direct involvement of decision makers, particularly public agencies, in the dispute resolution process. Of the site-specific disputes in which the negotiating parties had the power to decide and implement agreements (and for which an implementation result can be determined), agreements had been fully implemented 85 percent of the time. By contrast, agreements that were only recommendations to a party not at the table had been implemented only 64 percent of the time (figure 14). Agreements had been only partially implemented in 7.5 percent of the cases in which all the persons with the authority to implement the agreement were at the negotiating table but in 29 percent of the cases where those persons were not at the table. The percentage of cases in which agreements were not implemented at all was about the same in both categories. Finally, 23 percent of the cases in which all decision makers were at the table were still in the process of being imple-

Figure 14

Success in Implementing Agreements, by Whether the Parties Had Authority to Do the Implementing

	Overall	Authority to make decisions	Authority to make recommendations
Site-specific cases			
Fully implemented	80%	85%	64%
	(43)	(34)	(9)
Partially implemented	13%	7.5%	29%
	(7)	(3)	(4)
Not implemented	7%	7.5%	7%
	(4)	(3)	(1)
Subtotal— Agreements with known implementation results	100%	100%	100%
	(54)	(40)	(14)
Cases with unknown implementation results	(24)	(12)	(12)
Total— Cases in which agreements were reached	(78)	(52)	(26)
Policy cases			
Fully implemented	41%	0%	50%
	(7)	(0)	(7)
Partially implemented	18%	100%	0%
	(3)	(3)	(0)
Not implemented	41%	0%	50%
	(7)	(0)	(7)
Subtotal— Agreements with known implementation results	100%	100%	100%
	(17)	(3)	(14)
Cases with unknown implementation results	(8)	(1)	(7)
Total— Cases in which agreements were reached	(25)	(4)	(21)

Numerals in parentheses represent actual number of cases.

mented at the time this study was concluded, while implementation was still in progress in 46 percent of the cases in which some of the decision makers were not at the table.

These data should be viewed with some caution, however, because the sample sizes for the two categories are quite different. Still, these results do indicate that, when individuals or groups have the authority to influence a course of action, they usually use it. Exercising that authority within the negotiation process rather than after an agreement has been reached seems to make the outcome of environmental dispute resolution processes more stable.

Other factors may also have effects on the process of implementing agreements, but the data currently available are not sufficient to support firm conclusions. For example, those data indicate that neither the number of parties nor the kinds of issues in dispute is likely to significantly influence the chances for agreements to be implemented successfully. Some observers also suggest that the formality or enforceability of an agreement may increase the likelihood of successful implementation. Since nearly all of the cases in this study were concluded by putting whatever agreement was reached in writing, it is difficult to test the common-sense conclusion that a written agreement per se increases the likelihood that an agreement will be implemented, because it reduces misunderstandings about the terms to which the parties actually agreed. Also, the previously noted variation among the different types of documents into which agreements have been put makes it difficult to test the question of relative enforceability.

Finally, many mediators suggest that it is important to anticipate how an agreement would be implemented and what potential obstacles to implementation might arise before the negotiations are concluded. A prior agreement among the parties about how they intend to implement an agreement and about how they will deal with unanticipated problems during the implementation process may enable parties to reduce the number of implementation problems they eventually face. It also may encourage them to consider reopening their discussions when unexpected problems arise rather than allowing the implementation of the agreement to break down. In some cases, the parties have formed small committees to monitor and guide the implementation of agreements. In a few such cases—for example, the controversy surrounding the expansion of Interstate 90 in the

Seattle area (see chapter 1)—although not in all cases, such committees have made a significant difference in solving problems during implementation. In other cases, parties have incorporated a renegotiation clause into their agreements in which they have committed themselves to going back to the negotiation table if problems arose. So far, however, no evidence is available that any parties have used such clauses.

Policy Dialogues

The results of most policy dialogues to date have largely been informal suggestions that have relied for their implementation on the ability of the participants to gain the broad support of those who share similar interests and on their willingness and ability to bring new policy options to the attention of those making policy decisions. Implementation of the results of policy dialogues also is affected by the complex and changing context for making public policy decisions.

In contrast with the site-specific cases studied, in which all decision-making parties were represented in almost 65 percent of the cases for which the objective was to reach an agreement, policy dialogue or negotiation efforts examined for this report were conducted largely outside of government.[6] In only 12 percent of the policy-level cases studied in which the objective was to reach an agreement were all decision-making bodies represented in the dialogue or negotiation. In the remaining 88 percent, the objective was to agree on recommendations to a decision-making body that was not represented at the table. Thus, although the sample size to date is far too small for drawing reliable conclusions, the participation of representatives of all the parties with decision-making authority in policy dialogues again seems to affect the likelihood of success in implementing agreements (figure 14). Of the four cases studied in this report in which the parties at the table had the authority to reach decisions, implementation results are available for three of them. Although none were fully implemented, all three were at least partially implemented. Implementation results can be determined for 14 of the 21 dialogues that produced recommendations. Seven of those agreements were fully implemented, and seven were not implemented at all.

Current efforts to incorporate dialogue and negotiation into an agency's rule-making process may help solve such implementation problems.[7] It is too soon to draw conclusions, but the results appear promising.[8]

Because of its complexity, the normal, rocky course of implementing decisions on issues of state or federal environmental policy is difficult enough to describe with sensitivity and realism. Interjecting an analysis of factors that affect the likelihood of success in implementing policy recommendations or decisions, whether those policies are developed through dialogue or negotiation or are made by a public body, is even more difficult. The legislative, executive, and judicial branches of government each play important roles and each provide new forums for parties to attempt to modify policies to accomplish their objectives. Federal, state, and local levels of government also provide separate forums for action, with multiple agencies playing a role at each level. Perhaps, as a result of this complexity, although the hope has been that informal efforts at dialogue will help break the deadlocks that often plague the policy-making process, the actual results have been less successful than those for site-specific negotiations, at least in concrete terms.

In the future, greater attention needs to be paid to the problems of implementing policy dialogues. Other issues that must be considered, as those interested in environmental dispute resolution approaches look ahead to the increased use of these processes, are discussed in chapter 5.

REFERENCES

1. Gerald W. Cormick and Leah K. Patton, "Environmental Mediation: Defining the Process Through Experience" (Paper delivered at the American Association for the Advancement of Sciences Symposium on Environmental Mediation, Denver, Colorado, 1977).

2. Environmental mediators all report that they conduct many dispute assessments for each case that reaches the negotiation stage.

3. Roger Fisher and Michael Ury, *Getting to Yes: Negotiating Agreement Without Giving In* (Boston: Houghton Mifflin Company, 1981); and Roger Fisher, "Negotiating Power," *American Behavioral Scientist* 27 (1983):149-66.

4. Lawrence Susskind, "Environmental Mediation and the Accountability Problem," *Vermont Law Review* 6 (1981):1-47; Howard Raiffa, *The Art and Science of Negotiation*, (Cambridge, Mass.: The Belknap Press of Harvard University Press, 1982).

5. "Institute Named Lake Anna Mediator," *The Mediator*, Fall 1983; personal communication with Richard C. Collins, Institute for Environmental Negotiation, April 1984; and meeting minutes.

6. Sam Gusman, "Policy Dialogue," *Environmental Comment*, November 1981, pp. 14-16.

7. Philip J. Harter, "Negotiating Regulations: A Cure for Malaise," *Georgetown Law Journal* 71 (1982):1-118.

8. Henry H. Perritt, Jr., "Analysis of Four Negotiated Rulemaking Experiments," prepared for the Administrative Conference of the United States (draft), September 4, 1985.

Chapter 4

How Efficient Are Environmental Dispute Resolution Processes?

Perhaps the single most common assertion made about environmental dispute resolution processes—indeed, about alternative dispute resolution processes in general—is that they are cheaper and faster than litigation. No systematic attempt to test this claim by comparing litigation on environmental matters with environmental dispute resolution alternatives has ever been made, however, perhaps because very little evidence exists about how long it takes either to litigate or to mediate environmental disputes. Further, there are several conceptual problems in making comparisons between environmental dispute resolution alternatives and litigation. Through simple repetition, however, the notion seems to have become an accepted fact.

The very frequency with which claims are made that mediation is cheaper and faster than litigation is an indicator that people are interested in finding more efficient ways to resolve conflicts. Much has been written about problems in the American legal system and about potential reform measures. Legal scholars addressed judicial reform issues at least as early as the turn of the 20th century,[1] although concerns about resolving disputes in the courts go back to colonial times.[2] More recently, the American Bar Association's Action Commission to Reduce Court Costs and Delay released its findings on the effectiveness of measures to improve the efficiency of the judicial system.[3]

The reforms proposed in the report seem to fall into three categories—expedited court procedures, more efficient attorney practices, and alternatives to litigation. Although only the latter is discussed here, it is important to remember that alternatives to litigation are not the only ways to reduce the costs of resolving disputes through the judicial system.

Although this chapter focuses on questions of time and costs, it also is important to remember that from the perspective of those involved in environmental disputes efficiency is not enough. In looking for dispute resolution processes that will take less time and cost less money, the parties to disputes also are looking for processes that are more effective in producing satisfactory outcomes. Therefore, from the perspective of the parties in a dispute, the most important question is not so much whether mediation, in general, takes less time than litigation, in general. Rather, the parties' concern is a balancing one—how to achieve the best results most efficiently in each specific case.

Evaluating how individual cases might have been more efficiently mediated or litigated requires a level of detail that lies beyond the scope of this study, however. Even a general comparison between mediation and litigation is difficult, because of the lack of parallel data between cases that were litigated and cases that were mediated. Despite these limitations, this chapter does discuss the factors that would have to be taken into account if such a comparison were performed. Some statistics that are available about both litigation and mediation are presented, although it must be remembered that the data are not comparable in any way. The assumption that litigation of environmental issues is a problem is reviewed, as is the idea that some parties use delay as a strategy in their efforts to produce a satisfactory outcome to a dispute.

COMPARING MEDIATION WITH LITIGATION

Most individuals and organizations involved in environmental disputes can cite at least one dispute in which the parties became so locked in a legal stalemate that there seemed to be no way out. Such stories have helped build the case for the weakness in relying solely on litigation for settling disputes, but they also may have oversimplified the general public image both of litigation and of dispute resolution alternatives. A lawsuit that goes to trial may take a very long time, but few lawsuits go to trial. Some mediated environmental disputes may be resolved quickly, but voluntary dispute resolution processes are not necessarily fast if the issues are complex. In addition, although mediators generally charge less than attorneys, one is not necessarily a substitute for the other, and attorneys' and mediators' fees are not the only costs associated with resolving disputes. The costs of preparing for negotiation, for example, may be as high as or higher than the parallel costs of preparing for some kinds of litigation, particularly for public interest groups in cases requiring analysis of scientific information.

One example that is often cited as evidence that expensive, lengthy legal disputes can be better solved through mediation is a dispute that began in 1963 over a proposed pump-storage power station at Storm King Mountain in the Hudson River Highlands in New York.[4] During the course of the 17 years of litigation that ensued, three environmental groups, four public agencies, and five utility companies became involved at an estimated combined cost to the parties of over $6 million in legal fees and other court costs.[5] In April 1979, Russell Train, now chairman of the board of World Wildlife Fund and The Conservation Foundation and former administrator of the U.S. Environmental Protection Agency, was invited to step in as mediator, and, in December 1980, the parties formally signed an out-of-court settlement. The combined costs of the mediator's time and expenses, and the fees of the attorneys and technical people involved in the negotiations, must have been only a tiny fraction of the cost of the previous litigation—and an even smaller fraction of the total cost of the projects involved.

Such a simple comparison, however, although striking, can be misleading. Unlike the Storm King case, most civil disputes, including environmental disputes, never go to trial. In addition, in cases where all parties view the stakes as high, they are often not willing to negotiate until litigation has proved unable to settle the dispute in their favor. As a result, it is difficult to decide which costs to count in comparing litigation and environmental dispute resolution alternatives.

It may be unrealistic to begin counting the costs of mediation at the time that the parties agreed to negotiate, if the previous period of contention, litigation, or clarification of relative power contributed to the parties' willingness to negotiate a voluntary settlement. In the Storm King case, for example, the parties probably would not have agreed to mediation instead of litigation if the former had been available in the early 1960s. At the beginning of the dispute, the economic, environmental, and legal interests of all the parties did not give those parties sufficient incentives to compromise.

Filing a lawsuit also may be the only way that some of the parties to a dispute can get the others to talk to them. In almost 25 percent of the cases in this study, mediation was used to settle environmental disputes that were being litigated. In perhaps another 20 percent of the cases studied, there was the threat of a lawsuit. In a few cases, mediation actually occurred after a lawsuit had settled issues that were not easily negotiable.

A simple comparison of costs also leaves out perhaps the most important consideration in analyzing the worth of the settlement of a dispute—the nature and quality of the outcome itself. A more efficient process may not be more desirable if it leads to significantly poorer decisions in the view of one or all of the parties. The outcomes of litigation and environmental dispute resolution alternatives theoretically are very different. At the end of a trial, there is usually a winner and a loser. A clear win or loss may be the most desirable outcome in cases where what is at stake is a matter of principle or of law, because compromise may be neither possible nor desirable. In such cases, the publicity of even a hopeless fight might be better than an agreement that offers little or no real gain. Under other circumstances, however, neither the winner nor the loser really benefits. Sometimes, the decisions in lawsuits are made on procedural grounds. Such an outcome could produce an improved procedure, or perhaps an improved environmental assessment, but no substantial change in the proposed project, plan, or policy. By contrast, in a voluntary dispute resolution process, the parties are much more likely to deal with the substantive issues in dispute.

The goal of negotiation or consensus-building processes is an agreement among all of the parties at interest. Because everyone supposedly agrees voluntarily, it is assumed that everyone wins something—or, at least, that all parties feel that the outcome is better than it might have been without an agreement. In measuring the relative costs of litigation and environmental dispute resolution alternatives, therefore, one may be measuring the costs of two very different kinds of results. Choosing a winner and a loser in a lawsuit also may preclude the search for new alternatives that achieve important joint gains for all parties, if they are successful at engaging in creative problem-solving during the negotiations.

The final major conceptual problem in asking whether environmental dispute resolution processes are really cheaper and faster
than litigation is the difficulty of finding comparable samples of
cases. Many variables significantly affect the complexity and, therefore, the duration and cost of environmental disputes, independent
of the dispute resolution process used. As was noted in chapter 1,
some disputes involve particularly thorny scientific and technical
issues; others do not. Different statutes apply to different disputes.
The cases may or may not have precedential value. The number
and types of parties differ.

For example, a dispute over the siting of a new hazardous waste
facility differs significantly from a dispute over whether an existing
industrial facility is out of compliance with its water quality control
permit. Multiple parties are involved in the former; usually two—
the owner of the facility and the regulatory agency—are involved
in the latter. The technical resources available to the parties are
relatively even in the latter but unequal in the former. A local
community may benefit from the status quo in the former, but the
company probably benefits from the status quo in the latter. Despite
these differences, however, these disputes may have more in common
with each other than with disputes over plans for timber harvest,
oil and gas exploration, or mining on public lands.

Significant variation can exist even within a category of disputes.
For instance, it makes a big difference to the complexity of resolving
a dispute over forest management plans whether logging operations
are proposed in a potential wilderness area or in an area where
logging previously has taken place.

The comparison of litigation and voluntary environmental dispute
resolution alternatives can be further hampered by a misconception
that lawsuits and voluntary approaches are mutually exclusive
options. Most lawsuits never go to trial. In fact, it is commonly
estimated that over 90 percent of all civil cases are resolved out of
court through some form of voluntary settlement negotiations.[6] In
addition, mediated dispute resolution processes can begin with a
lawsuit or the threat of a lawsuit. Such overlap can easily blur a
comparison of the duration and cost of litigation and environmental
dispute resolution alternatives.

Moreover, the comparability of litigation and voluntary alternatives can be further confused because, in some disputes, either litigation or a voluntary approach simply is not a relevant alternative.

In some cases, in which parties are attempting to set legal precedents, informal negotiations may not be appropriate. Sometimes, a dispute must be settled first in an administrative process by a public agency responsible for planning, permitting, or regulatory decisions. Litigation may not be an option in such cases until after several levels of administrative appeals are completed. In other cases, where a dispute is over a controversial solution to a difficult environmental problem, the most likely alternative, although not the most desirable one from all points of view, to a voluntary dispute resolution process may be no action at all.

Thus, finding comparable cases with which to assess the efficiency of environmental dispute resolution alternatives and litigation presents a considerable challenge. One would like to find a sufficient number of similar cases, some of which were mediated and some of which were litigated. A large enough sample should nullify the effects of case variability, and it might even be possible to find correlations between certain factors and the processes by which disputes were resolved—for example, whether cases were litigated and went all the way to trial, whether lawsuits were resolved through negotiated settlements, whether mediation occurred, and whether mediation was used before or after lawsuits were filed.

Unfortunately, too few cases have been mediated in any one issue area to conduct such a comparison at this time. This should be possible sometime in the future, however.

IS LITIGATION REALLY A PROBLEM?

The search for more efficient dispute resolution alternatives to litigation presumes that problems exist with litigation. If there are problems, what are they? Is there too much litigation of environmental issues? Does it take too long and cost too much? Is the problem really one of inefficiency, or is it that litigation often may not be the most *effective* way to solve a problem?

A caution must be raised at the outset about the data in this section. Sources of information on litigation brought under environmental statutes are scattered, and different kinds of cases follow different paths. As a result, generalizations may be invalid. Not only are lawsuits filed under federal environmental laws, but each state has its own environmental laws and court systems. Even at the federal level, different kinds of environmental disputes are addressed by different adjudicatory bodies. Actions brought against federal agencies under the National Environmental Policy Act (NEPA) usually are filed in a U.S. District Court. Enforcement actions brought against private parties by agency officials also are filed in a U.S. District Court. Challenges to a rule-making process may be filed either in a U.S. District Court or directly in a U.S. Court of Appeals, depending on the statute. Also, because the "exhaustion of remedies" doctrine requires that many disputes with public agencies go through administrative review before becoming eligible for judicial review, many environmental disputes are initially brought before an administrative law judge or appeals board, not before the courts.[7] Decisions made in such proceedings can be appealed either to a U.S. District Court or directly to the U.S. Court of Appeals, again depending on the statute. Therefore, in looking at the data available for a particular court or appeals board on how long it takes to resolve disputes through litigation, one may not have a complete picture of similar cases brought in other court systems or an accurate picture of the duration of the particular cases about which one does have data, because one may not know how many times these cases have been appealed and from what forum.

Concerns about the overload on the judicial system are widespread, and statistics show that the overall burden on federal courts is increasing. The Administrative Office of the United States Courts reports that in the 12-month period ending June 30, 1983, 241,842 civil cases were filed in U.S. District Courts[8] and 29,630 appeals were filed in U.S. Courts of Appeals.[9] These totals constitute 74.3[10] and 56.6 percent[11] increases, respectively, over the same period five years previous.

Available figures, although limited, do not indicate that the number of environmental lawsuits has grown in a similar fashion, however (figure 15).[12] Rather, the Council on Environmental Quality's *Annual Reports* show that the volume of litigation under NEPA involving federal agencies actually declined slightly between 1974 and 1982—from 189 NEPA cases filed in 1974 to 157 filed in 1982.[13] In addition, the Judicial Conference of the United States, which keeps statistics about the federal courts, reports that between 1978 and 1983, the number of suits filed in U.S. District Courts under any environmental statute dropped from 519 in the 12-month period ending June 30, 1978, to 465 for the same period in 1982 and 1983.[14]

Figure 15

Number of Environmental Lawsuits from 1974-1983

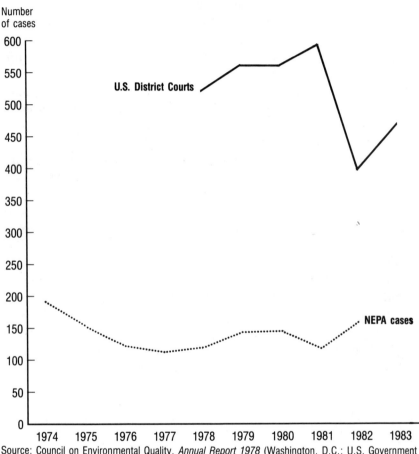

Source: Council on Environmental Quality, *Annual Report 1978* (Washington, D.C.: U.S. Government Printing Office).

Comparable information for U.S. Courts of Appeals is not available, but pieces of the picture can be put together. Most environmental cases in those courts, except for challenges to rule making, were appealed either from a U.S. District Court or from an administrative appeals proceeding. Between 1982 and 1983, the number of environmental cases in which a federal agency was the defendant, appealed from a U.S. District Court to a U.S. Court of Appeals, declined from 124 to 89.[15] Appeals to U.S. Courts of Appeals from administrative appeals processes throughout the federal government have declined overall since 1981;[16] trend information specifically for environmental cases appealed from administrative proceedings is unavailable. Information about the number of cases in U.S. Courts of Appeals involving rule making also is unavailable.

In addition, no trend information is included here for cases that involved neither a federal agency nor a federal environmental statute but that may have concerned environmental disputes in some way— for example, state or local land-use laws or regulations.

Opinions differ over whether decreases in the number of environmental lawsuits filed is a positive or negative trend. Litigation has been the principal way for those interested in protecting the quality of the environment to make gains, and that often continues to be the case. Thus, a decrease in litigation could be seen as a retreat from the vigorous pursuit of environmental objectives. Unless comparable achievements in protecting human health and the environment can be demonstrated to result from alternatives to litigation, environmental advocates will understandably remain skeptical about what the use of those alternatives really signifies.

If indications are that the number of environmental lawsuits is not increasing, is the problem with litigation instead that these lawsuits take too long to settle? Many think so. Among other factors, it is argued that environmental disputes often involve complicated facts, complex questions of causation, and scientific uncertainty, which can increase pretrial preparation time as well as time spent in court. A search of the literature, however, turned up no published information about how long it takes to litigate any kind of environmental dispute. Instead, many questions were raised about whether the question can be answered at all. Too much uncertainty exists over where one would start the clock. Environmental disputes generally involve considerable administrative action prior to the filing of a lawsuit. In addition, questions remain about whether it is possible to ascertain how representative any particular sample of cases might be, who keeps what kinds of data, whether those data are in comparable forms, and whether the complete duration of a case can be accurately measured, if the case has been appealed from one court to another.

Information on how long it takes to litigate general civil litigation is available, but, previously, such information has not been published for environmental disputes. For this report, the Judicial Conference of the United States conducted a special computer search of its data to determine the duration of environmental disputes filed in U.S. District Courts (figure 16).[17] These data assume that litigation began at the time of filing. They are limited to those kinds of environmental disputes that are brought to a U.S. District Court and, therefore, may not be representative of the broad range of environmental disputes.[18] Also, the data do not take into account whether the case had been heard previously in another administrative or judicial forum or, for those few cases that went to trial, whether the case was appealed further. These figures, therefore, should only be considered general indicators.

The information on the median number of months that it takes to dispense with a dispute in federal court indicates that cases are concluded relatively expeditiously and usually without going to trial. The range in the length of time it takes to conclude cases is great, however. On the average, the median duration of civil suits in U.S. District Courts terminated in the 12-month period ending June 30, 1983, was 7 months. The median time from filing to disposition of lawsuits involving environmental matters during this same period was 10 months. Only 5.8 percent of the civil litigation and 7.7 percent of the environmental litigation included in this sample went to trial, however. The remainder were terminated without court action or were terminated before or during pretrial proceedings. The median number of months from filing to disposition for cases that went to trial was 19 months for all civil disputes and 23 months for environmental disputes.

More interesting than the median duration of these lawsuits, however, is the range among the cases. Ten percent of all civil litigation in this sample took more than 28 months from the time of filing to disposition regardless of when and how the case was terminated, while 10 percent of the environmental litigation took more than 42 months. For those cases that went to trial, 10 percent of the civil suits took longer than 45 months to be decided, and 10 percent of the environmental suits took more than a whopping 67 months—or over five and one-half years. It is likely, therefore, that it is the *threat* of protracted litigation that is most significant in creating the incentives to find alternative ways to resolve disputes.

Figure 16

Time Interval from Filing to Disposition of Civil Cases in U.S. District Courts, by Nature of Suit and Method of Disposition during the 12-Month Period Ending June 30, 1983

	All civil cases[1]	Environmental matters[2]
Total cases		
Number of cases	184,427	416
Time interval		
Bottom 10%	<1 month	<0 months
Median	7 months	10 months
Top 10%	>28 months	>42 months
Cases involving no court action		
Number of cases	93,661	116
Time interval		
Bottom 10%	<1 month	<0 months
Median	4 months	3 months
Top 10%	>18 months	>32 months
Cases involving court action—disposed before pretrial		
Number of cases	54,057	204
Time interval		
Bottom 10%	<2 months	<0 months
Median	7 months	12 months
Top 10%	>24 months	>42 months
Cases involving court action—disposed during or after pretrial		
Number of cases	26,052	52
Time interval		
Bottom 10%	<6 months	<5 months
Median	16 months	22 months
Top 10%	>38 months	>47 months
Cases involving court action—disposed through trial		
Number of cases	10,657	32
Time interval		
Bottom 10%	<6 months	<7 months
Median	19 months	23 months
Top 10%	>45 months	>67 months

[1] All civil cases filed in U.S. District Courts other than land condemnation, prisoner petitions, and deportation reviews.

[2] Includes, among others, cases filed under the National Environmental Policy Act, Clean Air Act, Federal Water Pollution Control Act, and Federal Insectide, Fungicide, and Rodenticide Act.

THE STRATEGY OF DELAY

The length of time it takes to resolve a particular dispute through the legal system depends on the complexity of the dispute, how much is at stake, whether one of the parties is using the system to hold up the process, whether the case goes to trial, and whether the decision is appealed. Because some courts have larger backlogs than others, similar cases filed in different courts also may take more or less time to decide.

The use of the legal system to stop a project through delay has been blamed for many of the ills of environmental disputes. The implication seems to be that the motives behind these actions are cynical and, therefore, somehow suspect. A closer look at the strategy of delay, however, indicates that the picture is neither so simple nor so bleak as is often assumed. The reasons why parties use litigation to delay a decision vary, and no one type of party is uniquely "to blame." The effectiveness of voluntary dispute resolution processes to speed up the process, therefore, depends on a clearer understanding of what underlies the strategy of delay.

Although disputes are often escalated by accusations that one party or another is using litigation as a strategy to delay a decision, the reasons why parties attempt to block a decision are more important for creating a successful dispute resolution process than who the parties are. Sometimes, a party to an environmental dispute may benefit from the continuation of the status quo. Citizens' and environmental groups benefit, for example, when they delay a proposed project that is expected to discharge pollutants into the air or water, generate additional traffic, or threaten natural resources and wildlife habitat, unless the problems that could cause negative impacts on human health or the environment are solved. Delay is not always to the advantage of citizen and environmental groups, however, when they look to public agencies to solve problems such as the cleanup of abandoned toxic waste dumps or the reduction of pollutants in the environment. Delay also can work to the advantage of the party subject to regulation when stricter regulatory policies are being proposed or when enforcement actions are taken by a regulated agency. In such cases, change is likely to be expensive.

The longer a decision is delayed, the longer a regulated company can postpone paying those costs.

Obviously, delay can be an end in itself if a party—whether it be a citizens' group, an environmental organization, or a company—thinks that, if it waits long enough, the opposition will walk away. Environmental dispute resolution processes do not, by themselves, offer a magic solution to the use of litigation for delay. The incentives to cause delays also must be changed, or the parties either will not agree to participate or will use the mediation process as one more way to delay the eventual decision.

Usually, however, delay is only a means that parties in disputes use to satisfy their underlying needs and objectives. Occasionally, when a company faced with large expenditures for new pollution control equipment goes to court to block an agency's requirement, it can be satisfied if the agency can find ways to take the company's costs into account.[19] For example, allowing longer compliance deadlines may give the company a chance to achieve greater pollution reductions through plant retooling; "averaging" approaches such as the "bubble" concept, if properly used, can give companies the flexibility to reduce emissions further than required and at less cost.[20]

Similarly, active environmental litigators are concerned about accomplishing environmental goals and often would prefer to negotiate mitigation measures in project proposals or other changes in agency actions to protect the environment. They often file lawsuits or threaten to file lawsuits principally to persuade their opposition to sit down with them and negotiate. In one example, environmentalists who sued to stop construction of a proposed dam were most interested, not in totally preventing the dam, but rather in preserving habitat areas for water-dependent species. When proponents of the dam agreed to protect minimum in-stream flows, the environmentalists withdrew their lawsuit.[21]

One of the commonly cited strategies used by environmentalists to delay a proposed project has been to challenge the project on the grounds that an environmental impact statement (EIS) required under NEPA should have been prepared or that an existing EIS was inadequate. These suits, however, also illustrate the real dynamics behind the strategy of delay, described above. For the most part, environmental activists care more about the project and how to mitigate or compensate for environmental impacts than they do about EIS documents. It is not that they do not care about the value of environmental impact assessments in bringing out information that will be useful in sound project planning decisions but rather that they care most about the actual decisions that are reached. NEPA lawsuits can increase the incentives for project planners and public decision makers to respond to environmental concerns.

Realistically, however, not all issues are susceptible to compromise, either because matters of principle or of law may be at stake or because the parties are unable to invent new options that give each other more palatable choices and they remain opposed to an activity under any circumstances. In these cases, voluntary dispute resolution processes are not likely to be more efficient or more effective than litigation.

HOW LONG DO ENVIRONMENTAL DISPUTE RESOLUTION ALTERNATIVES TAKE?

To describe the time it takes to resolve environmental disputes through some form of negotiation or consensus building, one must first select beginning- and end-points. Because the scope of this study is limited to mediated processes, the date that someone first contacted a mediator serves here as the beginning point from which to measure the length of a mediation process. Some may prefer to measure environmental dispute resolution processes from the date of the first meeting; others may propose another point. There is sufficient variability in these processes that exceptions will be found to any choice.[22] However, because so much of a mediator's assistance is in helping the parties agree on the nature, ground rules, and agenda of the process, the point at which a mediator begins to provide this assistance seems the most logical beginning.

The end of the dispute resolution process is considered here to be the date of the last meeting or the date that an agreement was signed or ratified, whichever was later. There are times that the formalities of an agreement are worked out after the last meeting but that the agreement is signed without another meeting. At other times, as has been noted, environmental dispute resolution processes are relatively informal, with agreements not put into writing.

The results of this study indicate that, at least in site-specific cases, the duration of voluntary dispute resolution processes varies considerably.* Of the 78 cases for which information is available on the length of time the case took to resolve, the parties took from a single meeting to over two years to negotiate a resolution of the issues in dispute (figure 17). The variation can be explained easily by, among other factors, the variation in the complexity of issues, number of parties, and polarization among those parties. The median length of time these cases took to conclude was five to six months, whether agreements were reached or not. Over one third of the cases in which agreements were reached took less than four months to resolve; half the cases took less than half a year; and three quarters took less than a year. An encouraging note is that parties took significantly less time to conclude cases in which they failed to agree, indicating that, in calculating the risks of failure when considering a mediation option, parties need not be overly concerned about wasting their time. There appears to be no significant difference in duration among cases with different objectives.

Too little information is available on the duration of policy dialogues to draw reliable conclusions. A first impression, however, is that policy dialogues generally can be separated into two categories: those that took one or two meetings, one to three days long, with a few months of planning time before the meetings and a few months after for drafting a report; and those that involved a series of regular meetings over a period of nine months to two years.

HOW MUCH DO ALTERNATIVE DISPUTE RESOLUTION ALTERNATIVES COST?

Advocates of environmental dispute resolution alternatives also frequently assert that these processes are cheaper than litigation. At first glance, this seems reasonable. Cost is in large part a function of time, and mediators on the average charge less for their time than do attorneys. As was noted earlier, there are many more factors to the comparative costs of litigation and voluntary alternatives than

---

*Although the information available about how much time it took to resolve the environmental disputes examined for this study is incomplete, it is sufficient to provide general answers to some important questions about the duration of mediation-type processes. For about two thirds of the cases studied, information is available on when the mediators were contacted, how long the dispute assessments took, when the first meetings took place, how many meetings there were, the dates of the last meetings, when the agreements (if they were put in writing) were signed, and when any formal ratifications that might have occurred took place.

Figure 17

Duration of Dispute Resolution Process

(site-specific cases only)

| | All site-specific cases | | | Objective | | | | |
| | | | | To reach a decision | | To reach recommendations | | To improve communications |
	Total cases	Cases with agreement	Cases with no agreement	Agreement	No agreement	Agreement	No Agreement	
Over 2 years	4	2	1	2	1	–	–	1
18 months–2 years	4	3	–	2	–	1	–	1
13–18 months	5	5	–	4	–	1	–	–
12–13 months	5	5	–	4	–	1	–	–
11–12 months	3	3	–	–	–	3	–	–
10–11 months	4	3	–	2	–	1	–	1
9–10 months	1	1	–	–	–	1	–	–
8– 9 months	5	4	1	3	1	1	–	–
7– 8 months	1	0	–	–	–	1	–	1
6– 7 months	4	3	–	2	–	1	–	1

	5–6 months	5–6 months	2–3 months	6–7 months	1–2 months	5–6 months	2–3 months	6–7 months
5– 6 months	5	5	–	2	–	3	–	–
4– 5 months	6	4	2	2	1	2	1	1
3– 4 months	4	2	1	1	–	1	1	1
2– 3 months	11	6	3	3	–	3	3	2
1– 2 months	11	9	2	7	1	2	1	–
0– 1 months	5	3	2	3	2	–	–	–
Subtotal	78	58	12	37	6	21	6	8
No information	37	20	9	15	6	5	3	8
Total cases	115	78	21	52	12	26	9	16
Median duration of cases for which information is available	5–6 months	5–6 months	2–3 months	6–7 months	1–2 months	5–6 months	2–3 months	6–7 months

the relative cost of hiring mediators rather than attorneys or even the amount of time it takes to resolve cases.

It is important at the outset to consider who pays what costs. Taxpayers support the costs of the judicial system. To the extent that court reforms or alternatives to litigation reduce the burden on the courts, taxpayers benefit. If mediation services are adjuncts to the judicial system or are paid for by public agencies, the benefits are equal to the difference between costs of providing mediators and of supporting judges. The cost savings to the parties depend on (a) the extent to which the mediation reduces the use of attorneys, (b), whether or not the parties pay the mediator's fees, and (c) the difference between the expenses required for preparation for litigation or negotiation.

Mediators aren't always a substitute for attorneys. In some cases, parties may represent themselves directly in the negotiation process, thus avoiding legal costs. In other cases, parties in a mediation process may want the assistance of their attorneys during the negotiations and in reviewing any mediated agreement to ensure that its terms are in their interests, that the agreement itself is legal, and that it is adequately enforceable. The amount of time attorneys have spent participating in environmental dispute resolution cases has varied considerably, and it is not uncommon for the attorneys to represent their clients at the negotiating table. In such cases, the cost of the mediator generally does not offset the attorneys' fees.

Cases also vary considerably with respect to who pays the mediator. The first environmental mediation organizations were primarily financed by philanthropic foundations that paid their mediators' salaries, with corporate donations, government contracts, and in-kind support from citizens' groups and public interest organizations providing most of the remaining funding. In a few cases, fees were charged to the parties to a dispute resolution attempt, but, for the most part, the mediators' services were free of charge to the parties. This made sense at the time, because environmental dispute resolution alternatives were new, and, even without charging a fee for mediation services, it was difficult to convince all the parties to a dispute to attempt a voluntary resolution of the issues. Mediation services are available free of charge to the parties less frequently now than they used to be. In some cases, the parties must find ways to pay the mediator's fee; in many cases, however, the parties who pay are government agencies. Such arrangements are analogous to the support of the judicial system in that the dispute resolution process is paid for by the taxpayer.

Only a little information is available about how much it costs to employ environmental mediators. Average fees for the mediators' personal services in 1984 ranged from $250 per day to perhaps $700 per day, plus expenses. Under the earlier circumstances in which foundations supported most environmental mediation services, mediators often did not keep records about their time and expenses on individual cases. A few, however, were able to provide some figures on the costs per case for this report. Information about the cost of the mediator's time and expenses was available for 18 site-specific cases. In 9 of them, one mediator was involved; in the other 9, two mediators were involved (figure 18). The average cost for the cases with one mediator was $7,700. Half of those cases had costs below $5,000, and half had costs above $10,000. The range was from $1,000, for two cases involving two parties and one mediation session, to $26,000, for a case involving 10 parties over a 10 month-period. The average cost for the cases in which two mediators were involved was $23,000, with the range between $15,000, for a case involving six parties over a six-month period (including two and one-half months of intensive work), and $40,000, for a case involving 12 parties over a five-month period. Another case that cost about $38,000 involved 16 parties over a 12-month period. These figures, however, tend to come from organizations that still receive considerable grant support for general expenses. In addition, these figures, some of which are several years old, have not been adjusted for inflation.

Policy dialogues are estimated generally to cost somewhat more than site-specific disputes. Estimates range from $40,000 to over $100,000 per dispute, depending on the complexity and duration of the case.[23] A few particularly large cases have cost several hundred thousand dollars.

Environmental dispute resolution processes for both site-specific cases and policy dialogues tend to have substantial "indirect" costs for the parties, as well. The exact costs depend, of course, on a dispute's specific characteristics. In general, however, negotiation and other consensus-building processes usually require more direct— and therefore time-consuming—participation by the parties them-

Figure 18

Cost Estimates for Mediator's Time and Expenses
(selected site-specific cases only)

	One mediator	Two mediators
Agreement	9	9
Average costs	$7,700	$23,000
Average duration (in months)	3.8	8.8
Average number of parties	5.3	8.0

selves than may be required in litigation. The costs of participation by company executives, engineers, planners, citizens, environmentalists, and their technical experts may be considerable. Miscellaneous overhead costs can also be large. Citizens' and environmental groups can be hit especially hard, and some have found that the costs of these approaches to them may exceed the costs of litigation.

Even assuming that the advantages of a voluntary resolution of the issues outweigh the disadvantages, however, citizens' and environmental groups may still have a problem with lack of resources to participate. This can make it more difficult for these groups to choose negotiation. Not only may the investment in a lawsuit, if successful, set precedents for other similar cases; but, in addition, some kinds of legal action may be cheaper and faster for public interest groups than negotiation would be. For example, although the full process of preparing for and going to trial may be very expensive, procedural motions, injunctions, or other legal actions short of a trial may be sufficient to cause expensive delays for project proponents without large expenditures by the public interest groups concerned about the project's potential impacts. In contrast, precisely because of its advertised benefits, negotiation can demand significantly more time and expense for environmental groups.

The advantage of negotiation over litigation for environmental groups often is that the substantive issues can be addressed more directly. It is one thing, however, to argue in court that the responsible party has not provided sufficient information about the environmental impacts of a project. If one is successful, the expense for further studies is carried by the project proponent. It is another thing entirely in a negotiation to obtain sufficient evidence to persuade others at the table that adverse environmental impacts will occur and that alternative courses of action are justified. If environmental groups propose alternatives, they also may need resources for adequate scientific and technical studies to support the feasiblity of the proposed alternatives.

REFERENCES

1. Roscoe Pound, "The Causes of Popular Dissatisfaction with the Administration of Justice," American Bar Association *Reports* 29 (1906):395; reprinted in *Judicature* 46 (1962):55.

2. Jerald S. Auerback, *Justice Without Law* (New York: Oxford University Press, 1983).

3. American Bar Association, *Attacking Litigation Costs and Delay*, Final Report of the Action Commission to Reduce Court Costs and Delay (Washington, D.C.: American Bar Association, 1984).

4. Allan R. Talbot, *Settling Things: Six Case Studies in Environmental Mediation* (Washington, D.C.: The Conservation Foundation, 1983), pp.7-24.

5. Ibid., p.1.

6. The number of civil suits, filed in U.S. District courts, that reached trial has declined steadily from 10 percent in 1970 to 5.4 percent in 1983. See Judicial Conference of the United States, *Annual Report of the Director of the Admininistrative Office of the United States Courts 1983* (Washington, D.C.: U.S. Government Printing Office, 1983), p.142.

7. Will A. Irwin and Kathryn L. Russell, "Administrative Review of Environmental Decisions," *Environmental Law*, a quarterly newsletter of the American Bar Association Standing Committee on Environmental Law, Spring 1979, pp. 1-3.

8. Judicial Conference of the United States, "Analysis of the Workload of the Federal Courts during the Twelve Month Period Ended June 30, 1983," *Annual Report of the Director of the Administrative Office of the United States Courts 1983*, p.114.

9. Ibid., p.97.

10. Ibid., p.114.

11. Ibid., p.97.

12. Figure 15 only includes information on some cases in the federal court system and does not include any information on trends in the number of cases being heard by administrative law judges or cases heard in state courts, under whose jurisdiction many lawsuits involving environmental issues are brought.

13. Council on Environmental Quality, *Annual Report 1978* (Washington, D.C.: U.S. Government Printing Office); Council of Environmental Quality, *Annual Report, 1983* (Washington, D.C.: U.S. Government Printing Office).

14. *Annual Report of the Director of the Administrative Office of the United States Courts 1983*, p.122.

15. Ibid., p.103.

16. Ibid., p.100.

17. The author particularly would like to thank Joe Cecil and Eric Armen from the Federal Judicial Center for their assistance.

18. For example, lawsuits over many kinds of land-use issues more likely would be brought at the local or state level. The environmental lawsuits included in figure 16 involved a federal agency as either the plaintiff or a defendant; or if they did not involve a federal agency, the complaint cited a federal statute.

19. For example, the negotiated agreement in a dispute between the U.S. Environmental Protection Agency and the Brown Company over control of sulfur emissions at the company's pulp and paper mill in Berlin, New Hampshire resulted in significant economic gains for the company and in environmental gains for the agency. See David Gilmore, "Successful Regulatory Negotiation (The Brown Company Case)," in Lawrence Susskind, Lawrence Bacow, and Michael Wheeler, eds., *Resolving Environmental Regulatory Disputes* (Cambridge, Mass.: Schenkman Publishing Company, 1983), pp. 5-29.

20. For example, a Minnesota Mining and Manufacturing, Inc. (3M), tape coating plant in Bristol, Pennsylvania, reportedly can reduce its emissions of volatile organic compounds far below the levels required by conventional regulation, at far less cost, through use of a bubble. 3M is substituting water-based solvents as part of its bubble proposal. See Richard A. Liroff, *Reforming Air Pollution Regulation: The Toil and Trouble of EPA's Bubble*, (Washington, D.C.: The Conservation Foundation, forthcoming).

21. Lawrence S. Bacow and Michael Wheeler, *Environmental Dispute Resolution* (New York: Plenum Press, 1984), pp. 46-50.

22. For example, in the CREST case, the parties actually first contacted The Mediation Institute several years before the mediation process began. At that stage, the parties were able to proceed on their own in resolving many of the issues through the planning process. Ultimately, the parties reached an impasse, however, and returned for assistance from the mediators. In such cases, the mediation process will be measured from the later contact.

23. Testimony by Sam Gusman before the Senate Select Committee on Small Business, July 29-30, 1980, p.79.

Chapter 5

Looking Ahead to the Next Decade

During the first 10 years in which mediators helped resolve environmental disputes, most cases were mediated on an ad hoc basis. If the use of mediation and other consensus-building processes is to grow significantly during the next decade, however, reliance on the ad hoc approach probably will not be enough. Already, leaders in the environmental dispute resolution field have begun looking for ways to incorporate more systematically what has been learned thus far into existing institutions for public decision making. This growing attention to institutional mechanisms is intended to make voluntary dispute resolution processes more widely available, to increase the likelihood that disputes are resolved successfully, and to protect the parties to disputes from potential abuses of those processes. Still, not all observers view the development of institutionalized approaches favorably. Moreover, skeptics and optimists alike caution that accomplishing the intended goals without losing the flexibility that is a basic strength of voluntary dispute resolution processes will be a challenge.

In addition to developing institutional mechanisms, several important questions must be answered if alternative environmental dispute resolution processes are to continue their growth. How will the services of mediators be funded? How can mediation processes be made more affordable for citizens' groups and public interest organizations? To whom and for what should mediators be accountable, and how should such accountability be maintained?

Each of these concerns is discussed in this chapter. Although many observers raise questions about the relative strengths of different dispute resolution approaches, conclusions about what kinds of processes or techniques are most successful under different circumstances are not made, because this study's emphasis has been more on the track record of environmental dispute resolution attempts and the factors that affect success than on the differences among processes that parties used. As was discussed in chapter 2, current definitions of different dispute resolution approaches do not easily lend themselves to empirical comparisons, in part because no agreement has been reached on a single set of definitions that distinguish processes from each other and because actual cases do not easily fit the distinctions that are drawn. In practice, mediators tend to design processes to suit specific circumstances, not general definitions. Therefore, more detailed analysis of specific choices or strategies for responding to particular conflict resolution problems is needed before conclusions about techniques can be very helpful.

DEVELOPING INSTITUTIONAL MECHANISMS

Over the next decade, one of the most important issues in shaping environmental dispute resolution processes will be the choice of auspices under which such processes are used. Options include the continued practice of mediation on an ad hoc basis; court-referred or court-linked programs; mediation services provided by local, state, or federal agencies; and the incorporation of voluntary dispute resolution procedures into statutes or administrative procedures. Although these options are not mutually exclusive, the choices made will have important effects on how and how widely the processes are made available, on who pays the costs, on how flexible the processes are, on how and to whom the mediator is held accountable, and, ultimately, on the basic success of voluntary dispute resolutions processes as an innovation in public decision making.

In all likelihood, some environmental disputes will continue to be resolved on an ad hoc basis, as individual mediators and organizations with good reputations have cases referred to them by those who have worked with them in the past. This approach may allow the parties the greatest flexibility to design processes that most closely meet their needs in specific situations. But it may not be an efficient way to make the availability of mediation services widely known, nor is it likely to encourage significant change in existing institutions or procedures for public decision making.

The extent to which future cases are resolved on an ad hoc basis will be determined in part by whether the parties to disputes are able to pay for mediators' services or whether independent dispute resolution organizations are able to obtain funding from public or private sources. If funding continues at its current level, however, growth in the number of new, independent environmental dispute resolution organizations may be slow.

Second, mediation also may become a more frequent part of judicial approaches to settling environmental disputes. Courts in a variety of jurisdictions already routinely refer cases involving child custody, consumer complaints, and family and neighborhood disputes to mediation services.[1] Similar programs could be established for environmental disputes, with environmental mediators employed and funded by the courts. Cases also could be referred on a fee basis to independently funded mediation organizations. The availability and flexibility of the mediation process for a specific case would depend on the policies and procedures established by the referring court. The current experiment by the New Jersey Supreme Court, in which the state courts are to make greater use of alternatives to litigation in a wide range of disputes, including those that involve land-use and environmental quality issues, is an example of the ways that other courts could use mediation (see chapter 1).[2]

The expansion of court-related programs might satisfy some of the concerns that are raised about nonjudicial, voluntary dispute resolution processes.[3] Some critics argue that relying on processes other than litigation may lead to second-class justice. If alternatives to litigation are proposed principally because litigation is becoming so expensive, it is argued, discrimination against those who cannot afford to pursue judicial remedies may be perpetuated. According to this view, reforming the judicial system to increase the accessibility of the courts may be preferrable to nonjudicial dispute resolution options. By making alternative dispute resolution options a part of judicial reform, however, a link with the legal system could be preserved and the hazard of offering second-class justice to some might be mitigated.

Others are concerned about who represents the larger interests of the public when private parties resolve specific disputes. One of the outcomes of litigation is that the decision in one case can set precedents for other similar cases. For those who want to see broad changes in the way certain problems are solved, voluntary resolution of specific instances of a problem is flawed because little or no change results in the principles on which decisions are made. The most direct answer to this concern is that matters of principle or precedent should not be negotiated but, rather, should be settled legislatively or judicially. That response, however, does not address a related concern that agreements may not follow consistent standards in cases that set no major precedents but are similar to each other. Some critics, for example, ask whether public agencies that are parties to environmental dispute resolution processes should be required to reach similar agreements in similar cases. Others ask if mediators should be responsible for raising questions about whether agreements reached serve the public interest.[4] Although the concern about consistent standards can be satisfied in part by the assurance that voluntary dispute resolution processes must occur within the same legal and regulatory framework as other decision-making processes, it may be easier to ensure that individual mediated agreements are consistent with a broader public interest if voluntary dispute resolution processes are linked to the judicial system and thus are subject to judicial oversight.

Two arguments against court-related programs also have been raised. The first is that linking voluntary processes to formal institutions such as the courts might cause the loss of one of those processes' principal values—their informality—with the result that the use of these alternatives might become limited unnecessarily to problems that have already reached the stage at which litigation is an option. Second, critics of court-linked mediation programs contend that linking voluntary processes to the courts might reduce the benefits that result from giving the parties to a dispute the responsibility for and control over the dispute resolution process. Voluntary dispute resolution processes enable people to resolve their conflicts with each other directly, without recourse to external decision makers. Working together, particularly in disputes over local issues, parties can build new lines of communication and stronger bonds within a community. Such processes can empower individuals and groups, giving them a greater ability to solve problems and to influence the decisions that affect their lives. Linking dispute resolution programs to the courts, it is feared, may reduce opportunities for these informal community relationships to develop.)

Another way in which institutional mechanisms could be developed for environmental dispute resolution processes would be for local, state, and federal agencies to hire or assign staff to provide mediation as a government service. Two such models already exist in nonenvironmental government programs. Labor/management disputes are often mediated by the Federal Mediation and Conciliation Service (FMCS) or similar agencies at the state level. In addition, the Community Relations Service (CRS) of the U.S. Department of Justice sends mediators to help resolve disputes involving racial and ethnic minorities under Title X of the Civil Rights Act, particularly when the possibility of violence exists. Whether environmental disputes could also be resolved with the assistance of government mediators is yet to be tested, although some answers will eventually be provided by the statewide offices of mediation that were opened in 1984 and 1985 in Hawaii, Massachusetts, Minnesota, New Jersey, and Wisconsin (see chapter 1).

Clearly, if this is to be a viable option in increasing the availability of mediation for resolving environmental disputes, government agencies will need to appropriate sufficient funds to support mediation services on a continuing basis. In addition, they will have to decide whether to use public funds to cover all the costs of mediation services or to recover some of the costs through fees. Government agencies occasionally face financial obstacles to the use of mediation on an ad hoc basis. For example, in many cases involving public agencies today, an independent mediator's fee must come from the agency's limited discretionary funds, while the cost of an attorney for litigation is uncounted because it is paid from the budget of the state attorney general's office or the U.S. Department of Justice. Presumably, the availability of state-employed mediators as well as attorneys would help overcome this obstacle.

One important concern that must still be answered is whether publicly run mediation services can be sufficiently independent of other government agencies, especially in the many cases in which other government agencies are among the parties. Based on experiences with FMCS and CRS, there is reason to hope that they could be as independent as privately funded mediators, if appropriate legal and administrative structures establish and protect that independence. Several other factors must also be considered, however. Of particular importance are the perceptions of the nongovernmental parties to a dispute and whether they would consider government-employed mediators sufficiently neutral. In addition, the involvement of various levels of government, or of more than one state or local government, in a dispute might affect whether or at which level of government mediators should be employed.

In some cases, hybrids between private, nonprofit mediation organizations and publicly supported mediation services might be a useful option within a state. Environmental dispute resolution institutes already exist at several state universities, including the University of Michigan and the University of Virginia.[5] These institutes provide mediation and other services with partial state support through their universities, but they may have a more autonomous position than would other state employees.

Finally, mediation of environmental disputes could be made a more regular part of public decision making by incorporating alternative dispute resolution processes into statutes or administrative procedures. As was explained in chapter 1, several state laws already provide for negotiation, mediation, or arbitration of hazardous waste, city-county annexation, zoning, and coastal-zone management disputes. Similarly, some state and federal agencies are now searching for ways to incorporate mediation processes into their administrative procedures.

The hope is that incorporating provisions for voluntary dispute resolution processes into statutory or administrative procedures would establish general ground rules for negotiating or mediating certain kinds of environmental disputes, thereby increasing the overall use of such processes and reducing the opportunities for their misuse. In most disputes, the various parties' willingness to participate in an alternative dispute resolution process depends on many factors including, among others, (*a*) what is included in the scope of the issues to be negotiated, (*b*) who else is willing to participate in the negotiations, and (*c*) how committed the participating parties are to abiding by any agreements reached. With the current ad hoc use of negotiation, mediation, and other consensus-building processes to resolve environmental disputes, these decisions must be made anew with each case. Although this allows the greatest flexibility to tailor a process to the circumstances of a dispute, it also creates the greatest uncertainty for the parties about what benefits and risks a process has to offer. As has been discussed earlier in this study, case-by-case agreement on such ground rules for a dispute resolution process often takes considerable effort, and early uncertainty about what those ground rules will be sometimes seems to increase the parties' reluctance to participate.

Conscious attention, in developing institutionalized procedures, to the ground rules for resolving environmental dispute also may help reduce opportunities for abuse of these processes in comparison to the procedures' use only on an ad hoc basis. Specifying through institutional procedures which issues can legally be negotiated and which cannot, creating opportunities for groups to request that they be allowed to participate in the dispute resolution process, and establishing specific procedures for public review of agreements reached all may help institutionalized environmental dispute resolution processes to meet public standards of fairness and due process.

More needs to be learned, however, about the conditions under which laws or administrative procedures that authorize, or perhaps require, environmental dispute resolution processes are useful and about what specific procedures are most effective. Experience indicates that a series of questions must be answered each time such procedures are drafted, if the process designed is to be successful:

- Is explicit statutory authority or a defined procedure needed in this case, or can the obstacles to using voluntary dispute resolution processes be overcome some other way?
- Who will be able to initiate the process and under what circumstances?
- Will the process be voluntary or not?
- Who will participate in the process, and how will they be chosen?
- Will there be a limit on the scope of issues that can be negotiated, and, if so, what will it be?
- Will all other legal remedies remain open?
- Will the parties have access to mediators, and how will the mediators be selected and paid?
- Will negotiation sessions be open to the public?
- What will be the status of information and proposals exchanged during the process?
- If the negotiations are unsuccessful, where will that leave the

parties? How will they be able to withdraw from negotiations?
- Who will have the authority to decide that the negotiations have failed?
- How will a decision be made if the parties fail to reach an agreement?
- If an agreement is reached by the negotiators, who will have to ratify the agreement for it to be final?
- Who will have the responsibility for implementing agreements?
- Should the parties be required to deal with the possibility of unanticipated problems during the implementation of agreements or with other issues concerning their future relations?

Many of these questions are similar to those that must be answered in designing a dispute resolution process for a specific dispute, but they are more difficult to answer when writing general procedures because the variety among individual cases must be taken into account. One recent study suggested that, to be successful, any statutory or administrative attempt to establish generalized dispute resolution procedures would have to provide clear incentives for the various parties to negotiate in good faith, maintain sufficient flexibility for those parties to determine the specific ground rules for negotiating with each other, and obtain the involvement and support of those parties in the design of the specific procedures outlined.[6]

FUNDING MEDIATION SERVICES

As was explained in chapter 4, during the first 10 years in which mediators helped parties to environmental disputes to resolve issues, the mediators' services were paid for principally by private foundation grants and were free of charge to the parties to the disputes. The question of how these services will continue to be paid is pressing.

Several foundations continue to support existing environmental dispute resolution organizations, but even the most optimistic predictions indicate that future foundation grants will not be sufficient to support rapid growth in the use of mediation for environmental issues. Foundation officials and others in the field raise a legitimate question: If mediation has demonstrated some value, shouldn't society find a way to pay for it?

Some environmental dispute resolution organizations have begun, with moderate success, to charge fees for their services. Thus far, the most success with charging fees for individual cases has come in disputes involving public agencies. In various disputes—for example, rule-making cases, forest management decisions, water resource management problems, and annexation disputes—the services of mediators have been paid for in whole or in part by federal or state agencies or units of local government. Cuts in government spending, however, may limit the number of future cases paid for by agencies on an ad hoc basis.

Financial support from private corporations may also help to pay for mediation services. Only a few cases in this study were paid for by fees charged to corporations, but many environmental dispute resolution organizations with nonprofit tax status have received general support from corporations through corporate donations. In addition, during spring 1984, the National Institute for Dispute Resolution (NIDR) began planning for a new, national fund "intended to attract and pool funds not previously available to the environmental dispute resolution field, from corporations and corporate foundations."[7] This fund would be set up as a revolving fund and would be used to finance the resolution of individual disputes that could not be mediated otherwise.

As currently conceived, the fund would make two kinds of grants. The first, dispute assessment grants, would be available to mediators or to parties who wished to hire mediators to conduct dispute assessments. The second, participation grants, would be obtainable for the services of mediators under at least two different circumstances: (*a*) when the parties to a dispute are the only source of funds for a resolution process, some of the parties cannot pay their entire share of the costs of mediation, and concerns are raised about finding a neutral source of funding; or (*b*) when additional money is needed to supplement funding from other sources. In both types of cases, participation grants would be available not only for the mediators' services but also for technical assistance and other expenses incurred by the parties during the dispute resolution process.

Independent of the outcome, after a case was completed, those parties with the financial ability to do so would be expected to replenish the fund to provide support for future cases. The assumption here is that this would protect those involved in each case from perceptions of bias that might be associated with a mediator's being paid with money from some but not all of the parties to the dispute.

Despite the revolving fund concept's promise, several questions about it remain to be answered. If the problem is that there are too few funded environmental mediators or that those mediators are having trouble raising funds, aren't there other, less complicated methods for raising money? Does the payment for a mediator's services by corporations or others who have money and are parties to a dispute really affect a mediator's real or perceived neutrality? Would the fund draw general-support contributions away from dispute resolution organizations that already receive them directly? And, conversely, would corporations have any incentive to donate money to help start a revolving fund when they could support dispute resolution organizations directly?

Other options for funding mediation services are offered by each of the previously described institutional mechanisms that could be used to help resolve environmental disputes. For example, mediation might be funded as a service of the courts. Staff in the administrative offices of some courts, special masters appointed by judges to assist in the resolution or management of complex cases, and others already are playing this role to a limited extent in some environmental disputes.[8] Mediation might also be funded by state and federal agencies, either through contracts to independent mediators or by employing mediators in state or federal government.

These options, however, raise the same difficult questions about whether the source of funds affects the neutrality and accountability of the mediator as the revolving fund's planners have had to face. Some observers argue that the financial bases for paying mediators at least affect the *perceived* neutrality of the mediators and the bases on which they can be held accountable. Others hold that mediators establish reputations for neutrality throughout their careers and that those reputations are far more influential both on the parties' perceptions and on the mediators' behavior than are the sources of funds. Both sides of this issue make convincing arguments for their position. The issue of mediator accountability is discussed further below.

MAKING PARTICIPATION AFFORDABLE FOR CITIZENS' AND ENVIRONMENTAL GROUPS

Another issue that has been raised about environmental dispute resolution processes is whether citizens' groups and public interest organizations can afford—politically and financially—to participate in large numbers of mediated disputes. Politically, the success of environmental organizations usually has been closely related to their ability to generate publicity for their efforts. Legislative and judicial campaigns often attract substantial media and public attention; mediation tends not to. Financially, as chapter 4 explained, voluntary dispute resolution processes are not necessarily cheaper than litigation for public interest organizations.

In evaluating whether to participate in voluntary dispute resolution processes, environmental leaders must ask themselves what they may be giving up as well as what they may gain. When a group has less power than its adversaries, it may decide that it will gain less by negotiating on terms set by others than it will using adversarial processes to change the terms of the debate itself. The use of adversarial strategies has resulted in significant success for environmentalists over the past 20 years, and they may be cautious about giving up such approaches unless the alternatives offer real promise of something better. In addition, the wide-ranging consequences that legislation, litigation, and media coverage can have are very important to environmentalists, with their frequently tight financial and staff resources. Public interest groups concentrate their resources at the federal and state level, because legislation and regulatory policy decisions obviously have broad impacts. Litigation is an important tool because it has the potential to set precedents that may affect large numbers similar disputes. Further, simply the threat of litigation may cause public agencies or corporations to take environmental concerns into greater account, even though the public interest groups may not have to pay the costs of a lawsuit in each case. The media coverage that can accompany both litigation and battles over new legislation can also provide invaluable assistance in fund raising.

Even if citizens' and environmental groups perceive that the advantages of a voluntary dispute resolution process would outweigh the disadvantages in a particular dispute, however, those groups still may lack the resources to participate. As is discussed in chapter 4, public interest groups may find some kinds of legal actions to be cheaper than negotiation. One supporter of alternative environmental dispute resolution processes—Robert Golten, an attorney with many years of litigation experience on behalf of environmental groups in Washington, D.C., and the Rocky Mountain states— argues for the environmentalists' need for resources if they are to stay out of court:

> . . . the major obstacle to more negotiation (including mediation) and less litigation . . . is *not* the lack of mediation services but the lack of advocacy power (in the form of scientists, economists, and other technical resources) serving the "public interest" (environmentalists). Thus, I think if we had more resource power, we would be much more willing to negotiate; and our opponents would be more likely, also, to do so. We would . . . be able to get down to hard, credible facts—to everyone's benefit and satisfaction.
>
> We lack the resources to *stay out of court*. [There is an] imbalance in bargaining power that now works pervasively, and insidiously, as a disincentive to mediation.[9]

Golten cites numerous examples in which environmentalists need additional funds if they are to participate in problem-solving processes rather than merely to fight projects that can cause environmental problems. In the Metropolitan Water Roundtable process, for example, representatives of environmental groups questioned whether the proposed Two Forks dam really was needed and argued that a combination of conservation and other measures could make the same volume of water available for future use (see chapter 1). Others on the roundtable were skeptical and asked the environmentalists to document their claims. The environmental leaders agreed but lacked the money to hire a computer analyst. A donation from one of the business organizations on the roundtable, money from a technical assistance fund available to the mediators, and, eventually, a personal loan from one of the environmentalists allowed them to complete the study. Under the terms of the agreement that emerged, additional technical resources were made available to the environmentalists. Perhaps because the issues were so important to all concerned, an arrangement was made possible in this case, but the environmental groups' lack of money to generate needed information was not an easy obstacle to overcome. It would be foolhardy to assume that the problem of unequal resources for effective participation on complex technical issues could be resolved similarly in all environmental disputes.

In another case, public interest group representatives in a policy dialogue with leaders in the pesticide manufacturing industry jointly sponsored research on the use of symbols on pesticide container labels to communicate hazard warnings to illiterate farm workers in developing countries. Finding their share of the funds for this jointly sponsored study has been extremely difficult for public interest groups, and, as a result, the study is proceeding more slowly than scheduled.

Even expenses that might be regarded as minor and routine, such as travel to meetings, can pose problems for many citizens' and public interest organizations, particularly for environmental leaders participating in policy dialogues at the national level. In some policy dialogue efforts, the mediators have raised money for the expenses of private citizens and public interest group members as part of their general budget, although this has only seldom happened with site-specific disputes. To aid its own efforts at negotiated rule making, the U.S. Environmental Protection Agency has established a fund administered by the National Institute for Dispute Resolution to pay the expenses of public interest group participants and the costs of technical assistance jointly requested by all the participants. In none of the cases examined for this report, however, did participants receive any outside assistance to help pay for their time.

Two counterarguments have been made against the need for additional resources for citizens' and environmental groups. Environmentalists, it is argued, find money to pay for litigation; they should be willing to use those funds for negotiation instead of litigation in cases where negotiation could get them a better outcome. This argument, however, does not take into account those situations in which environmental statutes provide for reimbursement of attorneys' fees. Second, say some observers, too much money already is being spent on "adversarial science." In this view, the need is for joint scientific and technical studies, not for more funds for environmental groups to do their own studies. The parties to disputes should negotiate agreements on how necessary studies should be designed and on who should be hired to conduct them. The funds for those studies could come from either the corporations or the public agencies that would have had to do their own studies otherwise.

Finally, if negotiation and other consensus-building efforts are to be widely used, particularly for resolving national environmental policy issues, public interest organizations may have difficulty finding enough of their own leaders to participate in those efforts. Public interest groups typically employ relatively few individuals. Because negotiations can be time consuming, environmental groups may have an increasingly hard time being adequately represented in efforts to reach consensus on solutions to national environmental problems.

ESTABLISHING THE ROLE OF THE MEDIATOR

As the environmental dispute resolution field continues to grow and mature, it will be important to think about the appropriate roles and responsibilities of mediators. As a profession, the concept of mediation has been shaped, at least in this country, largely in the arena of labor/management relations. Environmental disputes, however, differ significantly from labor disputes in ways that have important implications for mediators and for the parties who use their services.

One of the most important differences is legal. Once unions are certified as representatives of groups of employees, unions and management are required by federal law to negotiate with each other. This, and the legalization of the strike for most workers, has given unions legitimized power to participate in decisions about labor issues. By contrast, citizen and environmental groups may or may not have sufficient power to get others to negotiate with them or to be willing to negotiate themselves.

In addition, because unions and management have this legally established and regular negotiating relationship, labor mediators usually enter disputes after the parties have begun to negotiate and are encountering difficulties, while mediators of environmental disputes typically enter disputes before negotiations have begun and often before the idea has even been suggested to all the parties. As a result, environmental mediators play a role in initiating and setting the ground rules structuring negotiating relationships, which traditional labor mediators usually do not play.

The mediators' responsibilities in helping the parties agree on the objective of the dispute resolution process are affected by differences in determining in whose interest it is to resolve a dispute. In labor disputes, it usually is in the mutual interest of both unions and management to have an acceptable contract and to keep a business in operation. The assumptions underlying negotiation of environmental issues are not always so straightforward, with the result that it may not always be clear initially whose interests are best served by negotiation. The controversy may be at the stage at which the assumptions that define the scope of the negotiations are themselves what is in dispute. In addition, the parties may not have interests as clearly in common as do labor and management in the viability of the business. At the national level, controversies may arise when environmentalists and others call attention to unsolved problems such as acid rain, lead in gasoline, and groundwater contamination. Their adversaries may question the data that suggests that there is a problem and may call for additional research. Engaging in negotiation at this stage in the controversy probably is more in the interest of those who call for action, if that negotiation is to be aimed at determining what course of action should be taken to deal with the problem. But, if the objective of the negotiation is to consider how to study the perceived problem further, it likely is more in the interest of those who are responsible for paying to solve the problem. Similarly, at the local level, in disputes over the siting of hazardous waste treatment facilities, negotiations based on the assumption that a facility will be sited may not be seen as neutral in the eyes of the potential host community.

In environmental disputes, mediators sometimes must consider whether the parties should seek a resolution in some way other than negotiation. Environmental mediators who wish to protect their reputations for neutrality must question how the issues are defined in each case and whether, simply by initiating and convening a negotiation, they are working to the advantage of some parties and not others. Also, as was noted in chapter 3, environmental disputes occasionally involve nonnegotiable items. In such cases, unless the issues can be redefined, mediation may not be the best way to settle the dispute.

In addition, environmental mediators potentially play a more important role than their labor counterparts in influencing who participates in a dispute resolution process. Because, in labor-management negotiations there is little question about who participates, labor mediators do not have to ask themselves whether their actions in this regard have nonneutral consequences. Environmental mediators, however, often play a major role in identifying the parties to disputes or the participants in dialogues. Their choices can directly affect both the fairness of a mediation process and the stability of an outcome since what satisfies one set of parties may not protect the interests of others who were not selected to participate directly in discussions. And, of course, any agreement that fails to respond to the interests of all affected parties is less likely to be perceived as fair or to be successfully implemented. Unlike most decisions in labor disputes, the choices made by those involved in resolving environmental disputes are likely to have important consequences affecting the interests of many hard-to-represent parties. Thus, whether they wish to or not, mediators of environmental disputes face questions about who should participate in the dispute resolution process, which have non-neutral consequences and which usually do not plague labor mediators.

The differences between labor and environmental disputes pose important questions about the ethics of environmental mediation: What are the ethical implications for mediators in how the issues are defined? Should the mediators be responsible for ensuring that all those affected by dispute resolution efforts are represented? Do the mediators have any responsibility to the public at large for those efforts' outcomes? Is there a way to structure some measure of accountability into how environmental mediation is practiced?

One of the oldest and most fundamental ethical principles of professional mediators is that they should always remain neutral. It is considered unethical to mediate disputes in which one has a personal stake in the outcome or to act in a biased fashion to the benefit of any particular parties or points of view. Mediators also have traditionally defined neutrality as the advocacy of no point of view and no specific solution to a problem. Neutrality, however, becomes a very complicated responsibility in resolving environmental disputes because some of the decisions that structure the dispute resolution process may have nonneutral consequences. One such decision is whether a mediator should agree to assist any negotiations between parties who wish to reach an agreement with each other, if those negotiations would exclude some affected interests. Some mediators report that this decision is made even more complicated depending on whether those interests actually are being excluded or whether they are choosing not to participate because they do not think the decision should be made by negotiation. Some mediators feel that they have no business interjecting their own views about who should be represented at a bargaining table. Other mediators, however, argue that their responsibilities extend to ensuring that all affected interests are represented as well as possible. Mediators who take this latter position do so largely because they believe the outcome will be more stable and that the process itself will remain neutral and therefore will be perceived as more fair.

Disagreement also exists over what responsibility mediators should have for ensuring that agreements are in the best interests of the participating parties. Some mediators assume no role in evaluating whether an agreement is in the parties' best interest, relying on the parties to act in their own best interests; other mediators raise questions about potential problems in the long-term stability of an agreement; and still others argue that mediators should take an active role in suggesting terms that will help the parties achieve joint gains that they may not have seen.

Finally, disagreement exists over whether mediators should take responsiblity for seeing that agreements are in the broader public interest. Some mediators assume that public agencies will represent the public interest in environmental disputes; others feel obligated to structure the process to make sure that negotiated agreements are subjected to the same public review that other public decisions receive; and others suggest that, because mediation of environmental controversies has broad social consequences, mediators should take more active, personal responsibility for questioning whether agreements are in the public interest.[10] This could be done by asking the parties to consider the effects of their agreements on those who are not directly represented in the process, by providing technical expertise, or, even, by acting as an advocate for elements of a solution that the mediator believes is in the public interest. This last option, however, obviously is a substantial departure from traditional mediator ethics. Also, the greater the responsibility assumed by mediators, the more their own experiences, expertise, and biases are likely to affect both the process and its outcomes.

The role of the mediator with respect to the public interest is already defined in many kinds of nonenvironmental mediation efforts, largely through the basic statutes that govern those issues. In labor relations, for example, keeping the peace between labor unions and management and avoiding the economic disruption caused by protracted strikes is the larger public interest that labor mediators serve. Similarly, in civil rights disputes, the underlying goals of Community Relations Service mediators are the protection of the rights of minorities and the avoidance of violent confrontations between different racial and ethnic groups. In the coming years, environmental mediators and those who use their services must determine what the equivalent public interest is in resolving environmental disputes.

Mediators must also consider how they can structure some measure of accountability into how environmental mediation is practiced. Traditionally, it has been assumed that mediators should be accountable to the parties in specific dispute resolution processes. To the extent that those parties share in paying the mediator's fee or can refuse without penalty to participate in a dispute resolution attempt, the parties do have some say over what acceptable behavior is for a mediator. In cases where mediators are expected to have some autonomy to raise questions about those who may not be represented in the negotiations, however, it is less clear that mediators should be accountable only to the parties that come forward initially or that are directly represented in the dispute resolution process.

The institutional mechanisms described earlier in this chapter may provide different answers to some of these questions about the appropriate neutrality and accountability of mediators. Fee-for-service arrangements would create direct acountability to the parties involved. Independent funding from foundations or other charitable sources might help establish necessary autonomy for environmental mediators, as might making those mediators, in effect, employees of either the judicial system or independent public agencies. Some of these arrangements, however, also raise uncertainties—for example, whether a court-paid mediator would be sufficiently accountable to the parties in a controversy; how that accountability would be affected by whether a judge appointed the mediator, recommended a mediator subject to the concurrence of the parties, or made a list of approved mediators available to the parties for their choice; and whether it would be necessary for any public agency that provided a mediator to be independent of the agencies involved in a controversy being mediated. Many mediators make the point strongly, however, that their neutrality and accountability are not directly linked to the source of financial support for their services.

They argue that mediators, like other professionals, must abide by professional standards and ethics or lose their credibility. Answers to the questions of mediator acountability must be explored in the years ahead.

CLOSING THOUGHTS

The first decade of experience with voluntary dispute resolution alternatives has demonstrated that they often are successful options for settling many environmental disputes. It still remains to be seen, however, whether the parties involved in environmental disputes will increasingly turn to negotiation, mediation, and other consensus-building processes and whether someone—the government or the parties themselves—will be willing to pay for mediators' assistance. Over the next 10 years, additional case experience, paired with the creation of institutional mechanisms to encourage the appropriate use of environmental dispute resolution processes, will provide a stronger basis for assessing how significant these processes can be in improving the processes for making decisions concerning difficult environmental issues.

REFERENCES

1. American Bar Association, Special Committee on Dispute Resolution, *Legislation on Dispute Resolution,* (Washington, D.C.: American Bar Association, 1984). In addition to the broad statutory authorization for court referrals to mediation in such states as California and Maine, many court referral programs are established by local court rule through, for example, small claims courts.

2. Sanford M. Jaffe and Linda L. Stamato, "Dispute Resolution: Complementary Programs and the Courts," prepared for the New Jersey Supreme Court and the Administrative Office of the Courts, (Trenton, N.J.: New Jersey Supreme Court, January 1983).

3. Richard L. Abel, *The Politics of Informal Justice* (New York: Academic Press, 1982).

4. Lawrence Susskind, "Environmental Mediation and the Accountability Problem," *Vermont Law Review* 6, no. 1, (1981); and Lawrence Susskind and Connie Ozawa, "Mediated Negotiation in the Public Sector: Mediator Accountability and the Public Interest Problem," unpublished manuscript, Program on Negotiation at the Harvard Law School.

5. The Project for the Study of Natural Resource and Environmental Conflict is located in the School of Natural Resources at the University of Michigan, and the Institute for Environmental Negotiation is part of the School of Architecture at the University of Virginia. The Mediation Institute in Seattle was formerly the Office of Environmental Mediation in the Institute for Environmental Studies at the University of Washington.

6. Jonathan Brock, *Developing Systems for the Settlement of Recurring Disputes: Four Case Studies, Analysis, and Recommendations* (Washington, D.C.: National Institute for Dispute Resolution, 1984).

7. National Institute for Dispute Resolution, "The Fund for Public Private Dispute Resolution," draft proposal, March 1986.

8. Recently, courts have appointed special masters to act as mediators and/or independent fact finders in environmental disputes. For example, U.S. District Court Judge Richard A. Enslen of the Western District of Michigan appointed Frances McGovern as special master in a case involving Indian fishing rights issues; Lawrence E. Susskind, through the New Jersey Center for Public Dispute Resolution, was appointed as special master by Judge Paul A. Lowengrub of the Superior Court Chancery Division in Camden County, New Jersey, in a dispute among 37 municipalities and the regional sewage authority over the construction of a new regional sewage treatment facility.

9. Personal communication with Robert Golten, formerly director of the Natural Resources Law Clinic at the University of Colorado, June 1984.

10. Susskind, "Environmental Mediation and the Accountability Problem," and Susskind and Ozawa, "Mediated Negotiation in the Public Sector."

Appendix

Selected Case Studies

ACCESS ACROSS SPORTING CLUB LAND

Site-specific
Objective: decision   Year concluded: 1980
Issue: land use   State: Colorado

Parties: **Mediator:**
Government: ACCORD Associates
U.S. Forest Service
Environmental groups:
coalition
Private citizens/landowners:
private sporting club (lessee)
landowner

The dispute: Access to a wilderness area across privately owned land, formerly used informally year-round, was closed when the landowner leased the land to a sporting club. A coalition of environmentalists, seeking to regain access for hikers, urged the U.S. Forest Service (which administers the wilderness area) to take action against the landowner. A confrontation between hunters and hikers on the property, reported in the media as an "armed conflict," drastically soured relations between the environmentalists and the sporting club. An attempt by the environmentalists to reassure the landowner was not successful, and the conflict strained the previously good relations between the landowner and the Forest Service.

The process: ACCORD sought to reduce tensions among the parties and to help the parties reach an agreement on access to the wilderness area. Because of the charged atmosphere, the mediators spoke with each of the parties separately. This process took several months, and several different mediators spoke with the different parties.

The result: The environmentalists agreed not to file a lawsuit, if the Forest Service and the landowner could reach an agreement on how to ensure access to the wilderness area. In addition, the environmentalists offered to help construct a new trail, since the existing trail was in poor condition. The landowner and the Forest Service reached an agreement on an easement, and the Forest Service flagged the route. Construction of the trail has not yet been completed.

AGRICULTURAL CHEMICALS DIALOGUE GROUP

Policy
Objective: recommendation
Issue: toxics

Duration: over 3 years
Years agreements con-
cluded: 1983, 1985
National/international

Parties:
Private citizens:
Interfaith Center for Corpo-
rate Responsibility*
Private companies:
American Cyanamid
Company
BASF Wyandotte
Corporation
Dow Chemical Company
Monsanto Company
National Agricultural Chem-
icals Association
Rohm and Haas Company
Union Carbide Corporation
Environmental groups:
Environmental Defense
Fund
National Wildlife Federation
Natural Resources Defense
Council

Mediator:
The Conservation
Foundation

The dispute: Concerns about the human health and environmental effects of agricultural chemicals exported by U.S. corporations to developing areas of the world were heating up in the press and in corporate circles. The Interfaith Center on Corporate Responsibility, which coordinates collective action by church stockholders to influence corporate policy, began its process to initiate stockholder action by sending letters of concern to several U.S. corporations. In early 1982, Union Carbide responded to one of these letters by suggesting a meeting to talk about the issues.

---

*Represented by individuals from two member churches: American Baptist Church-
es and the United Church of Christ.

The process: The company and the church groups both suggested expanding the dialogue to include the pesticide industry as a whole through the National Agricultural Chemicals Association and representatives from national environmental groups. The Conservation Foundation was invited to serve as facilitator of this expanded dialogue. Initial discussions led to an agreement to develop recommended guidelines for what corporations could do to reduce the misuse of their products in developing countries. The group has met six or seven times a year since May 1982.

The result: Two sets of guidelines have been adopted by the dialogue group and recommended by the National Agricultural Chemicals Association to its members that report export sales. Guidelines on advertising practices, which include recommendations for incorporating health and safety information into promotional communications, were adopted in 1983. Guidelines on labeling practices were adopted in 1985. The dialogue group has also cooperatively funded research on the development of symbols to communicate hazard warnings to illiterate agricultural workers and on pesticide safety education and training programs around the world. A plan to collect information on the implementation of agreements has been launched, and the group continues to discuss new issues.

ALEWIFE SUBWAY STOP

Site-specific
Objective: recommendation
Issue: land use

Duration: approx. 18
   months
Year concluded: 1977
State: Massachusetts

Parties:
Government:
Massachusetts Bay Transit
   Authority
Metropolitan Area Planning
   Council
City of Cambridge, Mass.
City of Arlington, Mass.
Massachusetts Secretary of
   Transportation
Massachusetts Department
   of Public Works
Private citizens/landowners:
represented on Alewife Task
   Force
Private companies:
represented on Alewife Task
   Force
Environmental groups:
represented on Alewife Task
   Force

Mediator:
Lawrence Susskind

The dispute: The Massachusetts Bay Transit Authority (MBTA) planned an extension of its Red Line subway from its terminal in Harvard Square, Cambridge, out to Route 128, a major suburban highway loop. An important stop was planned for the Alewife area in northwestern Cambridge, near Arlington. Residents, businesses, and environmental groups were concerned, however, about a variety of effects construction and operation of the subway stop would have in the Alewife vicinity, including: flooding, loss of open space, disruption of railroad freight service, positive and negative effects on the local economy, traffic flow, and safety. Others looked forward to increased economic development resulting from the transportation improvements.

The process: The government agencies involved agreed to form the Alewife Task Force to assist in resolving these concerns. Lawrence Susskind, a professor in the Department of Urban Studies and Planning at the Massachusetts Institute of Technology, was appointed as chairman. Much of the negotiation went on within the 54-member task force as it examined alternative designs for the subway stop at its biweekly meetings.

The result: The final plan was a negotiated agreement based principally on the work of a subcommittee formed to think about the opportunities created by the subway stop. A key feature of the plan was a linear park that would connect open space areas, soften the impact of automobile parking facilities, and attract pedestrians. Although implementation has been generally in accordance with this plan, some of the recommendations were based on the assumption that the Red Line would continue beyond the Alewife stop. After the negotiations had ended, however, the MBTA, for financial and other reasons, decided to make Alewife the northwest terminus of the extended Red Line. This caused changes in the implementation of the agreement, which significantly eroded the community's feeling that its needs had been met.

BANSHEE REEKS

Site-specific   Duration: 8 months
Objective: decision   Year concluded: 1983
Issue: land use   State: Virginia

Parties: **Mediator:**
Government: Institute for Environmental
Virginia Outdoors   Negotiation
  Foundation
Private citizens/landowners:
heirs to Banshee Reeks farm

The dispute: The terms of a will granting scenic easements to the Virginia Outdoors Foundation for the Commonwealth of Virginia were disputed by the heirs to a large farm. Some of the heirs sought to retain profitable development rights on the property, while the will could have been interpreted as requiring scenic preservation of the entire farm. Several lawsuits were filed.

The process: The Institute for Environmental Negotiation was approached in the spring of 1982 to assist in resolving the dispute. The process was complicated by at least two difficulties: disagreements among the heirs (represented by their attorneys at negotiations) as to the desired settlement and the need for the Virginia Outdoor Foundation's board to approve any agreement reached. An initial agreement was reached in October 1982, but the foundation's board, responding to concerns of neighboring landowners who had not been at the negotiating table, refused to approve it. Eventually, a second agreement was reached, with informal prior approval from the neighboring landowners, in the summer of 1983.

The result: The agreement permits certain development on the farm while clarifying and maintaining the easement, which ensures that an acceptable amount of open space will be preserved. The title to the property has been modified to reflect and codify the agreement. The lawsuits were dropped.

BARRINGTON SLUDGE-COMPOSTING FACILITY

Site-specific   Duration: 2 months
Objective: decision   Year concluded: 1981
Issues: land use, air quality   State: Rhode Island

Parties: **Mediator:**
Government: New England Environ-
Town of Barrington, R.I.   mental Mediation Center
Rhode Island Department
    of Environmental
    Management
Private citizens/landowners:
landowners abutting facility

The dispute: Residents near a town-operated sludge-composting facility complained frequently of odors from the plant. After several years of such complaints, the Rhode Island Department of Environmental Management ordered the facility closed. The town, believing that improved management practices could alleviate the problems, sought to keep the facility open.

The process: The New England Environmental Mediation Center assisted the state and town in negotiations with each other; the nearby residents chose not to participate, deciding that the state would represent their interests. In addition to convening the negotiations, the mediators helped the parties gather information on technical solutions to the odor problem that would be credible to all involved. The parties held one joint meeting, with a mediator present, on October 13, 1981.

The result: When the parties were brought together, the town and the Department of Environmental Management concluded that they had reached a point from which they would be able to negotiate without further mediator assistance. Both parties ultimately agreed to change operating and management practices of the composting facility to reduce odor and leachate problems, and the agreement was incorporated into an order written by a state hearing officer.

BLUEFIELD/TAZWELL COUNTY

Site-specific
Objective: decision
Issue: land use

Duration: less than 1 month
Year concluded: 1984
State: Virginia

Parties:
Government:
City of Bluefield, Va.
Tazwell County, Va.

Mediator:
Public Mediation Services

The dispute: Bluefield and Tazwell County were in dispute over a proposed annexation of county land by the city and over who would be responsible for the provision of water supply services.

The process: Three days of negotiations mediated by Roger Richman produced a signed agreement on the annexation and agreement on most of the issues involved in water supply.

The result: The annexation agreement was taken to the Virginia Commission on Local Government for approval. Further negotiations on the water supply issues, without a mediator, were continuing at the time this study was concluded.

BRAYTON POINT POWER PLANT

Site-specific
Objective: decision
Issues: energy, air quality

Duration: less than 18 months
Year concluded: 1978
State: Massachusetts

Parties:
Government:
U.S. Environmental Protection Agency
U.S. Department of Energy
Massachusetts Department of Environmental Quality Engineering
Private company:
New England Power Company

Mediator:
Center for Negotiation and Public Policy

The dispute: After the Arab oil embargo, the Federal Energy Administration (later part of the U.S. Department of Energy) ordered the New England Power Company to convert its Brayton Point power plant into a coal-burning facility. Both state and federal environmental officials insisted that if the conversion were to proceed, expensive pollution control technology be installed to reduce particulate and sulfur dioxide emissions associated with burning coal. The company argued that enforcing such pollution control requirements would render the conversion economically impossible.

The process: Mediation began at the initiative of the Center for Energy Policy (now the Center for Negotiation and Public Policy), which had completed a study of issues involved in conversion of power plants from oil to coal. Informal meetings, initially aimed at arranging a trial conversion and chaired by mediator David O'Connor, began in the winter of 1977. By April, the parties agreed instead to seek a plan for a permanent conversion. Eighteen more meetings were held, culminating in the signing of a memorandum of understanding in August 1978.

The result: The conversion to coal has proceeded, with limits set on the sulfur content of the coal to be burned and the requirement of electrostatic precipitators to reduce emissions of particulates, the pollutant that most concerned the Massachusetts Department of Environmental Quality Engineering in this case. The economic interests of the company were protected in two ways: first, despite the cost of the electrostatic precipitators, the state's agreement not to require sulfur dioxide-removing scrubbers limited the pollution control expense; second, the state agreed not to tighten the pollution restrictions for at least 10 years, enabling the company to plan for its coal supply and reducing the uncertainty of its investment. The final administrative barrier to the agreement was cleared in May 1979, when the U.S. Environmental Protection Agency formally approved the conversion plan.

BRIONES REGIONAL PARK

Site-specific   Duration: 10 months
Objective: decision   Year concluded: 1981
Issue: land use   State: California

Parties: **Mediator:**
Government: The Mediation Institute
East Bay Regional Park
  District
City of Martinez, Calif.
City of Pleasant Hill, Calif.
Contra Costa County, Calif.
Private citizens/landowners:
Martinez Horsemen's
  Association
five separate homeowners'
  groups

The dispute: Development of a new access point, road, and facilities for riding and hiking in Briones Regional Park was opposed by citizens in adjacent neighborhoods through which the road would pass.

The process: The Mediation Institute was first approached by officials of the East Bay Regional Park District in January 1978, by which time the conflict over Briones Regional Park was almost a year old. However, passage of the tax-cutting initiative Proposition 13 caused plans for the park to be put on hold. In early 1980, when the park district again began to plan the development, it formally requested the institute's assistance. Mediator Verne Huser met with dozens of individuals to determine who the interested parties were and how they could best be represented. Negotiations aimed at producing a development plan acceptable to all parties were then convened, with the first formal meeting held June 30, 1980. An agreement in principle was worked out by October; satisfactory implementation guarantees were then negotiated; and the agreement was signed in April 1981.

The result: The plan for development and management of the north part of Briones Regional Park, signed by representatives of all parties, provided for: a specific development plan for the park access point; means of reducing damage to natural features and scenic amenities; security measures; and a route for the access road that was acceptable to all the parties. A review committee was established to monitor implementation, which has proceeded on schedule.

CHARLES CITY COUNTY (WAYSIDE DISTRICT)

Site-specific
Objective: decision
Issue: water resources

Duration: 3 months
Year concluded: 1983
State: Virginia

Parties:
Government:
Board of Supervisors,
   Charles City County, Va.
Private citizens/landowners:
citizens of Wayside District,
   Charles City County

Mediator:
Institute for Environmental
   Negotiation

The dispute: A new water system was being constructed in the Wayside District of Charles City County. The county set a June 6, 1983 deadline for hookup, after which residents would be charged a $600 penalty as well as the basic connection fee. A number of residents felt the new system was unnecessary and that the connection fee would prove too expensive for the low-income residents of the area to pay. The threatened penalty exacerbated the residents' fears. They hired a lawyer and threatened to sue to stop the construction of the water system. The county, however, had made firm commitments to build the system in obtaining loans and grants to pay for it.

The process: At the advice of a person retained as an expert witness, the attorney for the citizens suggested mediation as a way to settle the dispute. Three joint meetings were facilitated by A. Bruce Dotson.

The result: An agreement was reached that permitted continued construction of the water system but eased the financial worries of the residents. The county agreed to extend the connection deadline by five weeks to avoid imposing the penalty and financial assistance was obtained from the nonprofit Virginia Water Project, Inc.

COLUMBIA BIKE PATHS

Site-specific
Objective: decision
Issue: land use

Duration: 8 months
Year concluded: 1979
State: Missouri

Parties:
Government:
Heritage Conservation and
  Recreation Service, U.S.
  Department of the Interior
Columbia, Mo., Department
  of Parks and Recreation
Boone County government
Private citizens/landowners:
abutters to proposed bike
  paths

Mediators:
ERM-McGlennon
American Arbitration
  Association

The dispute: The City of Columbia sought to acquire an old railroad right-of-way and convert it into an 8.5-mile-long park, including bike trails. A number of neighboring landowners argued that the proposed use was unacceptable because of problems of safety and security for abutting residents. Deed restrictions also clouded the city's title to the right-of-way.

The process: The Heritage Conservation and Recreation Service, eager to see the proposal become reality invited John McGlennon, who was working as a mediation consultant to conduct dispute assessments for the U.S. Department of the Interior through the American Arbitration Association, to attend a public hearing in August 1978. McGlennon then met separately with individuals and groups of affected parties over a period of eight months. The objective of these meetings was to answer questions, resolve issues for individual landowners, and obtain signatures to title documents.

The result: Acquisition and development of the park has proceeded along the right-of-way. Design of the trail was modified to respond to the concerns of abutting landowners, who also were compensated for signing a release on deed restrictions.

COLUMBUS, OHIO, NEGOTIATED INVESTMENT STRATEGY

Policy
Objective: decision
Issues: multiple

Duration: 9-10 months
Year concluded: 1980
State: Ohio

Parties:
16-member team of federal
  agency representatives
22-member team of state
  agency representatives
local team of municipal
  agencies, business, the
  city council, county representatives, and private
  citizens

Mediator:
The Kettering Foundation

The dispute: The Kettering Foundation had observed the need for more effective approaches to intergovernmental relations, particularly between the federal, state, and local levels of government with respect to urban development planning and decision making and the allocation and use of public funds.

The process: Between 1979 and 1981, The Kettering Foundation convened at least four negotiated investment strategy efforts, bringing together teams of government officials to develop coordinated plans for long-term urban development. One of these was in Columbus, Ohio, where mediators Lawrence Susskind, Frank Keefe, and William McCoy assisted negotiations that addressed seven major topics. These included transportation, human services, housing and historic preservation, leveraging private investment and minority participation in community development, water quality management and the control of urban sprawl, employment and training, and strategies for serving special needs populations. The negotiations began in August 1979, and the parties reached a 76-point agreement in May 1980.

The result: The majority of points in the detailed agreement have been implemented. Reductions in federal programs have precluded implementation of others.

COMMON GROUND

Policy
Objective: recommendations   Year concluded: 1983
Issue: land use   State: Illinois

Parties: **Mediator:**
14 organizations represent-   Illinois Environmental
  ing agricultural, environ-   Consensus Forum
  mental, and other public
  interest concerns

The dispute: Environmentalists and farmers in Illinois historically had differed on such land-use issues as protection of wetlands, agricultural lands preservation, and the impacts of soil erosion.

The process: To begin to bridge the gap, improve communications, and develop a clearer understanding of the issues, Philip Marcus of the Illinois Environmental Consensus Forum convened a policy dialogue called the Common Ground Task Force made up of representatives of the different perspectives on agricultural issues in the state. The first set of issues they addressed were tied to the budget bill then before the state legislature.

The results: The task force agreed on recommendations to the governor and the Illinois General Assembly to allocate funds for the state's share in a voluntary erosion and sedimentation control program, a county soil survey project, and additional technical staff for soil and water conservation districts in the state. These recommendations were implemented in the state's budget appropriations for that year.

CREST

Site-specific (regional)
Objective: recommendation
Issues: land use, natural
  resource management

Duration: 5 months
Year concluded: 1981
State: Oregon

Parties:
Government:
U.S. Fish and Wildlife
  Service
National Marine Fisheries
  Service
U.S. Army Corps of
  Engineers
U.S. Environmental
  Protection Agency
Oregon Division of State
  Lands
Oregon Department of Fish
  and Wildlife
Oregon Land Conservation
  and Development
  Commission
Oregon Department of
  Economic Development
Astoria, Oreg.
Warrenton, Oreg.
Clatsop County, Oreg.
Port of Astoria

Mediator:
The Mediation Institute

The dispute: Between 1974 and 1979, a long-range regional management plan for the Columbia River estuary was developed by the Columbia River Estuary Study Taskforce (CREST). Although informal consultation occurred between the taskforce, the members of which were local officials, and state and federal agencies, most but not all issues on which the local, state, and federal agencies disagreed were resolved. As a result, the plan was rejected by the Oregon Land Conservation and Development Commission (LCDC), which under a state law must approve local comprehensive plans, including those for estuaries. Specifically at issue were the plans for five potential port development sites and whether sufficient economic justification existed for proposed exceptions from requirements for water-dependent uses.

The process: CREST staff first contacted The Mediation Institute in 1977 to request a workshop on negotiation for task force members. In spring of 1981, after LCDC rejected the CREST plan, CREST staff asked the institute to mediate the dispute. After a preliminary assessment by mediators Verne Huser and Sam Gusman (on leave from The Conservation Foundation), those involved agreed to a negotiation process in which four federal agencies, four state agencies, and four units of local government would represent the various interests. Seven two-day meetings were held, and an agreement was reached by the parties' self-imposed deadline date, June 30, 1981.

The result: The parties signed a 35-page agreement, containing policies and maps detailing what kinds of development could occur at which locations on each site with what mitigation measures and specifying which site locations were to be protected for wildlife habitat. Land-use plans that incorporated the agreements were submitted by the local governments and were approved by LCDC. State and federal regulatory agencies are using the agreement as a basis for making permit decisions. The Port of Astoria has used the agreement as a promotional tool with potential clients who might be interested in developing projects on these sites, for whom predictability in regulatory decisions is an asset.

DELTA COUNTY QUALITY OF LIFE

Policy
Objective: improved
    communications
Issue: land use

Duration: approx. 15 months
Year concluded: 1978
State: Colorado

Parties:
Government:
6 unincorporated towns
Private citizens/landowners:
League of Women Voters
farmers and ranchers
other local citizens
Private companies:
Colorado Westmoreland
other coal companies

Mediator:
ACCORD Associates

The dispute: Delta County's population of approximately 19,000 was distributed between six relatively isolated towns and rural communities, and the county had no professional administrator or planner and only a volunteer planning commission. The county is rich in mineral resources, however, and the Delta County League of Women Voters was concerned about the county's ability to prepare in advance for the problems of rapid growth. Although a specific dispute did not exist, league members felt that there was a growing polarization between county residents who favored growth and those who opposed it.

The process: The league contacted Susan Carpenter and John Kennedy of ACCORD Associates in January 1977 to help them bring people together before a dispute erupted. After preliminary meetings, ACCORD and the league decided to cosponsor a one-day workshop. Planned in large part by a local steering committee, the workshop was held March 4, 1978, and attracted about 270 people.

The result: A wide variety of ideas for future action emerged from the workshop. The three most popular ideas for dealing with the anticipated problems of rapid growth were to begin a county planning process, to improve the education system in the county, and to increase citizen involvement in decisions. Subcommittees were formed and accomplished several of their goals. Most notably, the county also now has a professional county manager, county attorney, and new zoning ordinance.

EASTMAN-GELATIN COAL/OIL MIXTURE

Site-specific   Duration: less than 1 month
Objective: decision   Year concluded: 1983
Issues: Energy, air quality   State: Massachusetts

Parties: **Mediator:**
Government: New England Environmental
U.S. Department of Energy   Mediation Center
U.S. Environmental
   Protection Agency
Massachusetts Department
   of Environmental Quality
   Engineering
Private company:
Fuels Development Group
   (consultant to Eastman-
   Gelatin Company)

The dispute: Eastman-Gelatin Company wanted to test the conversion of its oil-fired boilers to a coal/oil mixture. Because the area around the plant had not attained the ambient air quality standard for particulates, and the test would at times cause increased particulate emissions, state and federal regulators were unable to permit the test. However, if the test were successful and permanent pollution control devices were installed along with the conversion technology, the change would in the long run greatly reduce emissions.

The process: The U.S. Department of Energy invited David O'Connor of the New England Environmental Mediation Center to attend a planned joint meeting of the parties.

The result: Eastman-Gelatin agreed to develop a plan for monitoring the test's effects on ambient air quality. The Massachusetts Department of Environmental Quality Engineering agreed that when it received the monitoring plan, it would ask the U.S.

Environmental Protection Agency (EPA) to change the status of the region near the plant from "nonattainment" to "unclassified," as long as approved monitoring tests also were conducted, as required for changing ambient air quality classifications. Such a change would permit the test to proceed. EPA agreed to do so when requested. The company is waiting for further reports from its consultant before deciding whether to attempt the test.

EAST WINDSOR TOWNSHIP ASBESTOS IN SCHOOLS

Site-specific
Objective: decision
Issue: toxics

Duration: 1-2 months
Year concluded: 1983
State: New Jersey

Parties:
Government:
East Windsor, N.J.,
  Township Board of
  Education
Private citizens/landowners:
Parents Against Asbestos

Mediator:
New Jersey Office of
  Dispute Settlement

The dispute: Parents in East Windsor Township became concerned that the local Board of Education was not promptly and adequately obeying U.S. Environmental Protection Agency regulations that the public be informed about school districts' plans to remove asbestos from schools. The board had received two separate engineering studies containing very different estimates of the magnitude of the problem, which were not widely available.

The process: The parents contacted mediators at the New Jersey Office of Dispute Settlement, who talked to the chairman of the school board. The mediators brought in a new and neutral expert to evaluate the technical aspects of the dispute. The parties met for about six weeks of joint meetings.

The result: The parties reached a written agreement based on the expert's recommendations. The board agreed to remove all the asbestos, which was located around pipes, before the school year began by a method that the parents accepted. The parties also formed an advisory committee to supervise the removal process. The agreement, though implemented, was never signed, because of a disagreement over one of the people to be named to the advisory committee.

EAU CLAIRE LANDFILL SITING

Site-specific
Objective: decision
Issue: land use

Duration: 5 months
Year concluded: 1978
State: Wisconsin

Parties:
Government:
Wisconsin Department of
  Natural Resources
City of Eau Claire, Wisc.
Wisconsin Public Intervenor
Town of Seymour, Wisc.
County of Eau Claire, Wisc.*
Environmental groups:
Northern Thunder
Trout Unlimited*
Lake Altoona Rehabilitation
  District*

Mediator:
Wisconsin Center for Public
  Policy (later became part
  of The Mediation Institute)

The dispute: The City of Eau Claire purchased land, located in the semi-rural Town of Seymour, planning to use it as a landfill for solid waste disposal. Seymour objected and initiated a court action as well as an administrative appeal asking the Wisconsin Department of Natural Resources (DNR) to require a full environmental impact statement (EIS) on the landfill; the DNR had already approved a simpler environmental impact assessment worksheet. The public intervenor, an ombudsman in the Wisconsin Department of Justice charged with protecting citizens' interests in government actions, argued for more careful consideration of alternative sites. His office, joined by Trout Unlimited and the Lake Altoona Rehabilitation District, also voiced concerns over possible stream contamination from the dump. Northern Thunder wanted recycling included in the plans. Eau Claire County was tangentially involved, primarily as owner of one of the possible alternative sites.

---

*Party had an interest in case and was consulted during mediation but was not a signator to the final agreement.

The process: The public intervenor, upon entering the case, invited Howard Bellman and Edward Krinsky, at the Wisconsin Center for Public Policy, to mediate the dispute. Mediation began on March 24, 1978, when Seymour petitioned the DNR over the EIS. The mediation effort occurred in two phases. After the City of Eau Claire and the DNR agreed to further study of alternative sites, the public intervenor dropped out of the case. Subsequently, Eau Claire, Seymour, and the DNR negotiated an agreement concerning the design and management of the landfill in Seymour. The agreement was signed on September 28, 1978, and was entered as a consent order on October 10, 1978.

The result: Seymour agreed to drop administrative and court challenges, allowing Eau Claire to operate the landfill in Seymour. Eau Claire agreed to close and surrender title to the dump after a limit of about 600,000 tons of waste had been deposited; to prohibit direct public access to the landfill, instead providing a transfer station in Eau Claire at which residents could deposit their refuse; to provide a dumping box in Seymour so that town residents could use the landfill as well; to restrict hours of both construction and operation of the dump; and to design the facility in such a way as to minimize the likelihood of polluting the nearby stream.

EMPORIA/GREENSVILLE COUNTY

Site-specific   Duration: 5 months
Objective: decision   Year concluded: 1982
Issue: land use   State: Virginia

Parties: **Mediator:**
Government: Public Mediation Services
City of Emporia, Va.
County of Greensville, Va.

The dispute: This dispute centered around the efforts of two
independent local governments—one to effect a merger and the other
an annexation. Greensville County sought an outright merger of
itself with the City of Emporia, under authority of state merger laws.
The city, however, challenged these laws as unconstitutional. In
addition to suing against the merger, the city initiated its own
annexation proceedings, seeking to acquire six square miles of land
from the county. The county countersued. In addition to the direct
question of control, at issue were the distribution of revenues and
service requirements between the localities.

The process: While the proposed merger was still in the courts,
the Virginia Commission on Local Government, under the authority
of its enabling statute, suggested mediation and nominated Roger
Richman of Public Mediation Services as mediator. Both the city
and the county eventually agreed to participate, and roughly five
months of meetings ensued.

The result: An intergovernmental agreement was approved by
both parties. It permitted the annexation of over four square miles
(about two-thirds the amount sought) of Greensville County by the
City of Emporia. In return, the city agreed to assume over 10 percent
of the county's outstanding long-term school debt and to provide
certain sewer and sanitation services to the county. The county
dropped any claims for tax revenues lost as a result of the annexation

and its pending antiannexation lawsuit. The earlier court case concerning the county's merger proposal was still pending when the agreement was signed. It was agreed that if the merger were upheld in court and approved by city and county voters, the merger would proceed and the annexation would not. However, if the merger were defeated at the polls or struck down in court, then the annexation would take place as agreed. The vote has been delayed in a court review of technical issues raised by a citizen review committee appointed by the court.

FITCHBURG WATER SYSTEM

Site-specific
Objective: decision
Issue: water resources

Duration: 6-7 months
Year concluded: 1980
State: Wisconsin

Parties:
Government:
Town of Fitchburg, Wisc.
Wisconsin Department of
　Natural Resources
Private citizens/landowners:
neighborhood association
Private company:
private developer

Mediator:
Wisconsin Center for Public
　Policy (later became part
　of The Mediation Institute)

The dispute: The Wisconsin Department of Natural Resources found high bacterial counts in wells serving about 100 houses in a subdivision of Fitchburg, near Madison. The housing development firm, which was no longer actively engaged in business, claimed it had no responsibility to maintain the wells or provide replacement service, because the residents' original 10-year water contract with the developer had expired. The town was willing to hook the subdivision into its own water supply system but only if the connections were paid for. The residents were unwilling to pay the connection fee, feeling it was the developer's responsibility.

The process: Three to four joint meetings were conducted by mediator Edward Krinsky.

The result: The town agreed to install a new water supply system in the subdivision. The developer agreed to compensate the town, partially in cash and partly by donating land for a park. The company also agreed to maintain and repair the old wells during the three years needed for connection to the town water system.

FOOTHILLS WATER TREATMENT PLANT

Site-specific
Objective: decision
Issue: water resources

Duration: 8 months
Year concluded: 1979
State: Colorado

Parties:
Government:
Denver Water Board
U.S. Environmental
    Protection Agency
U.S. Army Corps of
    Engineers
U.S. Forest Service*
U.S. Bureau of Land
    Management*
U.S. Fish and Wildlife
    Service*
Environmental groups:
Water Users Alliance*
National Wildlife
    Federation*
Trout Unlimited*

Mediator:
U.S. Representative Tim
    Wirth

The dispute: The Denver Water Board (DWB), responding to projected increases in population and per capita water demand, proposed building a new water treatment plant in conjunction with a 240-foot dam and 1.7-mile-long reservoir on the South Platte River, approximately 25 miles southwest of Denver. The federal government became involved because rights-of-way to federal land, as well as dredge-and-fill permits under the Clean Water Act, were needed for the project to proceed. Further, the federal permits could be granted only upon completion of an environmental impact statement. Both environmental groups and the U.S. Environmental Protection Agency (EPA) opposed the project, arguing that it would be unnecessary if Denver undertook appropriate conservation measures, that the dam would destroy valuable recreational and

---

*Parties involved in the negotiating process after December 15, 1978, meeting.

wildlife resources, and that the project (by encouraging rapid and dispersed growth) would contribute to air pollution and other environmental impacts.

The process: In June 1978—after several years of controversy, with one lawsuit pending, an earlier mediation attempt having failed, and conflict among federal agencies hampering the project—U.S. Representative Tim Wirth suggested that EPA and the DWB might be prodded to agreement by an impartial review of the Foothills project and possible alternatives. The Corps of Engineers conducted the study. After some dispute over the study and more negotiation, the Corps of Engineers, EPA, and the DWB reached an agreement at a meeting Wirth held December 15, 1978. Further negotiations then were held to satisfy the interests of the Bureau of Land Management (BLM), U.S. Forest Service (USFS), U.S. Fish and Wildlife Service, and the coalition of environmental groups that had meanwhile filed yet another lawsuit seeking to kill the project. At separate, but interacting, meetings held in January 1979, the DWB agreed on settlements with the environmental groups as well as the federal agencies.

The result: The parties agreed that the DWB would build the Foothills treatment plant and its feeder dam at the originally proposed site. Several steps were taken, however, to reduce environmental damage: the DWB agreed to establish a water conservation plan, enhance recreational and wildlife habitat features of other areas to replace values lost to the new reservoir, and ensure minimum stream flows below the dam. The DWB also paid the environmental groups' legal fees, established a citizens' advisory committee to help plan future water supply, and agreed to include the costs of environmental impact mitigation in such planning. In addition, the DWB agreed to prepare a systemwide environmental impact statement. Water conservation conditions imposed in the USFS and BLM right-of-way permits were allowed to stand.

The federal judge in Colorado in whose court the lawsuits were being tried, though he dismissed the DWB's lawsuit, cited numerous legal problems in the agreements and refused to sign them as a consent decree. Implementation of this complex agreement has continued into the Metropolitan Water Roundtable negotiations described in chapter 1.

FRANKLIN COUNTY CHEESE

Site-specific
Objective: decision
Issue: water resources

Duration: 1-2 months
Year concluded: 1982
State: Vermont

Parties:
Government:
Vermont Department of
  Water Resources
Private company:
Franklin County Cheese
  Corporation

Mediator:
New England Environmental
  Mediation Center

The dispute: A small cheese manufacturer, disillusioned with state environmental regulations, initiated its own process for handling whey and selling it as cattle feed. Although recognized by state government for its excellent waste management practices, the company refused to comply with state monitoring and reporting requirements and its discharge permit expired.

The process: Wishing to avoid litigation, the Vermont attorney general referred the case to the New England Environmental Mediation Center before filing suit. The mediator first met separately with the parties. State officials, with the mediator, toured the cheese plant and then met with the company to negotiate a solution to the problem. The agreement reached at that meeting was formally signed six to eight weeks later.

The result: The Vermont Department of Water Resources agreed to extend the company's permit. The company, in turn, agreed to contract with the local waste treatment plant for sampling the company's discharge and to report the sampling results to the department. In addition, the company and department agreed to work together to develop still more innovative approaches to waste management.

FREDERICKSBURG/SPOTSYLVANIA COUNTY

Site-specific   Duration: 1-2 months
Objective: decision   Year concluded: 1981
Issue: land use   State: Virginia

Parties: **Mediator:**
Government: Public Mediation Services
City of Fredericksburg, Va.
Spotsylvania County, Va.

The dispute: Fredericksburg sought to annex parts of Spotsylvania County, particularly a recently developed shopping center and industrial park and some additional lands ripe for development. The county opposed the annexation.

The process: The Virginia Commission on Local Government (the state body that approves annexations), under provisions of state law, suggested mediation. Representatives of the two parties met for six to eight weeks with the assistance of mediator Roger Richman. Critical to resolving the dispute was broadening the discussion to include not just the annexation but also problems that had been going on for years over provision of public services.

The result: Fredericksburg annexed 4.6 square miles of Spotsylvania County, including some prime land and part of the industrial park, though not including the shopping mall. The city also agreed to compensate the county for lost tax revenues and the value of existing infrastructure in the annexed area and not to seek any further annexations for 25 years. In addition, the city and county agreed to share water and sewer services. Both the Virginia Commission on Local Government and a special judicial panel approved the agreement. A lawsuit, seeking to prevent the annexation, subsequently was filed by a neighborhood group in the annexation area, but the state Supreme Court upheld the agreement.

HALEAKALA NATIONAL PARK

Site-specific
Objective: improved
   communication   Year concluded: 1980
Issue: land use   State: Hawaii

Parties: **Mediator:**
Government: ACCORD Associates
National Park Service
Private citizens/landowners:
Hana Community Improve-
   ment Association
Environmental group:
The Nature Conservancy

The dispute: In 1971, the National Park Service proposed that 800 additional acres be added to Haleakala National Park, on the island of Maui. Part of the land in question had been acquired by The Nature Conservancy, which intended to convey title to the land to the park service. Titles to some parcels were in question, and the park service began a condemnation action to clear the titles. A community of native Hawaiians, however, had recently found old taro patches on the land, which they were reconstructing as a way to pass on their culture to the younger members of their community, and opposed the transfer of land to the park service. They felt that their concerns were not being heard.

The process: Mediators Susan Carpenter and John Kennedy were called in to facilitate initial meetings to establish a new basis for communication about the problem. Meetings were held April 7-8, 1980.

The result: The parties agreed that they did share common goals regarding land protection and management and that they could work together to develop a joint management system. This planning process, which proceeded without additional mediation assistance, included the development of a community trust and discussions with elderly Hawaiians who knew where the old taro plots had been so that additional plots could be recreated.

HAZARDOUS WASTE SITING DIALOGUE GROUP

Policy
Objective: recommendations
Issues: toxics, land use

Duration: over 2 years
Year concluded: 1983
National

Parties:

Government:
National Conference of
State Legislatures
State of Colorado
Private companies:
Chamber of Commerce of
the United States
Chemical Manufacturers
Association
Dow Chemical, U.S.A.
E.I. du Pont de Nemours &
Company
Monsanto Company
National Solid Waste
Management Association
Environmental groups:
Environmental Defense
Fund
Legal Environmental
Assistance Foundation
National Audubon Society
National Wildlife Federation
Natural Resources Defense
Council
Sierra Club
Private citizens:
League of Women Voters
of the United States

Mediator:
The Conservation Foundation

The dispute: Although they did not select a specific policy dispute, in 1981 members of a Conservation Foundation steering committee had identified the problem of siting new and better hazardous waste facilities that could earn the public's confidence as a fruitful and important topic for dialogue.

The process: Individuals from industry, public interest groups, and state government were invited to participate in a policy dialogue facilitated by Sam Gusman. The group decided that a useful focus for its work would be to prepare a handbook on hazardous waste facility siting for citizens and developers, which would present their consensus on many of the basic questions that need to be addressed by all affected parties to evaluate the suitability of a proposed facility.

The result: After numerous drafts, written by the members of the dialogue group themselves, a handbook was published. The dialogue group stated that the handbook was intended to be an educational tool designed to promote public participation and to encourage the early exchange of information. Over 15,000 copies of the handbook have been distributed nationally by the National Audubon Society, Chemical Manufacturers Association, The Conservation Foundation, and others.

HETHWOOD SHOPPING CENTER

Site-specific
Objective: recommendation
Issue: land use

Duration: 2-3 months
Year concluded: 1983
State: Virginia

Parties:

Government:
Blacksburg, Va., Planning
    Department
Private citizens/landowners:
Haymarket Square Home-
    owners Association
Hethwood Foundation
Private company:
Lester Development
    Corporation

Mediator:
Institute for Environmental
    Negotiation

The dispute: Lester Development Corporation, having acquired the partially completed Hethwood Shopping Center in Blacksburg, Virginia, hoped to increase its profitability by adding a gas station, car wash, and convenience store. Town officials and local residents, however, opposed Lester's plans. The town sought development of a more comprehensive plan for the center, while nearby residents were concerned about increased traffic, hours of operation, and other associated effects of the proposed businesses.

The process: At the suggestion of the Blacksburg planning director, A. Bruce Dotson and Doug Frame of the University of Virginia's Institute for Environmental Mediation were asked to facilitate an agreement among the parties. A 12-point settlement was reached less than a month after the first meeting, which was held February 21, 1983.

The result: The agreement included: incorporation of the agreement itself in the site plan; permissible uses for an additional parcel; and a number of conditions relating to traffic flow, hours of operation, and lighting with respect to the gas station, car wash, and convenience store—the development of which all parties agreed to support. After a tentative agreement was reached on March 17, 1983, the town Planning Commission approved it on March 28, 1983, and final approval by the City Council was granted April 12, 1983. The construction was completed shortly thereafter.

HOMESTAKE PITCH MINE RECLAMATION

Site-specific
Objective: decision
Issue: natural resource
  management

Duration: approx. 12 months
Year concluded: 1981
State: Colorado

Parties:
Private company:
Homestake Mining
  Company
Environmental groups:
National Wildlife Federation
Colorado Wildlife
  Federation
Colorado Open Space
  Council
Colorado Mountain Club
Gunnison Valley Alliance
High Country Citizens
  Alliance
Gold Hill Committee on
  Mining and the
  Environment
Marian Skinner

Mediator:
The Mediation Institute

The dispute: The Homestake Mining Company proposed, in 1976, to open an open-pit mine at an elevation over 10,000 feet in the Gunnison National Forest, Colorado. Because the science of land reclamation at high altitudes is uncertain, environmentalists felt that the mine would cause substantial damage to vegetation, wildlife, land, and water resources. Before allowing the mine to open, the U.S. Forest Service, in its environmental impact statement, detailed procedures for reclaiming the mined land. However, a coalition of environmental groups opposed the mine, fearing among other issues that the reclamation measures stipulated by the Forest Service were insufficient.

The process: The Homestake mine began operating in 1978. Environmentalists used administrative avenues, and were prepared to go to court, to try and stop its continued operation. Both they and the company decided that mediating the dispute made sense and asked the Institute for Environmental Mediation (now The Mediation Institute) for assistance. After private consultations by mediator Orville Tice with the parties indicated that negotiations could be successful, the first joint meeting was held on June 15, 1980. The parties agreed at that time to focus on how best to reclaim the mine, leaving the sensitive issue of uranium milling for later discussion. After several informational meetings and negotiating sessions, a three-part agreement was signed, a little less than a year after negotiations began.

The result: The first part of the agreement, a "Statement of Understanding," commits Homestake to protect water quality, fill the mine pits in the manner stipulated, and use water quality and soil loss measures to help evaluate the success of reclamation efforts. To ensure enforcement of these provisions, they were added as stipulations to the relevant regulatory permits for the mine. In the "Mediation Agreement," Homestake agreed to make water quality information available to environmentalists, undertake a research program on high-altitude revegetation, and mitigate any adverse impacts on fish and wildlife which might arise from mine operation. In return for these concessions, the environmental groups entered into a "Covenant Not to Sue," which bound them to stay out of court on the issues discussed so long as Homestake did not violate the other two agreements.

ILLINOIS TOLLWAY

Site-specific
Objective: improved
   communication
Issue: land use

Duration: 7-8 months
Year concluded: 1984
State: Illinois

Parties:

Government:
Illinois Department of
   Transportation
Illinois Tollway Authority
Private landowners:
Morton Arboretum

Mediator:
Illinois Environmental
   Consensus Forum

The dispute: Officials of the respected Morton Arboretum were concerned about the effects of a new highway, proposed to be constructed next to the arboretum. Of particular concern were the effects of freeway lights on sensitive plants, of gasoline- and salt-polluted water runoff, and of traffic noise that might disrupt the peaceful atmosphere enjoyed by arboretum visitors.

The process: Although the parties did not meet formally to negotiate an agreement on the design and construction of the new highway, they did agree to meet informally with the assistance of Philip Marcus to identify and discuss issues, exchange information, and generate alternative solutions to potential problems.

The result: The ideas that emerged from the discussions were incorporated into project planning decisions.

INTERSTATE 90 HIGHWAY EXPANSION

Site-specific   Duration: 10 months
Objective: decision   Year concluded: 1976
Issue: land use   State: Washington

Parties: **Mediator:**
Government: The Mediation Institute
City of Seattle, Wash.
City of Mercer Island,
   Wash.
City of Bellevue, Wash.
Municipality of Metropoli-
   tan Seattle ("Metro")
King County, Wash.
Washington State Highway
   Department

The dispute: When a four-lane highway and floating bridge across Lake Washington connecting the cities of Bellevue and Mercer Island to Seattle became increasingly congested, the Washington State Highway Department proposed expanding the road to a 10-lane superhighway. The City of Seattle and neighborhood and environmental groups opposed the plan, arguing that, while it would serve suburban commuters from the cities of Bellevue and Mercer Island, it would increase congestion and cause major adverse impacts to neighborhoods in Seattle itself.

The process: After 12 years of dispute and the rejection of numerous alternate proposals, several of the parties approached the Institute for Environmental Mediation (now The Mediation Institute) for assistance. In March 1976, the mediators were officially appointed by the governor, the highway department agreed to abide by any feasible negotiated settlement, and negotiations were convened among the public entities involved. Neighborhood and environmental groups in Seattle decided to participate indirectly through the Seattle City Council representatives. Negotiations continued through the spring and summer, but a preliminary agreement was rejected by the Seattle City Council. At the last minute, however, a counterproposal by Seattle was accepted by the other parties, and an agreement was signed in December 1976.

The result: The agreement provided for expanding the existing four-lane highway to eight lanes, two of which would be for mass transit. The agreement also set out recommendations for solving related, regionwide transportation problems. To reduce the environmental impacts of the expanded highway, sections in Seattle and Mercer Island would be underground, access on local streets between Seattle neighborhoods separated by the right-of-way would be maintained, and a new park would be constructed along part of the highway corridor.

The environmental and citizens' groups that opposed the I-90 expansion opted to pursue their court challenge instead of accepting the mediated settlement, but the court ruled in favor of the highway expansion. By the late 1970s, however, the costs of the project had soared, and President Carter had frozen federal highway construction funds. Nevertheless, the parties continued to work toward implementation of their agreement, and by mid-1985 implementation of most parts of the agreement had been either completed or started. Construction of the I-90 improvements, begun in late 1983, were scheduled to be done by 1993.

LAKE ANNA

Site-specific
Objective: decision
Issues: water resources,
   energy

Duration: 4 months
Year concluded: 1984
State: Virginia

Parties:
Government:
U.S. Environmental
   Protection Agency
U.S. Fish and Wildlife
   Service
U.S. Nuclear Regulatory
   Commission
Virginia Game and Inland
   Fisheries Commission
Environmental group:
Environmental Defense
   Fund
Private company:
Virginia Electric Power
   Company

Mediator:
Institute for Environmental
   Negotiation

The dispute: Cooling water from Virginia Electric Power Company's (VEPCO's) nuclear power plant on Lake Anna was exceeding temperature standards for the lake, and therefore the company was out of compliance with its permit. VEPCO had filed a petition for release from these temperature standards, because under the Federal Water Pollution Control Act temperature levels can be exceeded if a study determines that no environmental damage is being caused. VEPCO proposed such a study, but the Virginia State Water Control Board (SWCB), which had granted the permit, had some objections to the study design the company proposed.

The process: SWCB appointed an expert panel consisting of members from state and federal agencies and environmental groups to design a study acceptable to all sides. Richard C. Collins, director of the Institute for Environmental Negotiation at the University of Virginia, facilitated meetings between the panel and VEPCO.

The result: The panel and VEPCO reached agreement on the study's design, which was subsequently approved by the SWCB. The expert group has been meeting approximately every six months to review progress on the study.

LAKE LEE DAM REPAIR

Site-specific
Objective: decision   Year concluded: 1979
Issue: water resources   State: Wisconsin

Parties: **Mediator:**
Government: Wisconsin Center for Public
Jackson County, Wisc.   Policy (later became part
nearby town   of The Mediation Institute)
Wisconsin Department of
   Natural Resources
Private citizens/landowners:
Lake Lee Property Owners
   Association

The dispute: Because a culvert running from Lake Lee under a Jackson County road was rusting, raising the possibility that the road would wash out, Jackson County imposed weight limits on vehicles that could use the road. The county felt that the only way to repair the culvert was to lower the lake level, but this raised two critical problems. First, altering the lake level might undercut the aging dam that created the lake and cause an even more serious washout. Second, raising and lowering lake levels required a permit from the Wisconsin Department of Natural Resources (DNR) issued to the dam owner, but neither the Lake Lee Property Owners Association, the county, or the nearby town was willing to assume ownership of the dam because it would then also assume ongoing maintenance costs of the dam. The impasse was preventing a solution to the road repair problem.

The process: At the DNR's request, mediator Edward Krinsky initiated a meeting among the parties. While this first meeting did not produce substantive results, the parties agreed that a town meeting, chaired by the mediator, should be held to decide what to do about the dam.

The result: At the town meeting, a citizen suggested the name of a company that might have an alternative way to repair the culvert. This idea proved acceptable to all parties. Prefabricated concrete was installed as a new culvert within the existing one, rendering it unnecessary to alter the level of the lake.

METROPOLITAN WATER ROUNDTABLE

Policy
Objective: recommendations
Issue: water resources

Duration: over 4 years
Year agreement in principle
  concluded: 1983
State: Colorado

Parties:
31 parties, representing east
  slope water providers and
  water users, west slope
  community interests, business interests, environmental and other public
  interest groups.

Mediator:
ACCORD Associates

The dispute: Water policy and planning issues have long been subjects of significant controversy throughout the West. Particularly intense in Colorado have been disputes, including protracted litigation, over proposals for meeting the future water needs of metropolitan Denver. A dispute over the Foothills treatment plant, mediated by U.S. Representative Tim Wirth, set the stage for conflict over a new water storage facility proposed by the Denver Water Board for the Two Forks site at the confluence of the north fork and main stem of the South Platte River in the foothills of the Rockies southwest of Denver.

The process: The initiative for the roundtable came from the Boettcher Foundation, located in Denver, and from the governor's office. Boettcher Foundation staff aproached ACCORD Associates in 1981, originally asking whether mediation on the Two Forks proposal might have a chance of success. After interviewing numerous parties, ACCORD staff informed the foundation that, while an agreement on that proposal alone was unlikely, a process enabling all the parties to take a more comprehensive look at how to meet Denver's future water needs was promising.

The result: In April 1983, after over 18 months of serious negotiations, the participants reached a series of agreements on east-slope water storage projects, water-use efficiency, groundwater use, and other general considerations that should be taken into account in water resource planning. This agreement was only the beginning, however. A roundtable task force set up to monitor the systemwide environmental impact statement (EIS) process mandated in the Foothills agreement has met on a weekly or biweekly basis with the U.S. Army Corps of Engineers since early 1984, providing direction as to the alternatives being considered in the EIS and the information needed for an assessment to be seen as adequate by all parties. The roundtable itself also has met perhaps eight times between April 1983 and fall 1985 to work on implementation of its agreements.

MIDDLEBURY HYDRO

Site-specific
Objective: recommendations
Issues: land use, energy

Duration: 6 months
Year concluded: 1982
State: Vermont

Parties:
Government:
Middlebury, Vt., Board of
   Selectmen
Private citizens/landowners:
Frog Hollow Crafts
   Association
Jessica Swift Park
   Committee
Frog Hollow Federation
Downtown Middlebury
   Business Bureau
Private company:
Central Vermont Public
   Services Corporation

Mediator:
New England Environmental
   Mediation Center

The dispute: Central Vermont Public Services Corporation wanted
to build a hydroelectric plant at the site of a natural waterfall on
Otter Creek in downtown Middlebury. Local residents, town
officials, and business proprietors were worried that both construction and operation of the plant would reduce the aesthetic appeal
of the downtown and thus hurt the tourist business, which is an
important part of the town's economy.

The process: The New England Environmental Mediation Center
was approached by representatives of the selectmen and the company
at a conference on environmental dispute resolution. The first
meeting occurred on January 7, 1982, two months after the initial
contact. After five formal sessions and much informal discussion,
mediated by David O'Connor and Tom Bean, an agreement was

reached formally among all but one of the parties on February 22, 1982. The agreement was presented at a town meeting on March 2, 1982, where the agreement was ratified by a slim margin. At a second town meeting in May, after additional discussions between the representatives involved in the negotiations and town residents, the agreement was approved by a substantial margin.

The result: In exchange for the town's support of the project, the company agreed that in whatever year it began building the plant, construction would start only after that year's fall foliage season and would be completed after affecting no more than one summer tourist season. The company also agreed to take reasonable noise and dust suppression actions, accept arbitrated settlements with any businesses claiming construction-related losses, provide some drainage and landscape improvements near its plant, and maintain a specified minimum flow over the waterfall at all times.

PAPAGO/TUCSON WATER RIGHTS

Site-specific   Year concluded: 1982
Objective: recommendation   State: Arizona
Issue: water resources

Parties: **Mediator:**
Government: Office of U.S. Representative
City of Tucson, Ariz.   Morris Udall
U.S. Government (as trustee
  for the tribe)
Indian tribes:
Papago
Private citizens/landowners:
Water Resources Coordina-
  tion Committee

The dispute: The 10-fold growth of the City of Tucson since the 1940s has put increasing pressure on the groundwater resources in the Santa Cruz basin from which it draws its water supply. Both the Papago Indians, for whom the basin is their traditional home, and the non-Indian water users feel that they hold legitimate rights to the water. As a result of the dropping water table, the Papago saw their traditional sources of both surface water and groundwater disappearing, and in 1975 the Papago brought suit seeking definition of the tribe's groundwater rights and general reserved rights for those portions of the reservation that are included in the basin.

The process: Representative Udall intervened in the dispute and Deborah Sliz of his staff held a series of separate meetings with different groups of parties. Eventually, specific settlement terms were agreed to by all the parties.

The result: Representative Udall embodied the agreed-upon terms, including quantitative allocation of water between Indian and non-Indian users, in the Southern Arizona Water Rights Settlement Act, which he introduced in Congress in 1981. Both houses of Congress passed the bill in the spring of 1982. However, President Reagan vetoed the bill on June 1, 1982, asserting that federal interests had been inadequately represented. A team of negotiators from the U.S. Department of the Interior was organized to develop a federal position on the dispute. The agreement was later revised, passed by Congress, and signed by President Reagan in October 1982.

PATUXENT RIVER NUTRIENT CONTROL

Site-specific
Objective: recommendation
Issue: water resources

Duration: 2-3 months
Year concluded: 1981
State: Maryland

Parties:
Government:
Several state and local
  agencies
Private citizens/landowners:
A group of scientists, fishermen, and other citizen
  leaders representing environmental and business
  interests

Mediator:
ERM-McGlennon Associates

The dispute: In June 1981, the Maryland Office of Environmental Programs issued a draft "nutrient control strategy" for the Patuxent River as a first step in preparing a regional water quality management plan for EPA. The state's strategy emphasized removal of phosphorus at large sewage treatment plants in the four upstream counties that make up part of the rapidly urbanizing area around Washington, D.C. In response, the Tri-County Council of Southern Maryland, which represented the interests of people dependent on fishing and recreation enterprises in the largely rural downstream counties closer to the Chesapeake Bay, challenged the state's plan in court. They viewed the draft plan as unsatisfactory because it would not have removed enough phosphorus from the sewage treatment plants and because it would have done nothing to reduce nitrogen loadings. The dispute threatened to block $29 million of EPA sewage treatment construction grants to Maryland.

The process: In October 1981, the Maryland Department of Health and Mental Hygiene invited John McGlennon and several of his colleagues to mediate the dispute, but gave the process only until the end of the year. After consulting with a steering committee representing key interests, the mediators convened a two-stage process. At a preliminary meeting, scientists and technical representatives of the various parties met to put together a common understanding of what was known, not known, and in dispute about the water quality of the Patuxent. A three-day meeting involving 40 people representing the diverse interests in the Patuxent River followed, from which a consensus nutrient control strategy emerged.

The result: Key portions of the long-term strategy included: reduction of both phosphorus and nitrogen loading of the river from sewage treatment plants, development of a plan for control of non-point-source pollution, and a major experiment of sewage disposal on land. A month after the agreement was reached, the Maryland Office of Environmental Protection issued its plan embodying the terms of the agreement, and implementation of the plan is underway.

RED CLIFF

Site-specific
Objective: decision
Issue: resource management

Duration: less than 2 years
Year concluded: 1981
State: Wisconsin

Parties:
Government:
Wisconsin Department of
  Natural Resources
Indian tribe:
Red Cliff Band of Lake
  Superior Chippewa

Mediator:
Wisconsin Center for Public
  Policy (later became part of
  The Mediation Institute)

The dispute: The Red Cliff Band of the Chippewa Indian Tribe asserted fishing rights, based on historical precedent and a century-old treaty, to lake trout and whitefish in Lake Superior. The Wisconsin Department of Natural Resources sought to regulate the fishery, but the Indians contested the state's legal jurisdiction to limit tribal fishing. Direct confrontations on the lake escalated the conflict, and the dispute was in court.

The process: The Department of Natural Resources initiated contact with mediator Howard Bellman in the fall of 1979 to see if he could assist the settlement negotiations. The state and the tribe reached their first agreement, covering subsistence fishing, in June 1980; in August 1981 an agreement covering commercial fishing was reached. Issues in the latter negotiations included how many fish the tribe could harvest, who had enforcement authority, protection of treaty rights, adequate catches for non-Indian sport and commercial fishermen, maintenance of an economically viable fishery, and protection of fish population levels.

The result: The subsistence fishing treaty protected and regulated the rights of tribal members to catch fish for home use. The commercial fishing treaty assigned a higher quota to the tribe than to non-Indian commercial fishermen and protected the Indians' fishing rights within limits set by the quotas, fishing seasons, and establishment of refuges and "sport fishing only" areas. The Department of Natural Resources also agreed to continue its stocking program and to participate in a cooperative enforcement program that would allow tribal wardens to enforce the regulations applying to tribal fishermen.

RIVERSIDE SANITARY LANDFILL

Site-specific
Objective: recommendation
Issue: land use

Duration: 11-12 months
Year concluded: 1981
State: California

Parties:
Government:
Jurupa Community Services
    District
Rubidoux Community
    Services District
Private citizens/landowners:
Citizens Against the Dump
City of Riverside Energy
    Committee
Friends of Riverside
League of Women Voters
Parents of Jurupa
Private companies:
Greater Riverside Chamber
    of Commerce
Jurupa Chamber of
    Commerce
San Bernadino and
    Riverside Counties
    Disposal Association
West Riverside Business-
    men's Association

Mediator:
The Mediation Institute

The dispute: Two sanitary landfills in Riverside County, California were scheduled to close in less than three years and the amount of solid waste had been growing. A new site was identified in Crestmore Heights for the replacement landfill, but intense opposition emerged.

The process: After several months of discussions with interested parties, mediators Jim Arthur and Alana Knaster determined that compromise on the Crestmore Heights site was unlikely. They suggested that the parties consider broadening the agenda to a comprehensive discussion of how the county should handle its growing solid waste disposal problems. In April 1981, the Riverside County Board of Supervisors endorsed this agenda and asked the mediators to convene what became known as the "Second District Task Force on Solid Waste," which included representatives of all the parties listed above. The parties began meeting formally in May and signed an agreement on October 26, 1981. A week later the Riverside County Board of Supervisors ratified the agreement.

The result: The parties recommended that the county use an existing landfill as the replacement for the two landfills scheduled to close do so in two to three years. Because the replacement site had a projected capacity of 10 additional years, the agreement included recommendations that the county use this time to develop waste reduction plans as part of a comprehensive solid waste management program. Other facets of the agreement were more stringent enforcement programs and establishing an ongoing citizen role in solid waste management planning.

ROGUE RIVER MANAGEMENT PLAN

Site-specific   Duration: 3-4 months
Objective: recommendation   Year concluded: 1984
Issue: resource management   State: Oregon

Parties: **Mediator:**
Government: The Mediation Institute
U.S. Forest Service
U.S. Bureau of Land
  Management
Private citizens:
Northwest River Rafters
  Association
recreational boater
Protect Our River Rights
Private companies:
A lodge owner
Summer and fall boating
  outfitters

The dispute: A permit system to control recreational boating use of a section of the Rogue River was administered by federal agencies only during the summer season, but heavy utilization on weekends in the fall was causing crowding, conflict among user groups, and generally less pleasant fishing and rafting conditions.

The process: Verne Huser of The Mediation Institute was contacted in December 1983 by a representative of the U.S. Forest Service. Early in January 1984, the parties, representing the agencies managing the river as well as diverse user groups, formed a working group to examine the problems of river utilization. After about two months of background work, two joint meetings held in early March produced an agreement, which was ratified by the parties and signed at the end of the month.

The result: The agreement affirmed the parties' dual goals of protecting the quality of the Rogue River for recreational use and allowing as many people as possible to enjoy using it. The parties agreed to start a cooperative education program on river etiquette and minimal impact camping techniques. New regulations on river use were also established, including requiring registration of all downstream float trips from mid-May through October, creating a weekend permit season from September through mid-October, and limiting all stays in the wild segment of the river to three nights.

ROLLINS TOXIC WASTE EXPLOSION

Site-specific
Objective: decision
Issue: toxics

Duration: 6-7 months
Year concluded: 1978
State: New Jersey

Parties:
Government:
U. S. Environmental
  Protection Agency
U.S. Occupational Safety
  and Health Administration
New Jersey Department of
  Environmental Protection
Logan Township, N.J.
three other townships
Gloucester County, N.J.
Private company:
Rollins Environmental
  Services
Private citizens/landowners:
Residents Against Rollins

Mediator:
New Jersey Office of
  Dispute Settlement

The dispute: In December 1977, a major explosion was ignited accidentally by a construction worker at Rollins Environmental Services' toxic waste treatment facility in Logan Township, New Jersey, killing six persons, injuring others, contaminating the site, and releasing unknown quantities of chemicals in the smoke plume from the resulting fire. The explosion seriously exacerbated existing tensions between municipal governments—which had trouble fighting the fire because they had insufficient information about the chemicals stored at the facility—and Rollins. State and federal agencies were faced with decisions about whether and under what conditions to allow the plant to reopen. Residents Against Rollins, which had been concerned about pollution problems at the facility, contacted the New Jersey Office of the Public Advocate asking that agency to sue the New Jersey Department of Environmental Protection to force a permanent shutdown of the plant.

The process: The Public Advocate's office, rather than suing immediately, suggested that the group consider mediation by the Office of Dispute Settlement (a branch of the Public Advocate's Office). Between January and June 1978, while litigation on some issues proceeded, mediator Ed Hartfield helped various combinations of the affected interest groups reach a series of negotiated agreements.

The result: The Rollins plant was permitted to reopen, but with numerous improvements in its operation. The agreement between Rollins and the Department of Environmental Protection concerned the cleanup itself, testing at the site, conditions under which the plant would reopen, and procedures each would follow if the plant were allowed to reopen. The company also agreed to provide additional information to local fire departments, conduct safety drills, install additional air and water quality monitors and involve itself more in community affairs. The Rollins plant reopened in June 1978, and Residents Against Rollins eventually disbanded.

SAN JUAN FOREST

Site-specific
Objective: recommendation
Issue: resource management

Duration: approx. 8 weeks
Year concluded: 1983
State: Colorado

Parties:
Government:
U.S. Forest Service
Private citizens/landowners/
  environmental groups:
Over 20 private parties and
  public interest groups

Mediator:
The Mediation Institute

The dispute: A proposed management plan for 40 square miles of the San Juan National Forest included several substantial timber sales. The area, which is located between the Weminuche Wilderness Area and the Piedra Wilderness Study Area, had also been considered as a possible wilderness area. Although passage of the Colorado Wilderness Act in December 1980 precluded it from further consideration for wilderness status, environmentalists and others felt strongly about the wilderness values of the area. The forest management plan was opposed by environmental groups concerned over disruption of elk and bighorn sheep migration routes as well as by local business leaders and residents who feared that logging would reduce tourism and that heavy equipment would damage roads in the town of Vallecitos.

The process: Several public meetings were held between February and June 1983, and most of the comments were in opposition to the proposed plan. An attorney for some of the opponents and the forest supervisor agreed that mediation might be helpful, and the supervisor contacted The Mediation Institute. A first meeting was held in early September 1983. A general consensus was reached at this meeting, but during the following weeks it became clear that several issues remained to be resolved. So, in early October representatives of the various interests rode through the area together. In subsequent meetings, the parties agreed to more detailed recommendations, and on October 11, 1983, the forest supervisor issued a decision notice on the management plan, which incorporated most features of the agreement.

The result: The final management plan ruled out four of eight controversial sales that had been part of the original proposal. In addition, road construction plans were significantly scaled down. The environmental effects of remaining timber sales and road construction will be assessed by an advisory group working with the U.S. Forest Service.

SAYREVILLE AND MIDDLESEX

Site-specific   Duration: 2-4 weeks
Objective: decision   Year concluded: 1980
Issue: air quality   State: New Jersey

Parties: **Mediator:**
Government: N.J. Office of Dispute
Borouch of Sayreville, N.J.   Settlement
Middlesex County, N.J.,
    Sewage Authority

The dispute: Odors emanating from a treatment plant operated by the Middlesex County Sewage Authority precipitated this dispute. Because the problem wasn't getting resolved, town officials from Sayreville refused to pay the fee due the authority and threatened to sue.

The process: Sayreville's attorney contacted the New Jersey Office of Dispute Settlement in the hopes that a suit could be avoided. Less than a month of meetings led to a consent agreement.

The result: The agreement set out procedures to identifying the substances causing the odors and where they were emanating from, a plan for eliminating the odors, and a timetable for doing so. Both the Sayreville Town Council and the Middlesex County Sewage Authority ratified the agreement, which has been implemented.

SCHILLER STATION

Site-specific
Objective: decision
Issues: energy, air quality

Duration: 17 months
Year concluded: 1982
State: New Hampshire

Parties:
Government:
New Hampshire Public
  Utilities Commission staff
New Hampshire Consumer
  Advocate
New Hampshire Air
  Resources Agency*
Maine Department of En-
  vironmental Protection†
Private citizens:
New Hampshire Community
  Action Programs
Private company:
Public Service Company of
  New Hampshire

Mediator:
New England Environmental
  Mediation Center

The dispute: The Public Service Company of New Hampshire had been ordered as part of federal energy self-sufficiency plans to convert three generating units at the Schiller Station (Portsmouth) from oil to coal. The New Hampshire Air Resources Agency was concerned about increased air pollution problems from burning coal. The Public Utilities Commission felt that the conversion was progressing too slowly. The company believed new rate mechanisms were needed to permit financing, particularly of expensive new air pollution control devices, while consumers were concerned about potential rate increases.

---

*Participation limited to air quality issues.
†Interested party not at the negotiating table.

The process: Mediators Bill Humm and David O'Connor of the New England Environmental Mediation Center were invited to help the parties negotiate a voluntary resolution of the issues at the urging of the Public Utilities Commission. After several months of preliminary discussions, formal mediation began on March 1, 1982 and ended on October 22, 1982, with an agreement.

The result: The agreement set forth an accelerated schedule for conversion, a creative rate mechanism to fund capital costs, financial safeguards for consumers and the company, and incentives for rapid conversion signed by the company, commission, the New Hampshire Consumer Advocate, and Community Action Programs. The Public Utilities Commission formally adopted the terms of the agreement the same day. In addition, letters of agreement exchanged by the company and the Maine Department of Environmental Protection indicated that the company, whose plant was located near the Maine border, would voluntarily meet Maine's more stringent particulate emissions standard. The conversion is incomplete but proceeding as scheduled, although the company has yet to take advantage of the creative financing mechanisms made available in the agreement, perhaps because capital costs so far have not been unusually high.

SNOQUALMIE DAM

Site-specific
Objective: recommendation
Issues: land use, resource
  management, water
  resources

Duration: 11-12 months
Year concluded: 1974
State: Washington

Parties:
Government:
U.S. Army Corps of
  Engineers*
Private citizens/landowners:
Representatives of farmers
  and other residents and
  business people in river
  valley
Environmental groups:
Representatives of local and
  national groups, including
  the Sierra Club

Mediator:
The Mediation Institute

The dispute: After a major flood of the Snoqualmie River in 1959, the Army Corps of Engineers studied the river system and, in 1968, suggested building large flood control dams on the river's middle fork. Environmentalists were concerned both about the flooding of the entrance to the Alpine Lakes Wilderness area and a high quality white-water rafting stretch of the river and about the likelihood that flood protection would not protect the valley's farmers but would induce sudden and inappropriate development downstream. These concerns persuaded the governor, in 1970 and again in 1973, to veto the dam projects, although he noted his continuing concern about the flooding problems.

The process: The mediators began inquiring into the appropriateness of the dispute for mediation late in 1973. After six months of investigation, including identifying suitable negotiators for the interests involved, mediation formally began with the governor's

---

*Participated as technical advisor, not direct participant.

appointment of Gerald W. Cormick and Jane McCarthy in May 1974. A tentative agreement was reached by the parties in September after six negotiating sessions and much informal discussion. It took two more months to ratify the agreement, which was endorsed by the governor.

The result: The agreement provided significant flood control benefits while protecting sensitive areas from development. A multipurpose dam would be constructed on the north fork, but the middle fork dam, which had most concerned environmentalists, would not be built. Raising the spillway at an existing Tolt River dam, and building a group of setback levees in developed areas of the middle fork valley, would provide further flood protection. Undeveloped areas along the middle fork would be kept rural by purchasing easements and development rights, imposing land use controls, and creating a major park at the confluence of the three forks. Restricting development in the floodplain would also reduce the costs of whatever flooding might occur. Finally, a commission would be established to coordinate planning in the basin.

Implementation of the agreement did not proceed smoothly, however. The basin coordinating commission was created and functioned for 10 years, but the flood protection measures agreed to were never built, in part because later technical studies indicated that the site chosen for the north fork dam was not geologically sound.

STORM KING

Site-specific
Objective: decision
Issues: energy, water
  resources, resource
  management

Duration: 20 months
Year concluded: 1980
State: New York

Parties:
Government:
U.S. Environmental
  Protection Agency
New York Department of
  Environmental
  Conservation
U.S. Nuclear Regulatory
  Commission
U.S. Federal Energy
  Regulatory Commission
Private companies:
Central Hudson Gas and
  Electric
Consolidated Edison
  Company of New York
Orange and Rockland
  Utilities
New York State Power
  Authority
Nigara Mohawk
Environmental groups:
Scenic Hudson Preservation
  Conference
Natural Resources Defense
  Council
Hudson River Fishermen's
  Association

Mediator:
Russell Train

The dispute: Opposition to Consolidated Edison Company of New York's plans to build a hydroelectric and pumped storage plant at the foot of Storm King Mountain in the Hudson River highlands first arose when the Scenic Hudson Preservation Conference was formed late in 1963. Over the years, the issues involved in the dispute spread from simply whether the plant would unacceptably mar the scenic beauty of the Hudson to broad questions of the total effect of several utility plants on the water quality and fish life of the Hudson River.

The process: After a decade and a half of litigation and administrative hearings, attorneys for the environmental groups and Consolidated Edison discussed negotiating face to face and, in March 1979, asked Russell Train to mediate the dispute. Train spent several months laying the groundwork for negotiations and began them in August 1979. On December 18, 1980, 11 parties signed an agreement that ended the dispute.

The result: Consolidated Edison forfeited its construction license for Storm King and turned the land over to the Palisades Interstate Parkway Commission. To protect striped bass and other fish species, the utilities agreed to establish a fish hatchery and to reduce, for 10 years, their withdrawals of water from the river during the summer months. They further agreed not to build any new power plants without cooling towers above the George Washington Bridge for 25 years, to endow a river research organization, and to reimburse legal fees to the environmental groups. In return for these concessions, EPA dropped its demands for expensive cooling towers at several of the existing plants, and the environmental groups dropped legal and administrative challenges against the utilities.

A year after the settlement, New York State issued discharge permits, incorporating the terms of the mediated settlement, to the utilities. All aspects of the settlement have been implemented.

SWAN LAKE

Site-specific
Objective: recommendation
Issues: energy, water
  resources

Duration: 6-7 months
Year concluded: 1979
State: Maine

Parties:
Government:
Town of Swanville, Maine
Private companies:
Maine Hydroelectric Development Corporation

Mediator:
New England Environmental
  Mediation Center

The dispute: Maine Hydroelectric Development Corporation was a small, new company established to generate electricity through small-scale hydroelectric projects. Its first project involved a series of small dams on the Goose River. The dam farthest upstream was at the mouth of Swan Lake. Residents and officials of the lakeshore town of Swanville feared that use of the dam for hydroelectric power would result in widely fluctuating water levels, impairing the reliability of their drinking water supply, greatly limiting recreational use of the lake, and, most important, seriously eroding the value of shorefront property (and thus the town's tax base). Swanville petitioned the Federal Energy Regulatory Commission (FERC) to deny the permit for the project and obtained standing in the company's license application.

The process: The dispute had gone on for nearly a year when the Maine Office of Energy Resources suggested mediation. FERC supported the idea, and mediator David O'Connor was invited to explore the idea with the parties. After several private discussions with the mediator, the parties met in early May 1979 and took a joint tour of the lake to explore what the problems might be. At this meeting, they also agreed to continue the process. The agreement that resolved the dispute was signed three months later.

The result: The settlement covered numerous areas of concern, including maintenance of lake levels, recreational opportunities, flood control, runoff management, dam maintenance, and management of the area around the dam. Perhaps the most critical feature was the specification of a 10-foot range within which the lake level would be allowed to fluctuate, with somewhat stricter levels mandated during the summer. This assured the town that it would not be flooded by excessive storage behind the dam nor left without a shoreline during droughts simply to keep the generators turning. The town therefore withdrew its opposition to the project, and FERC granted Maine Hydroelectric a license.

TERMAN MIDDLE SCHOOL

Site-specific
Objective: recommendation
Issue: land use

Duration: 11-12 months
Year concluded: 1981
State: California

Parties:
Government:
City of Palo Alto, Calif.
Palo Alto Housing
  Corporation
Private citizens/landowners:
Jewish Community Center
  of the South Peninsula
Terman Coalition
  (neighbors' group)

Mediator:
FORUM, On Community
  and the Environment

The dispute: The Palo Alto Unified School District closed the Terman Middle School after the 1977-78 school year and sought to dispose of the site. A joint Palo Alto Housing Corporation (PAHC)/Jewish Community Center (JCC) proposal called for mixed use of the site, including: construction by PAHC of subsidized and senior citizen housing, purchase and use of the school buildings by the JCC, and sale to the city of seven acres for athletic fields and playgrounds. When this plan was presented to the neighborhood in fall 1979, the Terman Coalition (which had declined an invitation to help plan the project) and most area residents opposed it. The residents, concerned that new housing would increase traffic, and feeling a need for more public recreational and library facilities, wanted the entire site to remain in public (i.e., city) ownership. The City of Palo Alto, wanting to ensure some public benefit from the site but unwilling to purchase the entire lot, supported the mixed-use idea but did not endorse the specific PAHC/JCC proposal.

The process: The Palo Alto City Council instructed its staff to work out a plan acceptable to all parties. The staff formed a working group including representatives of the city, JCC, PAHC, and the Terman Coalition, and facilitator Geoff Ball to assist the process.

Meetings began in May 1980 and were held weekly for over a year. The School District extended various deadlines for selling the property until agreement was reached in May 1981.

The result: All the desired uses were to some extent supported in the revised site plan. The city agreed to acquire, by purchase or lease, the entire school site. Most of the school buildings would then be leased to the JCC, with special provisions for use of the pool and gym by neighborhood residents. Two buildings, however, would be operated as a city library and community center. Most of the open space on the site (over 10 acres) would be city recreational facilities. The rest would be leased to PAHC for family and elderly housing at somewhat lower density than originally proposed. Other parts of the agreement specified buffer zones, traffic control, bike and pedestrian access, lighting restrictions, etc.

TEXAS HAZARDOUS WASTE SITING DIALOGUE

Policy
Objective: recommendations
Issues: toxics, land use

Duration: 12-13 months
Year concluded: 1983
State: Texas

Parties:
Government:
City of Galveston, Tex.
City of Taylor Lake Village,
    Tex.
Gulf Coast Waste Disposal
    Authority
Texas Air Control Board
Texas Department of Health
Texas Department of Water
    Resources
Environmental groups:
Gulf Coast Conservation
    Association
Houston Toxic Substances
    Task Force
Sierra Club
Texas Environmental
    Coalition
Private citizens/others:
Bay Area League of
    Women Voters
Oil, Chemical and Atomic
    Workers Union
several individuals and
    technical resource people
Private companies:
Gulf Oil Chemicals
    Company
Shell Oil Company

Mediator:
The Keystone Center

The dispute: The Gulf Coast Waste Disposal Authority (GCA) found itself confronted with a dilemma common to many agencies: it possessed the legal authority to site waste facilities but faced the likelihood of protracted court disputes brought by community and citizens groups when site selection took place. What GCA sought was a consensus decision-making process through which concerned citizens would have an opportunity for early and substantive input in the siting process.

The process: Early in 1982, GCA approached The Keystone Center to convene key decision makers from industry, public interest groups, and public agencies. The group met twice for multi-day sessions at The Keystone Center in the Colorado Rockies and consulted with each other between meetings. After the conclusion of its second meeting, the group appointed an eight-member executive committee to coordinate implementation of the recommendations. The committee worked with the League of Women Voters of Texas to plan regional training workshops at which their recommendations were introduced within the context of an effort to educate the public on hazardous waste disposal issues.

The result: The group developed two documents for use by municipalities, citizens, legislators, and regulatory agencies.

One of these has been published as *Siting Waste Management Facilities in the Galveston Bay Area: A New Approach*. The other, *The Keystone Siting Handbook*, was published by the Texas Department of Water Resources and the Texas Department of Health. The recommendations for how to establish effective consultation between a facility proponent and the potential host committee, now known as the Keystone process, have been written into recent revisions of the Texas waste siting law.

VIRGINIA TOXICS ROUNDTABLE (ad hoc committee)

Policy
Objective: recommendations
Issues: toxics, land use

Duration: over 2 years
Year concluded: 1983*
State: Virginia

Parties:
Government:
Virginia Municipal League
Virginia Association of
  Counties
Private companies:
E.I. du Pont de Nemours &
  Company
Virginia Chamber of
  Commerce
other business leaders
Environmental groups:
Environmental Defense
  Fund
other individuals
Private citizens/others:
League of Women Voters
Virginia Bar Association

Mediator:
Institute for Environmental
  Negotiation

The dispute: As in other states, leaders in Virginia recognized the need to anticipate conflicts over the siting of new hazardous waste treatment facilities.

The process: In 1981, the Virginia Toxics Roundtable, a group of business and environmental leaders who confer informally on toxics issues under the auspices of the Institute for Environmental Negotiation at the University of Virginia, formed a special committee to address hazardous waste siting issues. The committee reached agreement in 1982 on a draft bill for consideration by the Virginia General Assembly.

---

*Ad hoc committee only. The Roundtable continues to meet.

The result: The provisions of the bill include a state siting board whose decisions would override local zoning and a citizen participation and review process with options for negotiation. The bill was considered by the assembly along with a second bill prepared by the Virginia Solid Waste Commission. The assembly directed the commission to submit a new bill in the next legislative session, the members of the ad hoc committee were actively involved in the commission's deliberations, and a revised bill was adopted by the assembly in February 1984 and signed by the governor the following month.

WARRENTON TOWNHOUSE DEVELOPMENT

Site-specific
Objective: recommendation
Issue: land use

Duration: 8-9 months
Year concluded: 1983
State: Virginia

Parties:
Private citizens/landowners:
Representatives of neighbor-
  hood residents (with
  support of Warrenton
  Improvement League)
Private company:
Construction Management
  Systems, Inc.

Mediator:
Institute for Environmental
  Negotiation

The dispute: Construction Management Systems, Inc., sought to develop a cluster of townhouses on a vacant six-acre site bordering a residential neighborhood of Warrenton. Attempting to design a more sensitive project, the developer applied for a special permit. Area residents, concerned about the effects the development would have on their neighborhood, lobbied the town council against it. When the town council denied the permit, the company threatened to ram a conventional—and, to the neighbors, even less desirable—development plan through, certain it could win its case.

The process: An uninvolved party suggested privately to both the developer and the neighborhood that mediation be tried, at which point A. Bruce Dotson from the Institute for Environmental Negotiation at the University of Virginia was contacted. Private meetings, including selection of three neighborhood negotiators, were held in October 1982; the first joint meeting was held in November. An agreement was reached on March 4, 1983, and a permit incorporating terms of the agreement was granted by the town council three months later.

The result: During the course of negotiations, it became apparent that the original "compromise" proposed by the developer went precisely in the wrong direction from the neighbors' perspective. The developer, trying to reduce the impacts of the project, turned the focus of the development inward and separated the buildings from the street with landscaping. The neighbors, however, wanted the project to be as similar to existing structures as possible. The newly agreed-upon plans incorporated these concerns, for example, by placing homes about the same distance from the street as existing residences, including deciduous trees similar to those already lining neighborhood streets, lowering the density along the street (but making up for it in interior parts of the development), and specifying the architectural style of the homes.

WASHINGTON MOUNTAIN BROOK

Site-specific
Objective: decision
Issue: water resources

Duration: 4-5 months
Year concluded: 1982
State: Massachusetts

Parties:
Government:
Town of Lee, Mass.
Town of Lenox, Mass.
Massachusetts Department
  of Environmental
  Management
Massachusetts Water
  Resources Commission
U.S. Soil Conservation
  Service
U.S. Department of
  Agriculture
Private citizens/landowners:
League of Women's Voters
  of Central Berkshire
Environmental group:
Conservation Law
  Foundation of New
  England

Mediator:
The Mediation Institute

The dispute: The Conservation Law Foundation of New England (CLF) filed suit in February 1982 to stop construction of the Washington Mountain Brook dam project in western Massachusetts. Originally planned by the U.S. Soil Conservation Service as a flood control project, the project's emphasis had shifted over time to providing a protected surface water supply system for local municipalities. This shift was prompted by local community concerns about possible contamination of their groundwater supplies by pollution occurring along the Housatonic River. CLF was concerned about the precedent set by the destruction of part of a state forest in order to build the project.

The process: In June 1982, attorneys representing the federal, state, and local defendants and CLF began to meet, assisted by Orville Tice of The Mediation Institute. The meetings provided an opportunity for the exchange of technical information, and in August 1982, based on agreements reached, the parties jointly signed a motion for dismissal of CLF's action.

The result: The Department of Environmental Management agreed that any future municipal water supply projects that inundated state natural areas would be compensated for by land to be used for park or forest purposes, equal or greater in value than the land to be used for water supply.

WHITE OAK RIVER

Site-specific
Objective: improved
    communication
Issue: resource management

Duration: 2-3 months
Year concluded: 1980
State: North Carolina

Parties:
Government:
elected officials from the
    counties and towns
    bordering the estuary
U.S. Army Corps of
    Engineers
Private citizens:
fishermen
Environmental group:
Izaak Walton League

Mediator:
Public Mediation Services

The dispute: The U.S. Army Corps of Engineers had proposed a dredging project in response to a siltation problem in an inlet at the mouth of the White Oak River on the North Carolina coast. The Izaak Walton League opposed the dredging, arguing that deepening the channel would cause scouring of the bottom of the inlet and would change currents in the mouth of the river in such a way that the estuary would silt up more rapidly. Others disagreed, and conversations between competing experts were getting nowhere. In addition, the purpose of the dredging project was to open a channel for fishing boats, but, because local fishermen used boats made for shallow waters, they worried that a deeper channel would encourage competing fishermen from other harbors to come to their harbor.

The process: The Izaak Walton League approached John Clark of The Conservation Foundation, who suggested that mediation be tried. Clark and mediator Roger Richman visited the area and met with the parties. Richman continued separate meetings with the parties over the course of a week, getting an agreement on how to approach the mediation process. A first joint meeting was intended simply to create a forum to talk about the problem and to exchange information, but the parties also were able to reach an agreement to form a White Oak River Advisory Council and to undertake joint studies that would be credible to all concerned.

The result: The advisory council was formed, and funding for the joint study was subsequently obtained from the North Carolina Coastal Zone Management office.

Bibliography

Abel, Richard L. *The Politics of Informal Justice*. New York: Academic Press, 1982.

Alexander, Tom, ed. "A Promising Try at Environmental Detente for Coal." *Fortune* 97, no. 3 (1978):94-102.

American Bar Association. Action Commission to Reduce Court Costs and Delay. *Attacking Litigation Costs and Delay*. Washington, D.C.: American Bar Association, 1984.

Amy, Douglas. "The Politics of Environmental Mediation." *Ecology Law Quarterly* 2, no. 1 (1983):1-20.

Arnold, Ron. "Loggers vs. Environmentalists: Friends? or Foes?" *Logging Management*, February 1978, pp. 16-19.

Auerbach, Jerold. *Justice without Law?* New York: Oxford University Press, 1983.

Bacow, Lawrence S. *Bargaining for Safety*. Cambridge, Mass.: MIT Press, 1980.

Bacow, Lawrence S., and James Milkey. "Overcoming Opposition to Hazardous Waste Facilities: The Massachusetts Approach." *Harvard Law Review* 6, no 2 (1982).

Bacow, Lawrence S., Michael O'Hare, and Debra Sanderson. *Facility Siting and Public Opposition*. New York: Van Nostrand Reinhold, 1983.

Bacow, Lawrence S., and Michael Wheeler. *Environmental Dispute Resolution*. New York: Plenum Publishers, 1984.

Baldwin, Pamela. "Environmental Mediation: An Effective Alternative?" A report of a conference held in Reston, Virginia, January 11-13, 1978. Palo Alto, Calif.: RESOLVE, Center for Environmental Conflict Resolution, 1978. Available from The Conservation Foundation.

Ball, Geoffrey, Margorie Sutton, and Linda Brubaker. "Early Community Consultation in the EIR Process: New Opportunities for Environmental Professionals." *Environmental Professional* 2, no. 1 (1980):42-52.

Barich, Bill. "Playing Environmental Let's Make A Deal." *Outside*, February 1978.

Bartos, Otomar. *Process and Outcome of Negotiations*. New York: Columbia University Press, 1974.

Baur, E. Jackson. "Mediating Environmental Disputes." *Western Sociology Review* 8 (1977):16-24.

Bazerman, Max H. "Negotiator Judgment: A Critical Look at the Rationality Assumption." *American Behavioral Scientist* 27, no. 2 (1983):211-228.

Bellman, Howard S. "Siting for a Sanitary Landfill for Eau Claire, Wisconsin." *Environmental Professional* 2, no. 1 (1980):56-57.

Bellman, Howard S., Cynthia Sampson, and Gerald W. Cormick. *Using Mediation When Siting Hazardous Waste Management Facilities: A Handbook (SW 944)*. Prepared for the U.S. Environmental Protection Agency, Office of Solid Waste. Washington, D.C.: U.S. Government Printing Office, 1982.

Bellman, Howard S., et al. "Environmental Dispute Resolution: Practitioner's Perspective of an Emerging Field." *Environmental Consensus*, Winter 1981.

Bercovitch, Jacob. *Social Conflicts and Third Parties: Strategies of Conflict Resolution*. Boulder, Colo.: Westview Press, 1984.

Bernard, Jessie. "Parties and Issues in Conflict." *Journal of Conflict Resolution* 1, no. 2 (1957):111-121.

Bidol, Pat. "Designing Environmental Conflict Management Approaches for State Natural Resource Agencies." Ann Arbor, Mich.: University of Michigan, School of National Resources, 1982.

Bingham, Gail. "Does Negotiation Hold Promise for Regulatory Reform?" *Resolve*, Fall 1981.

Bingham, Gail, and Daniel S. Miller. "Prospects for Resolving Hazardous Waste Siting Disputes through Negotiation." *Natural Resources Lawyer*, 17, no. 3 (1984):473-90.

Bingham, Gail, Barbara Vaughn, and Wendy Gleason. *Environmental Conflict Resolution: Annotated Bibliography*. Palo Alto, Calif.: RESOLVE, Center for Environmental Dispute Resolution, 1981. Available from The Conservation Foundation.

Bleiker, Annemarie, and Hans Bleiker. *Citizen Participation Handbook for Public Officials and Other Professionals Serving the Public*. 3rd ed. Laramie, Wyo.: Institute for Participatory Planning, 1978.

Bosselman, Fred P. "Buying Off the Neighbors: Negotiated Private Settlements of Development Disputes in Japan." *Environmental Comment*, May 1977, pp. 12-13.

Boulding, Kenneth E. *Conflict and Defense*. New York: Harper, 1962.
———. "Conflict Management as a Learning Process." In deReuck and Knight, eds. *Conflict in Society*. Boston: Little Brown, 1966.
———. "Organization and Conflict." *Journal of Conflict Resolution* 1, no. 2 (1957):122-34.
Brock, Jonathan. *Bargaining Beyond Impasse: Joint Resolution of Public Sector Labor Disputes*, Boston, Mass.: Auburn House, 1982.
Brock, Jonathan. "Developing Systems for the Settlement of Recurring Disputes: Four Case Studies, Analysis, and Recommendations." Washington, D.C.: National Institute for Dispute Resolution, 1984.
Busterud, John. "Mediation: The State of the Art." *Environmental Professional* 2, no. 1 (1980):34-39.
Busterud, John, and Gail Bingham. "Environmental Conflict Resolution Update." *Environmental Professional* 2, no. 1 (1980):131-132.
Caldwell, Lynton K., Lynton R. Hayes, and Isabel M. MacWhirter. *Citizens and the Environment: Case Studies in Popular Action*. Bloomington: Indiana University Press, 1976.
Carnevale, Peter J.D. "Strategic Choice in Mediation." *Negotiation Journal* 2, no. 1 (1986):41-56.
Carpenter, Susan L. and W.J.D. Kennedy. "Conflict Anticipation: A Site-Specific Approach for Managing Environmental Conflicts." Paper presented to the Society of Mining Engineers of the American Institute of Mining Engineers, Tucson, Arizona, October 17-19, 1979.
———. "Consensus Building: A Tool for Managing Energy-Environment Conflicts." Paper prepared for conference on the Management of Energy-Environment Conflicts, Wye Plantation, Maryland, May 20-23, 1980.
———. "Developing a Conflict Management Strategy." Paper presented at the Wisconsin Coal Policy Conference, Madison, Wisconsin, May 21, 1980.
———. "Environmental Conflict Management." *Environmental Professional* 2, no. 1 (1980):67-74.
———. "Environmental Conflict Management in Western Communities." Paper presented at the Community Dispute Resolution Conference, Cherry Hill, New Jersey, June 18-19, 1979.

————. "Information Sharing and Conciliation: Tools for Environmental Conflict Management." *Environmental Comment*, May 1977, pp. 21-23.

————. "Managing Environmental Conflict by Applying Common Sense." *Negotiation Journal* 1, no. 2 (1985):149-62.

————. "ROMCOE Case Studies." 1979. Available from AC-CORD Associates, 1898 South Flatiron Court, Boulder, Colorado 80301.

Christian, Thomas F. "Should Dispute Resolution Be Attached to the Courts?" *Dispute Resolution Forum*, June 1984.

Cifrino, Deborah. "Tearing Down the Wall through Environmental Mediation." *Conservation News* 43, no. 19 (1978):8-11.

Clark, Peter B. "Consensus Building: Mediating Energy, Environmental and Economic Conflict." *Environmental Comment*, May 1977, pp. 9-12.

Clark, Peter B., and Wendy M. Emrich. "New Tools for Resolving Environmental Disputes." Paper prepared by the American Arbitration Association for the Council on Environmental Quality and the Resource and Land Investigations Program, U.S. Department of the Interior. 1980.

Clark-McGlennon Associates, Inc. *Final Report on Phase One of Developing Methods for Environmental-Energy Dispute Settlement*. Washington, D.C.: American Arbitration Association, 1978.

Coleman, James S. *Community Conflict*. Glencoe, Ill.: Free Press, 1957.

Colosi, Thomas R. "Negotiation in the Public and Private Sectors: A Core Model." *American Behavioral Scientist* 27, no. 2 (1983):229-54.

Colosi, Thomas R., and Arthur Eliot Berkeley. *Collective Bargaining: How It Works and Why*. New York: American Arbitration Association, 1986.

Cormick, Gerald W. "Comparing Processes for the Resolution of Environmental Conflict: Intervention, Issues and Timing." Paper presented to the Society of Mining Engineers of the American Institute of Mining Engineers, Tucson, Arizona, October 17-19, 1979.

————. "Environmental Mediation in the U.S.: Experience and Future Directions." Paper presented to the annual meeting of the American Association for the Advancement of Science, Toronto, Ontario, 1981.

――――. "The Ethics of Mediation: Some Unexplored Terri-
tory." Paper presented to the Society of Professionals in Dispute
Resolution, New York, New York, October 24, 1977.

――――. "How and When Should You Mediate Natural Resource
Disputes?" Paper presented to Alternatives to Litigation seminar,
Washington State Bar Association, Seattle, Washington, July 26,
1985.

――――. "Intervention and Self-Determination in Environmental Disputes: A Mediator's Perspective." *Resolve*, Winter 1982.

――――. "Mediating Environmental Controversies: Perspectives
and First Experience." *Earth Law Journal* 2 (1976):215-24.

――――. "Resolving Conflicts on the Uses of Range through
Mediated Negotiations: Answers to the Ten Most Asked Questions." Paper presented to the National Range Conference, Oklahoma City, Oklahoma, November 7, 1985.

――――. "Siting New Hazardous Waste Management Facilities
Using Mediated Negotiations." Paper presented to a conference
on Meeting the New RCRA Requirements on Hazardous Waste,
sponsored by Inside EPA and the Center for Energy and Environmental Management, Alexandria, Virginia, October 8, 1985.

――――. "The 'Theory' and Practice of Environmental Mediation." *Environmental Professional* 2, no. 1 (1980):24-33.

Cormick, Gerald W., and Jane McCarthy. "Environmental Mediation: Flood Control, Recreation and Development in the Snoqualmie River Valley." St. Louis: Washington University, Social
Science Institute, 1974.

Cormick, Gerald W., and Leah K. Patton. "Environmental Mediation: Defining the Process through Experience." Paper prepared
for the American Association for the Advancement of Science Symposium on Environmental Mediation Cases, Denver, Colorado,
1977.

――――. "Environmental Mediation: Potentials and Limitations." *Environmental Comment*, May 1977, pp. 13-16.

Coser, Lewis A. *The Functions of Social Conflict*. New York: Free
Press, 1956.

――――. "The Termination of Conflict." In Etzioni, Amitai,
and Eva Etzioni, eds. *Social Change: Sources, Patterns, and Consequences*. New York: Basic Books, 1964.

Craig, Robert. "The Keystone Process in Radioactive Waste Management." *Environmental Consensus*, Winter 1980.

Creighton, James L. *Public Involvement Manual: Involving the Public in Water and Power Resource Discussions.* Washington, D.C.: U.S. Government Printing Office, 1980.

—————. "A Tutorial: Acting As a Conflict Conciliator." *Environmental Professional* 2, no. 1 (1980):119-27.

Crohn, Madeleine. "Signs of Cohesion in Dispute Resolution." *Negotiation Journal* 1, no. 1 (1985):23-28.

Crowfoot, James E. "Negotiations: An Effective Tool for Citizen Organizations?" In "Negotiations for Public Interest Groups." *NRAG Papers* 3, no. 4 (1980):24-44. Available from the Northern Rockies Action Group, 9 Placer Street, Helena, Montana 59601.

Dahrendorf, Ralf. "Toward a Theory of Social Conflict." *Journal of Conflict Resolution* 2, no. 2 (1958):170-83.

Danzig, Richard, and M. J. Lowry. "Everyday Disputes and Mediation in the United States: A Reply to Professor Festiner." *Law and Society Review* 9 (1975):675.

Deutsch, Morton. *The Resolution of Conflict: Constructive and Destructive Processes.* New Haven: Yale University Press, 1973.

Dotson, A. Bruce. "Who and How? Participation in Environmental Negotiation." *Environmental Impact Assessment Review 4,* no. 2 (1983):203-17.

Doyle, Michael, and David Straus. *How to Make Meetings Work.* New York: Playboy Press, 1976.

Dunlop, John T. *Dispute Resolution: Negotiation and Consensus Building.* Dover, Mass.: Auburn House, 1984.

Ehrmann, John R., and Patricia A. Bidol. *A Bibliography on Natural Resources and Environmental Conflict. Management Strategies and Processes.* Chicago, Ill.: Council of Planning Librarians, 1982.

Emrich, Wendy. "New Approaches to Managing Environmental Conflict: How Can the Federal Government Use Them?" Paper prepared for the Council on Environmental Quality, 1980.

Fagence, Michael. *Citizen Participation in Planning.* Elmsford, N.Y.: Pergamon Press, 1977.

Fanning, Odom. "Environmental Mediation: The World's Newest Profession." *Environment* 21, no. 7 (1979):33-38.

Felstiner, William L.F. "Influences of Social Organization on Dispute Processing." *Law and Society Review* 9 (1974):63.

Felstiner, William L.F., Richard L. Abel, and Austin Sarat. "The Emergence and Transformation of Disputes: Naming, Blaming, Claiming." *Law and Society Review* 15 (1980-81):631.

Fieveson, H.A., et al, eds. *Boundaries of Analysis: An Inquiry into the Tocks Island Dam Controversy*. Cambridge, Mass.: Ballinger, 1976.

Fisher, Gary K. "The Colorado Joint Review Process: A Better Way." Paper prepared for National Bureau of Standards, Conference on Environmental Permitting, May 5-6, 1980.

Fisher, Roger. "Beyond *YES*." *Negotiation Journal* 1, no. 1 (1985):67-70.

—————. "A Code of Negotiation: Practices for Lawyers." *Negotiation Journal* 1, no. 2 (1985):105-10.

—————. *International Conflict For Beginners*. New York: Harper and Row, 1969.

—————. *International Mediation: A Practitioner's Guide*. New York: International Peace Academy, 1978.

—————. "Negotiating Power: Getting and Using Influence" *American Behavioral Scientist* 27, no 2 (1983):149-66.

Fisher, Roger, and William Ury. *Getting to Yes: Negotiating Agreement Without Giving In*. New York: Houghton Mifflin, 1981.

Fiss, Owen. "Against Settlement." *Yale Law Journal* 93 (1984):1973.

Folberg, Jay, and Alison Taylor. *Mediation: A Comprehensive Guide to Resolving Conflicts Without Litigation*. San Francisco: Jossey-Bass, 1984.

Folk-Williams, John A. "Negotiation Becomes More Important in Settling Indian Water Rights Disputes in the West." *Resolve*, Summer 1982.

—————. *What Indian Water Means to the West: A Sourcebook*. Vol. 1 of *Water In the West*. Santa Fe, N.M.: Western Network, 1982.

Folk-Williams, John A., and James S. Cannon. *Water for an Energy Market*. Vol. 2 of *Water in the West*. Santa Fe, N.M.: Western Network, 1983.

Folk-Williams, John A., Susan C. Fry, and Lucy Hilgendorf. *Western Water Flows to the Cities*. Vol. 3 of *Water in the West*. Santa Fe, N.M.: Western Network, 1985.

The Ford Foundation. *New Approaches to Conflict Resolution*. New York: Ford Foundation, 1978.

Fradin, David M. *The Moorhead Plant Dispute: Report of Minnesota's First Environmental Mediation*. St. Paul, Minn.: Environmental Balance Association of Minnesota, 1976.

Galanter, Marc. "Reading the Landscape of Disputes: What We Know and Don't Know (and Think We Know) about Our Allegedly Contentious and Litigious Society." *U.C.L.A. Law Review* 31 (1983):4.

—————. "Why the 'Haves' Come Out Ahead: Speculations on the Limits of Legal Change." *Law and Society Review* 9 (1974):95.

Gladwin, Thomas N. "The Management of Environmental Conflict: A Survey of Research Approaches and Priorities." Paper prepared for a conference on Environmental Mediation: An Effective Alternative?, Reston, Virginia, January 11-13, 1978.

—————. "Trends in Industrial Environmental Conflict." *Environmental Consensus*, September 1979.

Godschalk, D.R. *Participation, Planning and Exchange in Old and New Communities: A Collaborative Paradigm*. Chapel Hill, N.C.: Center for Urban and Regional Studies, 1972.

Goldbeck, Willis. "Mediation: An Instrument of Citizen Involvement." *Arbitration Journal* 30, no. 4 (1975):241-52.

Goldberg, Stephen B., Eric D. Green, and Frank E.A. Sander. *Dispute Resolution*. Boston: Little, Brown, 1985.

—————. "The Life of the Mediator: To Be or Not to Be Accountable." *Negotiation Journal* 1, no. 3 (1985):263-68.

Goldmann, Robert, ed. *Roundtable Justice*. Boulder, Colo.: Westview Press, 1980.

Golten, Bob. "Confessions of an Environmental Litigator." *Environmental Consensus*, Spring 1980.

—————. "Mediation: A 'Sellout' for Conservation Advocates, or a Bargain?" *Environmental Professional* 2, no. 1 (1980):62-66.

Green, Eric D. "A Comprehensive Approach to the Theory and Practice of Dispute Resolution." *Journal of Legal Education* 34 (1984):245.

—————. "Growth of the Mini-Trial." *Litigation* 9 (Fall 1982):12.

Green, Eric D., Jonathan M. Marks, and Ronald Olson. "Settling Large Case Litigation: An Alternative Approach." *Loyola of Los Angeles Law Review* 11 (1978):493.

Green, Eric D., Jonathan M. Marks, and Frank E.A. Sander, eds. *Disputing in America: The Changing Role of Lawyers*. New York: Harcourt Brace Jovanovich, 1985.

Greenberg, Michael R., and Donald B. Straus. "Up-front Resolution of Environmental and Economic Disputes." *Environmental Comment*, May 1977, pp. 16-18.

Gulliver, Philip. *Disputes and Negotiations: A Cross Cultural Perspective*. New York: Academic Press, 1981.

Gusman, Sam. "Policy Dialogue." *Environmental Comment*, November 1981, pp. 14-16.

————. "Policy Dialogue and Negotiation." *Environmental Professional* 4 (1982).

Gusman, Sam, and Verne Huser. "Mediation in the Estuary." *Coastal Zone Management Journal* 11, no. 4 (1984):273-95.

Harlow, Robert. "Conflict Reduction in Environmental Policy." *Journal of Conflict Resolution* 18, no. 3 (1974):536-52.

Harter, Philip J. "Negotiating Regulations: A Chance for Actual Participation." *Environmental Forum* 1, no. 6 (1982):8-11.

————. "Negotiating Regulations: A Cure for Malaise." *Georgetown Law Journal* 71, no. 1 (1982):1-118.

————. "The Political Legitimacy and Judicial Review of Consensual Rules." 1983. Accepted for publication by *American University Law Review*.

————. "Regulatory Negotiation: The Experience So Far." *Resolve*, Winter 1984, pp. 1ff.

Haynes, John M. "Matching Readiness and Willingness to the Mediator's Strategies." *Negotiation Journal* 1, no. 1 (1985):79-92.

Healy, Robert G. *Environmentalists and Developers: Can They Agree on Anything?* Washington, D.C.: The Conservation Foundation, 1977.

Henry, James F. "Mini-Trials: An Alternative to Litigation." *Negotiation Journal* 1, no. 1 (1985):13-18.

Hofrichter, Richard. "Justice Centers Raise Basic Questions." In Tomasic, R., and M. Feeley, eds. *Neighborhood Justice: Assessment of an Emerging Idea*. New York: Longman, 1982.

Huser, Verne. "Environmental Mediation: Resolution of a Site-Specific Dispute with Area-Wide Policy Implications." Paper presented to the Society of Mining Engineers of the American Institute of Mining Engineers, Tucson, Arizona, October 17-19, 1979.

Kinsey, David N. "The Coastal Development Review Process in New Jersey: Avoiding Disputes and Resolving Conflicts." *Environmental Comment*, May 1977, pp. 19-20.

Kriesberg, Louis. *The Sociology of Social Conflict*. Englewood Cliffs, N.J.: Prentice-Hall, 1973.

Kuechle, David. "Negotiation with an Angry Public: Advice to Corporate Leaders." *Negotiation Journal* 1, no. 4 (1985):317-330.

Lake, Laura M. *Environmental Mediation: The Search for Consensus*. Boulder, Colo.: Westview Press, 1980.

—————. "Mediating Electric Power Plant Options for California: A Case Study in Conflict Avoidance." Paper prepared for the Symposium on Environmental Mediation Case Studies, annual meeting of the American Association for the Advancement of Science, Denver, Colorado, 1977.

—————. "Mediating Environmental Disputes." *Ekistics* 4, no. 262 (1977):164-70.

—————. "Unifying the Concept of Third-Party Intervention in Environmental Disputes." *Environmental Comment*, May 1977, pp. 6-9.

Lambros, Thomas D. "The Summary Jury Trial and Other Alternative Methods of Dispute Resolution: A Report to the Judicial Conference of the United States on the Operation of the Jury System." *Federal Rules Decisions* 103 (1984):461.

Lambros, Thomas D., Eric D. Green, and Francis McGovern. "Addressing the Problem—One Court's Strategy." *State Court Journal* 8 (Winter 1984):19.

Laue, James, and Gerald Cormick. "The Ethics of Intervention in Community Disputes." In Gordon Bermant, Herbert Kelman, and Donald Warwick, eds. *The Ethics of Social Intervention*. Washington, D.C.: Hemisphere Publishing, 1974.

Lax, David A., and James K. Sebenius. "Interests: The Measure of Negotiation." *Negotiation Journal* 2, no. 1 (1986):73-92.

—————. "The Manager as Negotiator." Unpublished manuscript. 1985.

—————. "The Power of Alternatives or the Limits to Negotiation." *Negotiation Journal* 1, no. 2 (1985):163-80.

Lee, Kai N. "Defining Success in Environmental Dispute Resolution." *Resolve,* Spring 1982.

Lesnick, Michael, and James Crowfoot. *Bibliography for the Study of Natural Resource and Environmental Conflict*. Chicago, Ill.: Council of Planning Librarians, 1981.

Lewicki, Roy J. "Challenges of Teaching Negotiation." *Negotiation Journal* 2, no. 1 (1986):15-28.

Lewicki, Roy J., and Joseph A. Litterer. *Negotiation*. Homewood, Ill.: Richard D. Irwin, 1985.

Lieberman, Jethro. *The Litigious Society*. New York: Basic Books, 1981.

Lord, William B. "Water Resources Planning: Conflict Management." *Water Spectrum*, Summer 1980, pp. 1-10.

Lord, William B., et al. *Conflict Management in Federal Water Resources Planning*. Boulder, Colo.: University of Colorado, Institute of Behavioral Science, 1978.

Mack, Raymond W., and Richard C. Snyder. "The Analysis of Social Conflict: Toward an Overview and Synthesis." *Journal of Conflict Resolution* 1, no. 2 (1957):212-48.

Marcus, Philip A., and Wendy M. Emrich, eds. *Working Papers in Environmental Conflict Management*. New York: American Arbitration Association, 1981.

Marks, Jonathan B., Earl Johnson, Jr., and Peter L. Szanton. *Dispute Resolution in America: Processes in Evolution*. Washington, D.C.: National Institute for Dispute Resolution, 1984.

McCarthy, Jane E. "Learning from the Labor-Management Model." *Environmental Consensus*, Summer 1980.

—————. "Resolving Environmental Conflicts." *Environmental Science and Technology* 10, no. 1 (1976):40-43.

McCarthy, Jane E., and Alice Shorett. "Mediation to Resolve Environmental Conflict: The Snohomish Experiment." *Journal of Soil and Water Conservation* 31, no. 5 (1976):212-13.

—————. *Negotiating Settlements: A Guide to Environmental Mediation*. New York: American Arbitration Association, 1984.

McCarthy, William. "The Role of Power and Principle in *Getting to Yes*." *Negotiation Journal* 1, no. 1 (1985):59-66.

McCloskey, Michael. "Environmental Conflicts: Why Aren't More Negotiated?" Paper prepared for Aspen Institute meeting, Aspen, Colorado, July 18, 1977. Available from the Sierra Club, 530 Bush Street, San Francisco, California 94108.

McGillis, Daniel. "Minor Dispute Processing: A Review of Recent Developments." In Tomasic, R., and M. Feeley, eds. *Neighborhood Justice: Assessment of an Emerging Idea*. New York: Longman, 1982.

—————. "Who Should Pay." *Dispute Resolution Forum*, March 1984.

McNeil, E.B., ed. *The Nature of Human Conflict*. Englewood Cliffs, N.J.: Prentice-Hall, 1965.

Mellinkoff, Debra. "Mediation Settles Rhode Island Land Dispute." *Environmental Consensus*, Spring 1980.

Menkel-Meadow, Carrie. "Legal Negotiation: A Study of Strategies in Search of a Theory." *American Bar Foundation Research Journal* (1983):905.

—————. "Toward Another View of Legal Negotiation: The Structure of Problem-Solving." *U.C.L.A. Law Review* 31 (1984):754.

Mernitz, Scott. *Mediation of Environmental Disputes: A Sourcebook*. New York: Praeger, 1980.

Merry, Sally E., and Susan B. Silbey. "What Do Plaintiffs Want? Reexamining the Concept of Dispute." *Justice System Journal* 9 (1984):151.

Michael, Donald N. "Speculations on Future Planning Process Theory." In David R. Godschalk, ed. *Planning in America: Learning from Turbulence*. Washington, D.C.: American Institute of Planners, 1974.

Miller, William H. "Movement toward Environmental Peace." *Industry Week* 196, no. 4 (1978):20-22.

Moore, Carl, and Chris Carlson. *Public Decision Marking: Using the Negotiated Investment Strategy*. Dayton, Ohio: Kettering Foundation, 1984.

Murray, Francis X., ed. *Where We Agree: Summary and Synthesis*. Report of the National Coal Policy Project. Boulder, Colo.: Westview Press, 1978.

Nice, J. "Stalemates Spawn New Breed: The Eco-Mediators." *High Country News* 11, no. 6 (1979):6.

Nicolau, George. "Training in Community Conflict Resolution Skills." New York: Institute for Mediation and Conflict Resolution, 1973.

Nicolau, George, and Gerald Cormick. "Community Disputes and the Resolution of Conflict: Another View." *Arbitration Journal* 27, no. 2 (1972):98-112.

Nierenberg, Gerald I. *The Art of Negotiating*. New York: Cornerstone Library, 1968.

O'Connor, David. "Environmental Mediation: The State-of-the-Art." *EIA Review* 2 (1978):9-17.

——————. "The Use of Mediation to Resolve the Dispute Over Low-Head Hydroelectric Development of Swan Lake." Report of the mediator to the Maine Office of Energy Resources, 1980.

O'Gara, G. "Should This Marriage Be Saved?" *Environmental Action* 9, no. 21 (1978):10-13.

O'Hare, Michael. "Not on My Block You Don't: Facility Siting and the Strategic Importance of Compensation." *Public Policy* 25, no. 4 (1977):407-58.

Patton, Leah K., and Gerald W. Cormick. "Mediation and the N.E.P.A. Process: The Interstate 90 Experience." Paper prepared for a conference on Environmental Impact Analysis, University of Illinois, May 22-25, 1977.

Pruitt, Dean G. *Negotiation Behavior*. New York: Academic Press, 1981.

——————. "Strategic Choices in Negotiation." *American Behavioral Scientist* 27, no. 2 (1983):167-94.

Raiffa, Howard. *The Art and Science of Negotiation*. Cambridge, Mass.: The Belknap Press of Harvard University Press, 1982.

——————. "Creative Compensation: *Maybe* 'In My Backyard.' " *Negotiation Journal* 1, no. 3 (1985):197-204.

——————. "Mediation of Conflicts." *American Behavioral Scientist* 27, no. 2 (1983):195-210.

——————. "Post-Settlement Settlements." *Negotiation Journal* 1, no. 1 (1985):9-12.

Reilly, William K. "Who Should Pay?" *Dispute Resolution Forum*, March 1984.

Richman, Roger. "Structuring Interjurisdictional Negotiation: Virginia's Use of Mediation in Annexation Disputes." *Resolve*, Summer 1983.

Richman, Roger, Orion White, and M.H. Wilkinson. *Intergovernmental Mediation: Negotiations in Local Government Disputes*. Boulder, Colo.: Westview Press, forthcoming.

Riesel, Daniel. "Negotiation and Mediation of Environmental Disputes." *Ohio State Journal on Dispute Resolution* 1, no. 1 (1985):99-111.

Rifkin, Janet. "Mediation from a Feminist Perspective: Promise and Problems." *Law and Inequality* 2 (February 1984):21.

Rivkin, Malcolm D. "Negotiated Development: A Breakthrough in Environmental Controversies." *Environmental Comment*, May 1977, pp. 3-6.

——————. *Negotiated Development: A Breakthrough in Environmental Controversies (An Issue Report)*. Washington, D.C.: The Conservation Foundation, 1977.

Ross, Jerome. "Should the Mediator Raise Public Interest Considerations during Negotiations." *SPIDR: Ethical Issues in Dispute Resolution*. 1983 Annual Proceedings, p. 50.

Roth, Alvin E. "Some Additional Thoughts on Post-Settlement Settlements." *Negotiation Journal* 1, no. 3 (1985):245-48.

Rubin, Jeffrey Z. "Negotiation: An Introduction to Some Issues and Themes." *American Behavioral Scientist* 27, no. 2 (1983):135-48.

Rubin, Jeffrey Z., and Bert R. Brown. *The Social Psychology of Bargaining and Negotiation*. New York: Academic Press, 1975.

Sampson, Cynthia. "The Mediator's Role in Environmental Disputes." *Environmental Consensus*, July 1979.

——————. "The Roles of Environmental Professionals in Mediation." *Environmental Professional* 2, no. 1 (1980):53-55.

Sander, Frank E.A. "Varieties of Dispute Processing." *Federal Rules Decisions* 79 (1976):111-34.

Sander, Frank E.A., and Frederick E. Snyder. "Alternative Methods of Dispute Settlement—A Selected Bibliography." Prepared for the American Bar Association Special Committee on Resolution of Minor Disputes, Washington, D.C., 1979.

Saunders, Harold H. "We Need a Larger Theory of Negotiation: The Importance of Pre-negotiating Phases." *Negotiation Journal* 1, no. 3 (July 1985):249-62.

Schelling, Thomas C. *The Strategy of Conflict*. Cambridge, Mass.: Harvard University Press, 1960.

Sherman, Harris D. "Colorado's Joint Review Process: More Involvement, Better Decisions, and Less Delay." *Environmental Consensus*, Fall 1980.

Shonholtz, Raymond. "Neighborhood Justice Systems: Work, Structure, and Guiding Principles." *Mediation Quarterly* 5 (1984):3.

Shorett, Alice J. "Environmental Mediation at the Port of Everett." *Environmental Consensus*, December 1978.

——————. "The Role of the Mediator in Environmental Disputes." *Environmental Professional* 2, no. 1 (1980):58-61.

Simkin, William E. *Mediation and the Dynamics of Collective Bargaining*. Washington, D.C.: Bureau of National Affairs, 1971.

Singer, Linda R. "Nonjudicial Dispute Resolution Mechanisms: The Effects on Justice for the Poor." *Clearinghouse Review* 13 (1979):569.

Stein, Robert E. "Environmental Mediation of Transboundary Issues." Paper prepared for the annual American Pollution Control Association meeting, Montreal, Quebec, June 22-27, 1980.

Stockholm, Nan. "Environmental Mediation: An Alternative to the Courtroom." *Stanford Lawyer* 15,no. 1 (1980):21-25.

Straus, Donald B. "Managing Complexity: A New Look at Environmental Mediation." *Environmental Science and Technology* 13, no. 6 (1979):661-665.

————. "Mediating Environmental and Economic Tradeoffs, A Case Study of the Search for Improved Tools for Facilitating the Process." Paper prepared for the Symposium on Environmental Mediation Case Studies, annual meeting of the American Association for the Advancement of Science, Denver, Colorado, 1977.

————. "Mediating Environment, Energy and Economic Tradeoffs." *Arbitration Journal* 32, no. 2 (1977):96-110.

Straus, Donald B., and Peter B. Clark. "Bigger Problems Need Better Tools: Guidelines to Identify, Manage and Resolve Environmental Disputes." Prepared for the annual conference of the National Association of Environmental Professionals, Washington, D.C., April 21-23, 1980.

————. "Computer Assisted Negotiations: Bigger Problems Need Better Tools." *Environmental Professional* 2, no. 1 (1980): 75-87.

Straus, Donald B., and Michael R. Greenberg. "Data Mediation of Environmental Disputes: Converting Facts from Weapons into Tools." New York: American Arbitration Association, Research Institute, 1978.

Stulberg, Joseph B. "The Theory and Practice of Mediation: A Reply to Professor Susskind." *Vermont Law Review* 6, no. 1 (1981).

Sullivan, Timothy J. *Resolving Development Disputes through Negotiations.* New York: Plenum Press, 1984.

Susskind, Lawrence E. *Citizen Involvement in the Local Planning Process: A Handbook for Municipal Officials and Citizen Involvement Groups.* Cambridge, Mass.: Massachusetts Institute of Technology, Laboratory of Architecture and Planning, 1976.

—————. "Court-Appointed Masters as Mediators." *Negotiation Journal* 1, no. 4 (1985):295-300.

—————. "Environmental Mediation and the Accountability Problem." *Vermont Law Review* 6, no. 1 (1981).

—————. *The Importance of Citizen Participation and Consensus-Building in the Land Use Planning Process.* Cambridge, Mass.: Massachusetts Institute of Technology, Laboratory of Architecture and Planning, 1978.

—————. "Mediating Public Disputes." *Negotiation Journal* 1, no. 1 (1985).

—————. "Mediating Public Disputes: A Response to the Skeptics." *Negotiation Journal* 1, no. 2 (1985).

—————. "Resolving Environmental Disputes through Ad Hocracy." *Environmental Consensus*, Summer 1980.

—————. "Scorable Games." *Negotiation Journal* 1, no. 3 (1985):205-10.

Susskind, Lawrence, Lawrence Bacow, and Michael Wheeler. *Resolving Environmental Regulatory Disputes.* Cambridge, Mass.: Schenkman Publishing, 1983.

Susskind, Lawrence, and Jeffrey Cruikshank, "Dealing with Differences: Approaches to Resolving Important Public Issues." Unpublished manuscript. 1986.

Susskind, Lawrence, and Michael Elliott. *Paternalism, Protest and Co-Production: Learning from Citizen Action and Citizen Participation in Western Europe.* New York: Plenum Publishers, 1984.

Susskind, Lawrence, and Denise Madigan. "New Approaches to Resolving Disputes in the Public Sector." *The Justice System Journal* 9, no. 2 (1984).

Susskind, Lawrence, and Gerard McMahon. "The Theory and Practice of Negotiated Rulemaking." *Yale Journal on Regulation* 3 (1985):133-65.

Susskind, Lawrence, and M. O'Hare. *Managing the Social and Economic Impacts of Energy Development.* Summary Report, Phase 1 of the Massachusetts Institute of Technology Energy Impact Project. Cambridge, Mass.: Massachusetts Institute of Technology, 1977.

Susskind, Lawrence, and Connie Ozawa. "Mediated Negotiation in the Public Sector: Mediator Accountability and the Public Interest Problem." *American Behavioral Scientist* 27, no. 2 (1983).

—————. "Mediating Public Disputes: Obstacles and Possibilities." *Journal of Social Issues* 41 (1985):151ff.

Susskind, Lawrence, and Alan Weinstein. "Towards a Theory of Environmental Dispute Resolution." *Environmental Affairs* 9 (1980):311-57.

Susskind, Lawrence, et al. *Resolving Environmental Disputes: Approaches to Intervention, Negotiation, and Conflict Resolution.* Cambridge, Mass.: Massachusetts Institute of Technology, Laboratory of Architecture and Planning, 1978.

Talbot, Allan R. *Environmental Mediation, Three Case Studies: The Island, The Highway, The Ferry Terminal.* Seattle, Wash.: Institute for Environmental Mediation, 1981.

—————. *Settling Things: Six Case Studies in Environmental Mediation.* Washington, D.C.: The Conservation Foundation, 1983.

Thomas, Kenneth W. "Conflict and Conflict Management." In Dunnette, Marvin D., ed. *Handbook of Industrial and Organizational Psychology.* Chicago: Rand McNally, 1976.

Tribe, Lawrence H., Corrine S. Shelling, and John Voss, eds. *When Values Conflict: Essays on Environmental Analysis, Discourse and Decision.* Cambridge, Mass.: Ballinger, 1976.

United States. Department of Justice. *Paths of Justice: Major Public Policy Issues.* Washington, D.C.: National Institute for Dispute Resolution, 1984.

Vaughn, Barbara J. "Environmental Mediation: Fighting Fair." *Planning* 46, no. 8 (1980):16-18.

Wald, Patricia. "Negotiation of Environmental Disputes: A New Role for the Courts?" *Columbia Journal of Environmental Law* 10, no. 1 (1984):17-25.

Waters, Elizabeth. "Talking Things Over: The Subtle Art of Environmental Negotiation Can Solve Preservation Disputes." *Historic Preservation*, March/April 1982.

Watts, Sylvia. "The Connecticut Negotiated Investment Strategy Experiment: The Uses of Mediation in Inter-governmental Negotiations." Master's thesis, Massachusetts Institute of Technology, Department of Urban Studies and Planning. 1983.

Weingarten, Helen R., and Douvan, Elizabeth. "Male and Female Visions of Mediation." *Negotiation Journal* 1, no. 4 (1985): 349-58.

Wehr, Paul. *Conflict Regulation*. Boulder, Colo.: Westview Press, 1979.

—————. "Environmental Peacemaking: Problem, Theory and Method." In Louis Kriesberg, ed. *Research in Social Movements, Conflicts and Change*. Vol. 2. Greenwich, Conn.: JAI Press, 1979.

The Work Group on Conversion to Coal at Brayton Point. "Conversion to Coal at Brayton Point Power Plant for Somerset, Massachusetts." Final Report to the New England Energy Task Force, 1978.

Yost, Nicholas C. "The Governance of Environmental Affairs—Toward Consensus." New York: Aspen Institute for Humanistic Studies, 1982.

—————. "New N.E.P.A. Regulations Stress Cooperation Rather Than Conflict." *Environmental Consensus*, March 1979.

Zartman, I. William, and Maureen K. Berman. *The Practical Negotiator*. New Haven, Conn.: Yale University Press, 1982.

Index

Italicized numbers represent figures.